Conflict Through Consensus

CONFLICT

THROUGH

CONSENSUS

United Nations Approaches to Aggression

JULIUS STONE

The Johns Hopkins University Press, Baltimore and London

Published in the United States of America, 1977, by The Johns Hopkins University Press, Baltimore, Maryland 21218

Published in Australia by Maitland Publications Pty. Ltd., 1977,
  88 Brighton Street, Petersham, N.S.W. 2049

Published in India by N. M. Tripathi Private Ltd, 1977,
  164 Samaldas Gandhi Marg, Bombay-2

Library of Congress Cataloguing in Publication Data

Stone, Julius, 1907—
  Conflict through consensus.

  Includes indexes.
  1. Aggression (International law) 2. United Nations.
3. International relations. I. Title.

JX4471.S82   1977   341.5'8   77-3984

ISBN 0-8018-1989-X

Printed in Australia by Hogbin, Poole (Printers) Pty. Ltd., Sydney

To
GEOFFREY CHEVALIER CHESHIRE
my former tutor and longtime mentor
for his
ninetieth birthday

Table of Contents

Preface

This book examines the significance, at the present stage of world affairs, of the Consensus Definition of Aggression promulgated by the United Nations General Assembly in 1974. The meanings of that definition in terms of the search for peace and in terms of international law are of course considered here. The main concern, however, has been to assess its actual and potential meanings for the cardinal strategic, ideological, political and economic struggles which mark (and mar) the contemporary international community.

As the work proceeded there emerged also, as a rather fascinating by-product, a case study of the authenticity (or perhaps I should say *in*authenticity) of the notion of "consensus," so much in current fashion as an approach to the management of conflict. The study suggests that problems may be looming here for the international community, as fateful as those raised by Rousseau's exploration of "the general will" for free municipal societies.

The present book therefore has an ambit very different from that of my *Aggression and World Order,* first published in 1958 and recently reprinted by Greenwood Press of Westport, Connecticut. Apart from the changed perspectives and constellation of forces brought by the intervening decades, that earlier work was more theoretically focused on the logical, semantic, political-philosophical and jurisprudential aspects of the definitional enterprise. While, as already observed, the present focus is on its meanings for strategic, ideological, political and economic struggles which pervade the present world of states.

In the full and close documentation I have sought to afford, I have had in mind the needs of general and specialised libraries and research institutes. On the other hand, the contents of most of the chapters may engage the interests of students of international relations as regards the substantive strategic, ideological, political and economic issues central to the main theme; of students of international organization as regards "parliamentary diplomacy" and the relations between the United Nations Security Council and the General Assembly; of students of conflict resolution; and (of course) of international lawyers and officials, diplomats, and those involved in foreign policy and defence planning.

I am indebted to colleagues in New York, in Washington, D.C., and at the Department of Foreign Affairs in Canberra for help with documentation, to my friend Professor Upendra Baxi of the University of Delhi for reading the manuscript and making valuable suggestions. I also owe much to Dr. Gabriel Moens, Research Officer, and Zena Sachs, Senior Research Assistant (both of the University of New South Wales) for their faithful and fruitful assistance in bringing the manuscript to completion, and to the Australian Research Grants Committee for financial support of the research tasks involved.

JULIUS STONE

University of New South Wales
Sydney, Australia, January 1977

Adequate recognition of "aggression" is of preeminent concern to all people and peoples, and not merely to lawyers and political leaders, much less merely to international lawyers. It was therefore a notable achievement when the 29th General Assembly, its Sixth Committee and its fourth (thirty-five State) Special Committee on the Question of Defining Aggression, arrived, by "consensus" of all these bodies, at the definition now embodied in A/Res/3314. It was the more notable because of fifty-odd years of frustrating failures under both the League of Nations and the United Nations which preceded it.

It was to be expected, therefore, that the Definition would be hailed as reflecting "the spirit of true *détente*",[1] as providing objective criteria for identifying aggressors, strengthening the Security Council and deterring aggression.[2] M. Adjoyi (Togo) thought that "there was no reason to harbour any misgivings regarding the interpretation of any article of the draft definition".[3] For this fifty-year triumph, credit was claimed for the Soviet Union and socialist and non-aligned countries,[4] and also for Greece, in title of the final success of the formula offered by M. Politis under the League of Nations in 1933.[5] As to the means whereby the brand of definition was snatched from the fifty-year old flames, some orators in the General Assembly and its Committees also had very clear views. Apart from the role of *détente* already mentioned, they thought it resulted from "a firm common will",[6] from "completeness" and "balance" produced by a process of reciprocal concession,[7] or (in the inimitably polite phrase of Japanese representative Iguchi) from "a precise, well-balanced and reasonably satisfactory synthesis of the wide range of positions expressed by Member States".[8] It is an intriguing rider on these credits that, at the same session where consensus was reached, and Greece claimed her credit, the Greek and Turkish representatives were in bitter altercation over the Cyprus crisis of 1973-74, each State claiming that the other was an aggressor *within the terms of* the just agreed and much-hailed definition. That such a definition, at the very moment of its triumph, could be so barren of objective guidance for a crisis current during its very elaboration, is but one of the mysteries demanding explanation.[9]

The lack of guidance from the definition for contemporary acute threats to the peace, such as the Middle East and Cyprus, actually in course at the moment of universal consensus, does not in itself negate its value. Those particular threats may be so unusual as still to leave the definition useful for "normal" situations. A number of delegations thought the contrary. Canadian representative Lee thought "it remained to be seen whether that definition . . . would prove workable".[10] Quentin Baxter of New Zealand questioned whether the proclaimed balance of the Definition was stable and "not achieved by merely papering over the differences". As between "hard-edged law" and "soft-edged law", he thought it was the latter. The "edge", moreover, as will be shown, covers much of the whole ambit of the Definition.[11] M. Wehry of the Netherlands thought that the effect of the main Articles 2 and 3 was to leave it wholly to the Security Council's psychological and political wisdom in placing the search for a solution above attempts to establish the culpability of the parties.[12]

The United Kingdom representative, Mr. Steel, thought that whatever the adequacy of the formula as a working out of Article 2 (4) of the Charter, it did not define self-defence and thus preserved the "differences of opinion" as to Article 51 on that matter. He also thought that absence of a definition had not, in any case, been a serious handicap to the Security Council's primary function, the finding of aggression guilt not being its major concern, nor should it be. On these points, he thought that the new definition simply preserved whatever was already in the Charter.[13] Even Soviet bloc representatives dressed their obvious doubts about the sanguine laudations of the definitions (including their own) in a cloak of illusory praise.[14] The representative of Ruanda, M. Bararwerekana, thought that definition was likely to be overtaken by events, and the United Nations might find itself dealing again with the same question in the near future, but now, under the heading "need to redefine aggression" or "need to review the definition of aggression".[15] M. Eustathiades of Greece thought that the definition would be of little use to the Security Council, which had not yet and was not likely in the future to pass on whether an act of aggression had been committed. And this was not for lack of a definition.[16]

Those who praised were often, when the rhetoric is stripped away, also the skeptics. After expressing firm belief that the definition would "undeniably" deter aggressors, and assist prompt Security Council action, M. Camara of Brazil went on to doubt the value of the crucial "priority" provision of Article 2. For, he said, "it was usual in armed conflicts for all parties involved to exchange reciprocal accusations of being the first to resort to force".[17] M. Jaipal of India observed a little inconsequentially that though the definition has "no magic formula for the maintenance of world peace ... it would have the effect of deterring aggressors."[18] M. Kurukulasuriya of Sri Lanka agreed with Iran and the Federal Republic of Germany that the definition was not a legal definition since it did not "contain the whole thing and the sole thing", but he still thought it was a "triumphant conclusion". Pakistan's M. Mahmud, while thinking that the definition would be "an authoritative legal basis" for the Security Council, still feared that it "would provide an excuse" for delays in the Council's response to breaches of the peace.[19]

What is to be made of a text to which such simultaneously momentous *and* vacuous imports are attributed by those whose consensus it embodies? A full answer to this will require a close examination of the nature of the definitional problem in general, and of the major provisions of the Consensus Definition itself and their interrelations. Some preliminary hints may be gleaned from two of the more sophisticated statements of position following the consensus. Yugoslavia's M. Petric listed the blessings which "would" ensue from a precise, impartial and workable definition of aggression, as well for the Security Council's functions, as for deterrence of potential aggressors, for the protection of victims of aggression, particularly developing and non-aligned States, for the promotion of peace, the codification of international law, and the guidance of public opinion.[20] From this list of benefits to ensue from a *hoped-for* definition, the orator turned to the *actual* definition before the Committee, and spoke of the "insurmountable differences" overcome by the triumphant consensus on which it was based. The apparent inference is, of course, that the actual contents of the Consensual Definition would yield the benefits he had attributed to the hoped-for definition. Yet he was concerned to add immediately that the differences among States which preceded the consensus still continued after the consensus, and *would now be manifest in differences of interpretation.* So that perforce the Yugoslav delegation now had to state its own interpretation (which he proceeded on a number of points to do).

The representative of the People's Republic of China, M. An Chih-yuan, obviously agreed with the final Yugoslav point. But he did not beat so long about the bush. He observed that there was no basis for the recital, in paragraph 9 of the Preamble, of the many achievements of the definition. For, he explained, this definition would not change the pre-existing position. "The Super Power engaged in frantic expansion everywhere" (i.e. the U.S.S.R.) would conceal this lack of courage by apparent enthusiasm for the Definition and boast of its own success in this peace initiative. It would "use the definition to dub itself a standard-bearer in the struggle against aggression."[21] After the Sino-Soviet hostility is subtracted, the point has obvious applicability to other major Powers and even to minor Powers who enjoy protection from any one of these.

In face of such confrontations of semblance and reality, it is perhaps not surprising to find interwoven threads of the mystical. Without particularising how, the New Zealand delegate thought that the definition might deepen the sense that the Security Council was acting on principles rather than expediency;[22] nor did he say that this sense would prove warranted. M. Boulbina of Algeria thought that "naturally, the definition would be seen as perfect if the competent bodies *were never called on to apply it.*"[23] M. Rakotoson thought that "the text would achieve its real goal when the United Nations no longer needed to cite it".[24] M. Mai'Ga of Mali asserted that "definition" must "not give rise to contradictory interpretations", ignored the obvious fact that this was precisely what *this definition* did, and then asserted roundly that *this definition* was one of the "essential elements of the new international order". Similar mixtures of mystical flights characterised the attitudes of delegates towards the very act of adoption by "consensus" itself. M. Reshetnyak of the Ukraine thought that "even the slightest alteration of the present text would disrupt the balance of the definition and vitiate the results of many years' work."[25] M. Steel of the United Kingdom thought that all States should record their views and reservations and allow the Assembly to adopt the definition without amendment *and by consensus*. For though the definition would not serve much purpose, frustration of the efforts at definition *would harm the reputation of the Sixth Committee and its associated bodies*. Czechoslovak representative, Mme. Slamova thought that since three special United Nations committees had failed in earlier decades, the results of the present Special Committee, *whatever its imperfections*, must be considered to be successful.

The very virtues which Mme. Slamova then enumerated as redeeming *this* definition's imperfections, are themselves most illuminating.[26] They were that the Consensus Definition—(1) was the result of many years of effort; (2) was an elaborate structure which could collapse if tampered with; (3) was consistent with international law and the Charter; (4) preserved the prerogatives of the Security Council; (5) continued to permit liberation struggles; and (6) would have moral influence contributing to international peace. Be it noted that, apart from the speculative "moral influence" to be later examined, none of these virtues even if agreed at face value, offer any functional improvement in the use of the aggression notion, over what existed before. Some authorities on the Charter might even think that the effect of Nos. 3, 4 and 5 is to preserve some elements of prior State and Security Council practice to the modification rather than the preservation of which efforts to define aggression have mostly been directed.

This summation by the Czech representative no doubt expressed as euphoric as possible a view of an outcome with which the Soviet Union and the Soviet bloc could be associated. It is of interest to compare it with the summation by the Canadian representative, Mr. Wang, which bears a similar relation to the general Western view of the outcome.[27] He hailed the text as "due above all to a sense of realism in the Committee as to what could be demanded of a definition and the purposes that it might serve".[28] He thought consensus had eluded the world for over 50 years because the question of the limits of lawful force was "one of the most important and at the same time most controversial problems of international law, touching upon the vital interests of States and the foundations of international peace and security." And, as if to reconcile the implicit contradiction here, he added that the Consensus Definition "reflecting as it did compromise on all sides, inevitably opened the door to differing interpretations." He was careful *not* to assert that this compromise so open to different interpretations, would in any way make more clear or more effective the limits of lawful force.

Indeed, he proceeded immediately to suggest why this substantial outcome should *not* be expected. Delegations in the past, he said, had tended to press for definitions which were as restrictive as possible with regard to the use of force by certain States whose cause was not favoured, and yet as permissive as possible with regard to the use of force by other States whose cause was favoured. Naturally, as the decades brought changes in State relations, these also brought changes of emphasis in the various proposals, but he offered no reason for believing that the above tendency in State attitudes did not still continue. "The ambiguities in the present definition were therefore an inevitable reflection of the complexity of the real world . . . and a reflection of a realistic desire to develop guidelines which would be generally acceptable and widely applied to future conflicts."[29] Mr. Wang himself left it ambiguous whether this last reference to "wide application" merely described the aspiration of the Committee, or stated his own prediction about the actual effect of the Definition on future decision-making.

Which he meant emerges, however, clearly enough from his immediately following list of the advantages afforded by the new Consensus Definition. First, it required the determination whether aggression had been committed to be made in the light of "all the circumstances of each particular case."[30] Second, Article 2 and other articles make clear that the Security Council's "ultimate discretion" on these matters under the Charter was in no way "prejudiced". The Security Council had in all its 29 years of activity never made a determination of aggression, and nothing in the Definition alters its proper practice of avoiding judgments of aggression which might be harmful to the task of terminating hostilities.[31] In this and other respects it allowed full flexibility to the Security Council, rather than imposed guidelines on it. Third, said M. Wang, the Definition is "in no way inconsistent with the Charter, and was in fact founded upon the Charter."[32] Fourth, the Definition "avoided being so general as merely to repeat the Charter, and yet avoided being so specific as to suggest that it was exhaustive". He did not specify which particular added specificity increased ease or certainty in determining who was the aggressor.[33] Fifth, it covered "both direct and indirect uses of force", and "embraced the prohibition under the Charter of the use of force, as well as the exceptions . . .".[34] (Here again he listed no respect in which long controverted lines between prohibition and exceptions had been in any way clarified.) As in the Czechoslovak representative's speech of praise of the Consensus Definition, all these substantial benefits attributed by M. Wang to it, add up to little more than that the Definition has preserved the preexisting position under the Charter, or that at least it has not made any problems worse than they were. Whether even this last modest claim is justified is part of the inquiry here entered upon.

Finally, M. Wang gave praise to the procedure of adoption of the

Definition by consensus. Without such general consensus, including acceptability by the Permanent Members, a definition could be brushed aside. He, therefore, hoped the General Assembly would similarly act by consensus, and that to this end his and other delegations would refrain from proposing other amendments, which would upset "the carefully-devised (*sic*) and hard-won balance and consensus which would enable the definition to become a useful contribution to international law and to the maintenance of international peace and security."[35] Yet his own summation had not revealed any respect in which, however immaculately unamended, it could in any case make such a useful contribution.

The succeeding Chapters of this work will consider in detail whether these rather typical assessments of the Consensus Definition were unjust by the modesty of what they claimed it had achieved. They will explore what United States Representative Rosenstock perhaps meant when he said that the Consensus Definition had some of the strengths and all the weaknesses of a compromise, and how far his further view that it was "a hopeful sign of a growing spirit of international cooperation and understanding" is to be regarded as more than polite rhetoric.[36] Above all, however, they will be concerned with the bearing of the Consensus Definition, one way or another, on the prospects of peaceful resolution of the main contemporary conflicts.

CHAPTER 1

The United Nations Charter Context

I

Chapter 7 of the United Nations Charter deals with peace enforcement by the Security Council, and it is clear from its opening Article 39 that all the powers of the Security Council can be activated by a finding under that Article of a threat to the peace, breach of the peace *or* an act of aggression. A vast range of powers is conferred on the Security Council consequential on *any* of these determinations, so that a finding of *aggression* is in no way a prerequisite for effective peace enforcement. Measures which the Security Council can take after such a determination include all kinds of pressures ranging from mere economic and diplomatic sanctions to the most rigorous use of military power on the part of United Nations forces, provision for the establishment of which also appears in Chapter 7. When the Charter was adopted, in short, the Security Council was designed as an executive organ with teeth in it. Yet, even then, the founders of the United Nations did not feel it necessary to *require* any finding of *aggression* before the Security Council could act. For otherwise they would not have conferred the same vast powers on the Security Council even on a mere finding of a "threat to the peace" or "breach of the peace".[1]

This means that the Security Council *does not have to enquire* in a particular case as to which State is the aggressor, or otherwise at fault, before it is empowered to act. All that it need do is to determine that there has been a threat to the peace or a breach of the peace, either of which can exist even if no protagonist is more blameworthy than the other, or if it is doubtful which is more blameworthy. Once it determines that such has occurred, the Security Council is legally empowered to act without making any further judgment even as to which side is morally responsible, a judgment certainly involved in the notion of aggression. And this no doubt was one reason why the founders found it unnecessary to include any definition of aggression in the Charter.

The exercise of these powers did, of course, require *decisions* on the part of the Security Council, and in the taking of such decisions Article 27(3) of the Charter required that no Permanent Member vote in the negative, or in the common phrase, exercise its veto. And the critical nature of this voting requirement became fully apparent after the Security Council resolutions of 1950 initiating the Korean Action. These were adopted in the absence of the Soviet Union, which was then boycotting the Council's proceedings owing to differences about the representation of China. After the Soviet Union representative returned to his seat in August, it was obvious that that State would never again risk by its absence a hostile vote in the Security Council, which if present it could have vetoed. It thus became clear (even for those who might still have entertained illusions on the matter) that the Security Council, despite its theoretically great powers, could not be an effective *peace-enforcing* organ *in any conflict involving grave interests or allies or protégés of any of the Permanent Members.* The organ with "the teeth" was destined for some years at any rate to fade into the background, taking on at times the semblance of the Cheshire Cat's grin.

II

At about this same time, the General Assembly, representing all Members of the United Nations on the basis of one-State-one-vote, attempted to organise alternative devices for performing the peace-enforcing functions which might be frustrated by use of the veto in the Security Council. The Membership of the General Assembly in 1950 was less than half the present number. Decolonisation had then scarcely begun, and the United States and other Western Powers hoped that, as the General Assembly was then constituted, its majorities would usually favour policies acceptable to them. On this basis, the United States and other Western States sponsored and supported the Uniting for Peace Resolutions, which provide that the General Assembly should, when a threat to the peace, breach of the peace or act of aggression occurred, and the veto prevented the Security Council from acting, be convoked in Emergency Session. That body might then make certain recommendations to Members concerning the situation, and even invite Members to contribute units to a force for use in the emergency.

There was (and still remains) at least one vital difference between such action of the General Assembly in relation to a threat to the peace, breach of the peace, or act of aggression, and peace enforcement action by the Security Council under Chapter 7. As already seen, the Security Council does under the Charter have clear legal authority, made explicit by Article 25, to bind all Member States (including any violator of the peace) by such decisions as it may take by way of peace enforcement action under Chapter 7. The Council also has clear legal power to enforce those decisions by such United Nations forces as it may have at its disposal. We may term its powers "magisterial" in these respects. It is, however, clear, despite many surrounding controversies, that *the General Assembly* has no power by *its* resolutions to impose any legal obligations on the Member States, not even on any States which a majority of Members regard as engaged in committing a threat to the peace, breach of the peace, or even an act of aggression.[2]

It follows that the legal basis of "quasi-peace-enforcement" by the General Assembly (or as it is usually called "peace-keeping operations") is different from the Security Council's magisterial powers. In General Assembly operations the actions involved must be voluntarily undertaken by the Member States, and also voluntarily submitted to even by the very States involved in the alleged threat to the peace, breach of the peace, or act of aggression. For example, one of the principles which affected the first United Nations Emergency Force in the Middle East or similar forces sponsored by the General Assembly, is that they could only engage in operations on any territory with the consent of the Government of the State to which that territory belongs, though that State might, of course, bind itself to permit such a force to remain for any agreed period. (Of course, the Security Council *may* also organise *voluntary* forces—as with the Second United Nations Emergency Force in the Middle East—which would then be subject to similar limits.)

A system of peace-keeping which thus depends upon voluntary co-operation of Members, including those involved in the disturbance of the peace, must obviously seek to secure this voluntary cooperation by some kind of inspiration which will motivate the Members not involved in the disturbance to such cooperation. And since crisis action is here involved, this motivation must be such as to trigger instantly converging voluntary decisions of many Members, perhaps even to the point of contributing forces and incurring dangers in a common cause. It is reasonable to suppose that one purpose, at any rate, of the campaign for an agreed authoritative definition of "aggression" which came to be revived after the Korean Affair in the Security Council in 1950, was the search for such an activating symbol. Once the magisterial power of the Security Council was blocked, the hope was to marshal the voluntary actions of Members against "the aggressor" through the General Assembly. A consequential point is this. To serve as such a symbol, triggering readiness to incur sacrifices and risks by the co-operating Members to meet a crisis, it seemed (and still seems) to many that "aggression" has to be "defined" in terms sufficiently clear and comprehensive for instant application in crisis. Otherwise the judgments of Members will not concur, and may even conflict in the particular case; nor will their wills be galvanised into rapid and effective action.[3]

It is to be noted, even at this outset, that this seemingly sensible and desirable objective has proved endlessly elusive during the first twenty-four years of United Nations efforts, when it engaged successively no less than four Special Committees of the General Assembly. Does the Consensus Definition of 1974 mean that the objective was finally achieved? The answers to this are complex and will concern many of the Chapters which follow.

III

Even, however, before we approach such answers in relation to the Consensus Definition, we need to bring to mind a number of serious obstacles to fulfilment of such an objective in general. We begin with the question, what kind of content of definition would be necessary to inspire positive crisis action of third States by way of voluntary co-operation against "the aggressor". A main desideratum is that the definition's criteria must be simple rather than elaborate, precise rather than vague, and clear rather than indeterminate. Nearest to these re-quirements, for example, would be the criterion of movement of forces across international frontiers; and we may perhaps illustrate from this the problems which arise.

From the League of Nations onwards, this criterion of the armed crossing of a State's frontiers without its consent has been a constant favourite of definers of aggression. It is certainly difficult to deny that such a crossing plays some part in the criteria of aggression. Is it not instantly clear, for instance, that China was an aggressor on India's northern frontier in the 1960's when Chinese forces descended deep into North-East India? Or that Soviet or Chinese armed crossings of their disputed frontiers would be aggression by the State which first committed it? These very cases, however, bring out very sharply one kind of reason why the criterion of crossing frontiers has proved simplis-tic and inadequate. For while, for example, India might say that China committed aggression by crossing the international frontier by force of arms, it was also true that China challenged the frontier which India claimed to be the correct one, and claimed that the line was really further south. So that in China's view, under such a definition, any forceful reaction by India across the line of frontier *as China claimed it to be*, would be equally an act of aggression by India.

In other words, in a very typical kind of dispute about territory a definition of the word "aggression" in terms of crossing the frontier will not do, because the very question over which the trouble arises is as to *where the frontier is* according to the existing rules of law. The issue in the Sino-Indian Case was whether those rules of law included, as China claimed, a rule making "unequal" treaties void. There are many such cases on which reasonably strong arguments can be made on both sides of a boundary dispute: and which side is an aggressor by this simple test then depends on whose argument prevails. Such matters, on which arguments can be made both ways, are by their nature *arguable*. They are unlikely to be determinable in a day or two, let alone by instant and commonly shared intuitive judgments of all third States. In such cases, however simple the test of armed crossing of international frontiers may *seem*, it cannot serve as a basis of quick action in future crises. It cannot work even for such comparatively simple conflicts as those about frontiers. In fact it became clear quite early in the aggression debate, and remained agreed under the 1974 Definition, that even if such a simple criterion were sometimes applic-able, it would not be so in cases of invasion by a State which had some claim of right to sovereignty over the invaded territory.

IV

It might be said that, nevertheless, if sovereign title in territory is undisputably vested in the *State* victim of the alleged aggression, then at any rate invasion of it must always constitute aggression. A State which is satisfied with its frontiers will, of course, favour this simple test of forcible frontier crossing, as did France after the post-World War I territorial settlement. Such a simple test, had it been adopted, would have bolstered French security against "revisionist" claims, by subjecting any invader to whatever additional sanctions flow from commission of aggression. So with Soviet support of this kind of test after the Second World War. The Soviet Union made great territorial gains after World War II, the legality and/or morality of which were far more questionable than the French gains after World War I. A definition of "aggression" centred on armed crossing of frontiers would have given her a kind of cachet of moral approval and even of international political guarantees of her expanded domains, including her satellite buffer zone. In short, States which are content with their present frontiers, especially if they fear challenges to these, favour this kind of definition.

By the same token, however, other States resist this simple test, not only when the territorial gain has been made at their expense, but also when, as third States, they morally disapprove or politically resent the particular expansions. They are thus not willing to give either moral approval or political guarantees to them. Such resistant States, before they will voluntarily incur risks and commitments in relation to an alleged aggression by invasion, react to all the circumstances in which the crossing of the frontier occurred before they make a judgment of aggression. Such deliberations can rarely yield instant decisions triggering voluntary cooperation of many States in a crisis.

The difficulties with the simplistic crossing of frontiers test went, however, even deeper. It was increasingly confronted by doctrines about "wars of liberation" and "struggles for self-determination", which clamoured for the licence to use armed force against putatively "oppressive" sovereign States. They demanded that the use of armed force by third States in support of such struggles be exempted from the definition of aggression; and this necessarily implied that the test of armed crossing of frontiers was to be no longer valid for such cases. The political motives operating are obvious in the very short shrift given by Soviet bloc or black African or Asian States to former colonial Powers of the last thirty years which tried to protect their sovereignty in territory from anti-colonialist activity of third States supporting rebel movements against those Powers. This matter, as we shall see in Chapters 5 to 8. remains a main point of dissension, even after the formulation of the 1974 Consensus Definition. It is likely to remain so for the future, since there is every prospect that the use of the "wars of liberation" doctrine as a weapon of political warfare will continue long after all "colonies" in the traditional sense have disappeared. And the hankering for such simple physical facts as a touchstone of aggression was further confounded by demands of States with such political interests that the target sovereign States which resist such use of armed force against their domains be stigmatised as aggressors.

V

When the search for criteria of aggression moves away from simple physical models such as invasion of territory, or disobedience to cease-fire orders, and tries to allow for other kinds of factors and the circumstances surrounding them, the reasons for decades of frustration become ever clearer. The wide range and variability of the elements to be considered set up increasing tension with the exigencies for triggering quick voluntary cooperation of nations in crisis. For this last, not only quick decision of third States is required: their decisions must also concur. This means that the terms of definition must be clear and precise enough so that its application in any future circumstances is immediately obvious and even self-evident. They must be such that States will have been confident enough about the outcomes to agree *in advance* to accept their application in circumstances which may conceivably affect their own vital interests.

One reason why the hopes of meeting these desiderata are so desperate is that the facts and circumstances of a future international crisis are often quite unforeseeable, and increasingly so as the future becomes long-term, and the pace of global change increases. A "good" definition should cover what should be covered, and cover nothing that should not be covered, and to remain "good" in a future crisis, it must in this sense not prove disconcerting to apply whatever the circumstances of that crisis. For if it proves disconcerting, its application will involve deliberation and debate which will thwart the quick response for which crisis calls. To avoid this, draftsmen would have to envisage in advance all the situations to which the definition will in future have to be applied; and this *ex hypothesi* is not possible.

The Governments of most States, for their part, which are asked to commit themselves to the terms of a definition, are conscious, even in a world less changeful than that of 1977, that they cannot now predict either their own action, or their relations with other States, in future unforeseen circumstances. States have been (and remain) very wary of accepting as authoritative for them any present definition whereby, three or thirty years later, they might find themselves exposed to the rapacious or treacherous designs of other States (because the definition does not forbid some kind of coercion then used against them). They are no less wary about finding themselves forbidden, by terms to which they now commit themselves, to respond to such rapacity or treachery by what may turn out to be the only effective way of protecting themselves. It is thus as much the unpredictability of future relations, as any present Machiavellian intentions, which holds States from committing themselves in advance to simple, precise and unqualified criteria of aggression, capable of instant clearcut application in crisis. These reasons are not unrelated to those which hold many States (including practically all Communist-bloc States, and most new African and Asian States) from committing themselves in advance to third-party settlement of their disputes with other States. They are even closer to those which hold States from placing standing armed forces at the disposal of either the Security Council or the General Assembly for use against some as yet unidentified State in a future crisis.

VI

The flow of time in which alleged aggression occurs is another main reason for the illusoriness of the hope that a clear definition of aggression could trigger instant voluntary repressive action among Member States of the General Assembly. The circumstances of any alleged aggression are part of a shorter or longer span of history. The aggression emerges from what has gone before in a series of historical contexts.

How much before? In the 1974 Cyprus crisis, was the critical time when Greek military officers joined in ousting President Makarios? Or when the Turkish expeditionary force was landed on the island? (It was a classic of ironies when in 1974 the Greek and Turkish representatives bitterly accused each other of "aggression", *in terms of the "balanced" Consensus Definition which was a triumph of "fragile" consensus*, in which both had just joined.) In the Middle East crisis of 1973, was the context limited to the concerted Egyptian-Syrian armed attack on Israel in October 1973? Did it extend to Egypt's earlier "War of Attrition"? Or to her repudiation of the 1967 Cease-Fire? Or the 1967 hostilities or Cease-Fire? Or the attacks of Arab States in 1948? Or the 1947 Partition Resolution? Or the Balfour Declaration and the McMahon and related pledges during the First World War? Did it embrace even the Arab conquest of Palestine in the 7th century? Or the Israelite conquest of this land two thousand years earlier? Or even (for where does history begin?) even with the Covenant reported in the Pentateuch between God and Abraham? The irony of each antagonist fresh from joining in the "consensus" confidently invoking the Consensus Definition to support its charge of aggression against the other was seen here also.[4]

Even in less complex and long-standing conflicts than these, the seamless web of history has no self-evident line of section which is obviously the only critical one for determining culpability in the particular conflict. To allot responsibility, the decision-maker must go back at least to the first point of distinct relevance; and to fix that first point requires the canvassing of a much wider historical context. He cannot begin arbitrarily at any random point. On the other hand, to go thus into the fuller merits must prolong the inquiry. And such prolongation defeats the whole object of triggering by advance definition instant voluntary cooperation of United Nations Members for handling a crisis requiring speedy measures. There is thus an inbuilt contradiction between the ostensible purpose of finding a definition for General Assembly operations (facilitating instant voluntary cooperation in crisis), and the nature of any rational inquiry into aggression between States (complex, problematical and requiring deliberation in most cases). While the notion of aggression, and a definition of it, may thus be valuable for other purposes, like the trial of individuals for crimes against the peace, they are not effective for marshalling immediate voluntary cooperation of Members in the context of General Assembly "Uniting for Peace" operations.

VII

Here, too, we meet a further paradox. The aggression notion seems at first sight to offer a strongly emotive symbol, apt for inspiring quick community decisions for managing an armed crisis. Yet some of the very elements of the aggression notion which make it promising for this purpose also defeat that very purpose. It is the "moral" (evaluative and emotive) components of the judgment of aggression which make it promising as instant trigger for State decisions; but it is also these same components which (by the width and complexity of inquiry they entail) will usually prevent quick decisions. United Nations organs cannot, as a practical matter, delay action in a crisis until there has been sufficient investigation and deliberation to fix moral responsibility.

The point is not merely speculative. In historical fact, neither the General Assembly nor (as already seen) the Security Council has ever used a finding of aggression as an effective basis for peace-keeping action. When we look at the terms of either Article 39 (as regards the Security Council) or of the Uniting for Peace Resolutions (as regards the General Assembly) it is plain that any action that can be taken under the Charter or the Resolutions on the ground of "aggression", can also be taken on the ground of simple threat to the peace or breach of the peace. The immediate business in a crisis is to damp down the hostilities. And even after it is recognised that the General Assembly's lack of magisterial power (that is, of power of taking legally binding decisions) creates a special problem of inspiring voluntary cooperation of Members in crisis action, the fact remains that the aggression symbol has not, and cannot fulfil its promise as such an inspirational trigger. What has produced the degree of voluntary cooperative action by Members in a number of crises has been rather the common fear of a general (and even thermo-nuclear) war, unless the particular conflict is contained.

VIII

The painful footdragging of nations on the fifty-year trail towards definition of aggression thus has many explanations. Certainly, the reason is not any lack of urgency of achieving a definition which would really produce voluntary cooperation at moments of crisis, *if only one could be found which would work in this way.* One could, indeed, summarise these explanations by saying that it is the very high stakes depending on the contents of any definition adopted which inhibit States from committing themselves to a text that will, as it were, hold water. The paradox that States have been so reluctant to commit themselves to precise formulations of so important a conception as international aggression is only an apparent one. The truer point is that States were so reluctant *just because what the formulation contained or omitted is so important, once they do commit themselves in advance to a precise formulation.*

All this begins to clarify why the task of definition set for the diplomats and publicists was no mere exercise in logic or philosophy, much less of mere taxonomy or lexicography—of placing the aggression notion at its proper point within the matrix of knowledge or stating accurately the usages of the word "aggression". The task was not merely to find, describe or classify linguistic knowledge or usage, but (as will be later elaborated) *to prescribe rules* for the relations of States.

The United Nations undertaking, as most participants conceived it until shortly before the Consensus Definition came onto the horizon, was to provide a definition with a double virtue. By what it included, it would clearly brand and repress certain activities as "the greatest crime against mankind". By what it omitted, it would leave all other conduct as licensed or (even when it is clearly violative of international law) subject only to the mild and often impotent processes of traditional international law. In the nature of things, this prohibition, branding and repressing of specified activities (for instance, of armed invasion of territory) would have a more restricting effect on States with greater capacity for such activities (on those, for instance, with greater military capacity). And it would have this effect even if, in the particular conflict, the militarily stronger State was the victim of the grossest violations of its legal rights by the militarily weaker State, so long as these violations were not by activities caught within the definitional prohibition. In such a case, the particular terms of the definition would strip the militarily wronged State of remedies of self-help against legal wrongs hitherto legally enjoyed by it. Correspondingly, it would transfer from that State to the violating State those legal rights which the wronged State cannot protect except by the responses now stigmatised as aggression. This effect is clearly seen, even in relation to the branding as "aggression" of military invasion of territory, an activity with which most of us have little sympathy. What applies there, applies *a fortiori* to other more ambiguous activities of which the "aggressive" nature has been so much debated. Numerous examples will inevitably emerge from the succeeding Chapters.

It must be asked, at this point, whether the fact that a Consensus Definition was reached in 1974 does not belie the above reasons for believing that no definition can be found which will fulfil the functions for which it is sought. A main purpose of this whole work is to answer this question. Yet we may note, even at this early stage, an important part of the answer implied in Professor Schwebel's able analysis of the work of the fourth Special Committee *as at 1972*. He observed that what seemed in that year rather unusual progress became possible because at that time the advocates as well as the opponents and sceptics of definition came to *"see less importance in a definition of the type currently proposed than formerly. . . ."* (Italics supplied.)[5] This change in turn was due to it becoming agreed on all hands that the definition would *only guide* the Security Council. All three competing drafts at that stage, the learned writer pointed out, reserved all the powers of the Security Council. This meant that, *whatever the terms of the definition*, the "essential discretion of the Security Council" was to continue; and this reduced "both the importance and the contentiousness of a definition of aggression".[6]

The corollary from this moderation of expectation is also notable, and will warrant considerable study in subsequent Chapters. He thought it conceivable that at that stage an acceptable definition would be found, but one as to which it would remain to be seen "how valuable such a definition would really be."[7] This, of course, still remains to be seen, after the 1974 Definition. And the point rather parallels the main point of the present thesis. This is that while hopes are understandable that instant recognition of "aggression" could be a useful trigger of voluntary cooperation of States, a definition of aggression which would ensure such instant recognition is rather unattainable, and may even not be worth searching for.

CHAPTER 2

The Story of the Fourth Special Committee on Defining Aggression

I

It was in 1967—significantly, perhaps, shortly after the dramatic Six-Day War in the Middle East—that the Twenty-Second General Assembly established the last Special Committee on the Question of Defining Aggression.[1] This was the fourth Special Committee on that general subject. The first Committee of 15 States was appointed in 1952, in continuance of work of the International Law Commission on the Draft Code of Offences against the Peace and Security of Mankind. In the course of this, the Commission had listed aggression as a crime against the peace and security of mankind. It also, however, decided that aggression could not be defined more specifically than to say that it was the use of armed force by one State against another other than for purposes of "national or collective defence", or pursuant to decision or recommendation by competent United Nations organ.[2]

The General Assembly, declaring that it was nevertheless "possible and desirable" to define aggression further, appointed successively the first Special Committee of 15 States which did substantial work from 1953 to 1956,[3] and the Second Special Committee of 19 Members which worked even more intensively, especially in a series of 19 meetings from October 8 to November 9, 1956, against the dramatic background of the prevailing Suez Crisis.[4] Out of this setting, perhaps, came new questionings as to the "possibility" and "desirability" of the enterprise. Had the General Assembly foreclosed the preliminary questions about the feasibility of the whole enterprise of definition, on which the Committee members were now deeply divided?[5] The gist of the Second Special Committee's Report was that its members were unable to agree either on the question whether it was desirable to define aggression, or whether it would be feasible to define it. The General Assembly (XII) was sufficiently infected by these doubts so that when it established its Third Special Committee in 1957, the task it imposed was essentially that "of determining *when* it shall be appropriate for the General Assembly to consider again the question of defining aggression". This Committee found at meetings of 1959, 1962, 1965, and 1967, that the time was not yet ripe.[6]

The fourth and final Special Committee on this subject was established on a new Soviet initiative in 1967. If the 1956 Middle East Crisis blunted (as it did) the search for definition, it would be an intriguing subject for a Ph.D. thesis to ask why the 1967 Middle East Crisis should have reactivated it? At any rate, of all the committees on the matter under the League of Nations or the United Nations, the Fourth Special Committee has the longest, most diligent, as well as most successful record. Even to 1973, at which point the prospects of success were still rather uncertain, the Fourth Special Committee had already held 100 meetings, of which the 100th, in May 1973, was at a five weeks session. And before the conclusion of its work in 1974 the time spent in meetings, had it been consolidated, was equivalent to a conference lasting without a break nine solid months.[7]

Even as its 100th meeting approached close students were uncertain, if not sceptical, about the outcome of its proceedings and those of its Working Group. This latter consisted of States representative of those which had offered the three principal drafts put forward. These were the Soviet Union (which had submitted its own draft),[8] five States from the sponsors of the Thirteen Power Draft,[9] and two from the sponsors of the Six Power Draft—all six of these last (apart from Japan) being Western States.[10] As late as 1972, B. B. Ferencz has observed, progress on the major issues was so small that a number of delegates "began to question whether it was really productive to continue the effort."[11] He also thought, however, that part of the difficulty was the excessive turnover of personnel from meeting to meeting and from year to year. He points out that the number of persons who had participated in all five of the five week sessions from 1968 to 1973, was only five. This meant that of the 80 or so participants *at each session,* the majority came to the deliberations more or less inexperienced in negotiation, if not ignorant of the issues, involving an excessive number of new and false starts.[12] And even though moves were made at this stage to expand the Working Group informally from 8 to 13, and Chairman Xenon Rossides of the Special Committee took steps to promote informal consultations between the representatives between sessions, the outlook for arrival at an agreed definition was still bleak.

II

Mr. Ferencz entitled his stocktaking study of this stage, rather hopefully—"Defining Aggression—The Last Mile". He based his hopefulness on the small numerical proportion of the paragraphs of the 7 Articles of the Consolidated Text drawn up by the Working Group of the Committee, on which there continued to be disagreements. He did not attempt, as will later be stressed, to give any weighting to the question how many of the really hard choices which had hitherto baulked agreement had already been built into the agreed terms, and how many more were finally concentrated into that "last mile", that is, into that comparatively few disputed paragraphs.

At its 103rd meeting on April 30, 1973, the Special Committee established a Working Group open to all delegations with the same rights of participation and decision, thus extending the informality of the work of that Group,[13] of which the Chairman was Finland's representative, Mr. Bengt H. G. A. Broms. Within this flexible frame of the

Working Group, use was made of "Contact Groups" of Member States representative of the main points of conflict concerning certain broad divisions of the proposed definition.[14] And out of these procedures there emerged by the 106th meeting, on May 28, 1973, a report including, in addition to the original Soviet, Thirteen Power and Six Power drafts, a Consolidated Text of the reports of the Contact Groups. In this text, the extent of emergent agreement was presented by way of a draft of seven articles, followed by a series of notes indicating points of persisting disagreement and competing or additional proposals,[15] from the various delegations on the Special Committee.[16] At the final meeting (109th) of the 6th Session on May 30, 1973, the Special Committee took pains to emphasise that "in the absence of agreement on a draft definition, each proposed article must be read together with the comments thereon".[17]

The four "Contact Groups" and "Drafting Group" working still under the supervisory Chairmanship of M. Broms of Finland, proved to be a highly efficient device. These drew up the Consolidated Text, notes, and table of State proposals, available towards the end of the Special Committee's Session on May 24, 1973. As will be seen in the next section, these documents disclosed continuing conflicts of position on many fundamental questions. These Groups and their members, and Chairman Broms himself, worked informally to move the text in the succeeding year to the point when it would accommodate these conflicts, and to persuade or cajole particular States to tolerate the accommodating text.[18] That achievement was considerable even if, as will have to be considered, the triumph was often rather a verbal *tour de force* than a miraculous conversion of strategic political and economic conflicts into a harmonious consensus.[19]

III

After numerous further meetings and great activity among members of the 35-member Special Committee, its Working Group and Contact Groups, not to speak of the Sixth (Legal) Committee of the 29th General Assembly, a text emerged which was adopted at all stages by *consensus*. Great pressures were exerted on members not to disturb this "consensus" by even the slightest offer of amendments. Despite sharp protests by a number of States concerning non-consultation and disregard of their views,[20] the text produced by the Working Committee was in due course adopted by the General Assembly (also by consensus) in Resolution 3314(XXIX) on December 14, 1974(A/Res. 3314 (XXIX)). The text was said to be so "delicately balanced" that the least tampering would destroy consensus and text. Its achievement was hailed as a triumph culminating fifty years of high efforts of statesmen and lawyers, and even as a kind of fitting fruit of the new era of *détente*.

Appreciation, indeed, was not left in these vague terms, but was set out by various participants in terms of the following specific gains.

First, it would deter potential aggressors. Second, it would enlighten States as to the limits of lawful use of force and thus promote peaceful coexistence. Third, it would by its guidance assist the Security Council to maintain and restore peace, and even (some thought) ensure that that Council acted on legal principle rather than political expediency. (There was little suggestion, curiously, in these discussions, that the General Assembly either needed or would receive similar guidance from the Consensus Definition to act on legal principle rather than political expediency!) Fourth, one or two Members thought it might even prevent Permanent Members of the Security Council from being tempted into aggression in reliance on their legal capacity to escape the consequences by veto. Fifth, it would provide new impetus for more successful codification of international law in furtherance of "the rule of law" among nations. Sixth, it would make it possible to resume the work of the International Law Commission on the Code of Offences against the Peace and Security of Mankind, suspended in the 'fifties for lack of an accepted definition of aggression.[21] Seventh, it would allow work to be resumed for the establishment of an International Criminal Court for the trial of offences against such a code, also suspended for related reasons in the 'fifties.[22]

Only the course of international relations in the next decade or so will finally decide how far such predictions are based on sober judgment, and how far on naive euphoria or the grateful ritual rhetoric of the concluding sessions of these hard-working bodies. Yet it is also possible even now to inquire what basis there was for such predictions. The prediction of the above gains, for example, must proceed on the assumption that pre-existing conflicts in the positions of States *as to the definition of aggression,* were the cause of the evils which these gains overcame. It assumed that it was resulting uncertainties which gave rise to the risks of delinquency or default referred to in the first, second, third and fourth anticipated gains; and to the lack of progressive development of international law referred to in the fifth, sixth and seventh items. Insofar as this is the basis of the predictions, it is immediately possible to ask how far the terms of the Consensus Definition have removed the uncertainties from which these risks and defaults have supposedly sprung. Insofar as they have, there may be some rational basis for predicting the listed benefits (though we would still have to wait on the years for actual outcomes). However (and this is the present point), insofar as the Consensus Definition *has not removed the conflicts in the positions of States, and resulting uncertainties, but has merely incorporated them into the Consensual Definition itself,* the absence of any rational basis for such predictions would immediately appear. We would have to try to explain them as proceeding from naive euphoria or ritual rhetoric, or as directed to other objectives than those implied in the list of claimed achievements or both.

A practical way of proceeding for the above purpose is, first, to identify the critical conflicts between States as to the nature and scope of aggression which seemed to block agreement on definition in the earlier years of the Fourth Special Committee, say, up to 1972. Thereafter the Consensual Definition can be examined to see what solutions, if any, it brought to these conflicts. If this examination shows that on these critical matters the same conflicts continued to prevail after the Consensus Definition by way of conflicting interpretations of its terms, the above enumerated claims made for the Consensus Definition would seem to fall *ab limine*. For if the Definition did *not* resolve the critical conflicts but rather codified or otherwise preserved them within the intricately interwoven equivocations, contradictions or silences of what its authors presented as a "delicately balanced" text, based on "fragile" consensus, such claims would lack any serious basis.

The Consensus Definition might then represent a triumph of verbal skills in using such devices to conceal conflicts. It would certainly, as will be seen, illustrate the role in definitional debates of the strategy and tactics of political warfare, as well as the role of "consensus" on verbal formulae as a triumph of face-saving for the Fourth Special Committee and the Twenty-Ninth General Assembly, to avoid adding still another failure to the half-century of vain efforts to define aggression which had gone before. But by the same token, the bearing of the Consensus Definition on prescribing or even guiding conduct of Member States in their mutual conflicts, or that of United Nations organs in handling such conflicts, would, alas, be insubstantial to the point of vacuity.

One main object of the Chapters which follow, then, will be to examine the interpretations placed on key provisions of the Definition by States who joined in the Consensus adopting it. A comparison of the conflicting interpretations thus exposed with the conflicting State positions which had *up to then been such as to make agreed definition unattainable,* will indicate the respects and extent to which the Consensus Definition had really resolved the conflicts, or (which is perhaps only the other side of the coin) how far "consensus" was, on critical points, a genuine one.

For the purpose of this decisive comparison, it is fair to choose, for exposing the pre-existing conflicts of position, the latest point in time before the "consensus" emerged, at which the prospect of reaching an agreed definition still seemed slight. In the Chapters which follow I have chosen for this purpose the point in the Fourth Special Committee's work when the Soviet, Thirteen Power and Six Power drafts had already been well canvassed, and when the "Consolidated Text" and its notes of persisting conflicts of State positions, based on careful Reports of the Working Group and its Contact Groups, had just been presented. This, as seen in Section II above, was in April-May 1973. At this point of time, delegates were still questioning whether it was worthwhile continuing the effort.[23] At the other side, this point of time was also within a year of the Fourth Special Committee's adoption by consensus of the present text on 12th April, 1974.[24] In Chapter 9, as I approach my conclusions, I shall attempt to draw together the results, in the main areas of conflict, of the comparisons made in the intervening Chapters.

CHAPTER 3

Standing and Force of Resolution 3314 (XXIX) and the Annexed Consensus Definition

I

As long ago as 1952, a Report of Secretary-General Hammarskjoeld[1] set the terms which continue to dominate debate as to the legal standing and effects of any General Assembly definition of aggression. This is that insofar as definition did not go beyond basic elements found in the Charter, its provisions would obviously draw legal force from the Charter. On the other hand, insofar as it would prohibit conduct not prohibited by the Charter, the General Assembly lacked power legally, at any rate, to impose it on Members or on the Security Council. Some participants, nevertheless, demanded that this dichotomy be somehow transcended, so as to make good gaps, ambiguities and other Charter defects. It was, they urged, just because the Charter spoke in too general terms, that further definition by the General Assembly was sought.[2]

Resolution 3314(XXIX), by which in December 1974 the General Assembly adopted the Consensus Definition attached thereto, and called it to the attention of the States and the Security Council, seems to stay within the frame offered by the 1952 Report. For, in calling upon States to refrain from acts of aggression, numbered paragraph 3 scrupulously refrained from even referring to the annexed Definition itself. They were to refrain from such acts *"contrary to the Charter of the United Nations* and the Declaration . . . concerning Friendly Relations . . . among States *in accordance with the Charter of the United Nations."*[3] Whatever may be thought of drafting style, clearly no claim is being made by this resolution to add to or vary obligations already imposed by the United Nations Charter.

The different issues involved in the question of "legal standing" or "binding force" of a General Assembly definition are classically illustrated by the early debates concerning "economic" and "ideological" aggression. The sequel on these substantive matters in the 1974 Consensus Definition will be examined in Chapter 7. At this point they are considered merely to introduce the confusion of issues involved in the question what legal standing and force is to be given to Resolution 3314, and the attempt in this Chapter to disentangle them.

II

The question what relation the definition bears to existing Charter provisions is perplexing enough as to the conventional "armed aggression".[4] The difficulties were even more dramatic with the Asian, Latin American and Soviet proposals of 1953 as to "economic" and "ideological" aggression which made noteworthy an earlier Committee's pioneering discussion.

A majority of the Committee saw its mandate as limited to defining aggression "in the sense of the Charter". This raised immediately the issue whether this sense extended beyond "armed" aggression.[5] The Bolivian delegate inferred a Charter prohibition of "economic aggression", from the three Charter principles of "political independence", "sovereign equality" and "non-interference in the domestic affairs" of States. Political independence was so "closely linked with economic independence", that a threat to the latter was "as much an act of aggression as was armed aggression".[6] M. Adamiyat (Iran), too, classed "economic aggression" as an important form of "indirect" aggression. Its essence was "coercive economic and political measures taken against a State ... designed to impede the exercise of its sovereignty over its natural resources or its efforts towards economic development", tacitly included by the Charter under "acts of aggression".[7] They might have added that Article 2(4) of the Charter forbids not only use of *armed* force, but force of any kind.

The United States delegate, Mr. Maktos, pointed out some of the *non sequiturs* involved in this view of the Charter, as well as the danger that the widening of the notion of aggression to include the "economic" would "weaken the whole concept of aggression" in its primary application to armed aggression.[8] And at least one State, the Argentine, which thought that a definition to be of value must cover "economic" and "ideological" aggression, nevertheless regarded definition as undesirable in part because of this very fact.[9] All this, of course, was at a time when charges of economic aggression were being levelled only against Western States, two decades before the oil boycott of 1973. It would be surprising if the resistance of the United States to the new notion were ever again, after the 1973 oil boycott, as firm as it was in 1953.[10] Yet, as will be observed in Chapter 7, it is a fact that when the Consensus Definition was being settled in 1974, United States policy had not yet adjusted to the changed situation.

Similar differences affected the proposal as to "ideological aggression" pressed by Soviet delegate Morozov. It was to include particularly "war propaganda", propaganda for the use of atomic, bacterial, chemical and other types of weapons of mass destruction, and "also the promotion of the propaganda of fascist-nazi views, racial and national exclusiveness, hatred and contempt for other peoples".[11] M. Adamiyat (Iran), as well as others, saw "ideological aggression" also as a form of "indirect aggression", of intervention in another State's internal or foreign affairs, including "direct or indirect incitement to civil war, threats to internal security, and incitement to revolt by the supply of arms or by other means".[12] And here, too, the United States stressed the danger of weakening the application of the aggression notion to "armed aggression" by such an extension, as well as collateral dangers to freedom of the press, and of opinion.

On one of the few points of general agreement, it is difficult to think that the Committee in 1953 meant quite what it said. Its members were reported as substantially agreed that any definition adopted by the General Assembly resolution could have only the status of a recommendation, and would not have a binding character. M. Röling (Netherlands) even thought that a definition "could play only a negligible part in the maintenance of international peace and security, since it would bind neither the Security Council nor the General Assembly of the United Nations."[13] Insofar, however, as a definition merely brands as "aggression" what is already so branded by the Charter (as its proponents claimed, for example, that "economic aggression" was) the definition would surely be legally binding on competent organs for that reason. The question whether it *is* already so branded by the Charter, remains debated through and after the Consensus Definition of 1974.[14] The following sections indicate that even this point, proceeding from the Secretary-General's 1952 Report, is in need of much further refinement.[15]

III

Within the overall question of what is the legal standing and binding force of the Consensus Definition embodied in Resolution 3314 (XXIX), a number of other issues need to be identified, in addition to the issue as to how far the definition merely expressed obligations already express or implicit in the United Nations Charter. It is important, at the outset, to bring all these issues clearly to mind, and their bearing on the answer to the overall question.[16]

(1) *Precision of Terms.* Moving from narrower to wider issues the first is how far the Consensus Definition is framed in terms sufficiently precise to set clear directives for States and other decision-makers. It cannot, for instance, have much binding force if at critical points it uses terms which can only be applied to a concrete situation by a virtually discretional decision. Such terms would have this disarming effect whether they appear either in the prescribed constituent of aggression as stated, or in the grounds of exculpation of such acts, or additional inculpation of other acts.

(2) *Whether Terms Merely Hortatory or Peremptory.* Even if (as is of course unlikely) all terms of the Definition were precise enough to control all concrete situations, its binding force would still depend on whether they purport to impose them on Members and on United Nations decision-makers, rather than merely to exhort, recommend, and guide. And this question also has to be asked concerning Resolution 3314 itself, adopting and transmitting the Definition to Members and to the Security Council.

(3) *Constitutional Power of the General Assembly to Bind Members.* Even assuming sufficient precision of terms, clearly purporting to bind, it still has to be asked whether such a General Assembly resolution can be binding on Members, in view of the fact that that body's power

under Articles 10-12 of the Charter in relation to matters of international peace and security are powers of discussion and recommendation, and not of decision.

(4) *Constitutional Power of the General Assembly to Bind the Security Council.* Whatever the answer to these first three questions, the further question would still arise whether the constitutional power of the General Assembly extends to making norms *binding on the Security Council in the exercise of its exclusive powers in relation to a threat to the peace, breach of the peace or act of aggression under Articles 39-51 of the Charter.* This, of course, is especially so in view of the terms of Article 39 and the "primary responsibility" of the Security Council on these matters expressed by Article 24 of the Charter. (It would so remain, even if the controversial interpretation of Articles 24 and 25 in the *Namibia Advisory Opinion* were accepted as correct. For that Opinion is directed to the binding legal effect of Security Council decisions *on Member Nations,* and not to that of the binding legal effect of General Assembly decisions *on the Security Council.*)[17]

(5) *Definition Declaratory of Charter Provisions.* Even if (as seems clear) the immediately preceding question has to be answered in a sense denying General Assembly power, a resolution of that body might still draw binding force from the truism of the 1952 Report of the Secretary-General mentioned in Section I. Insofar as the acts caught by a General Assembly definition are also caught by prohibitions of the use of "force", "aggression" or "armed attack" in the Charter, that definition would legally bind Members and all United Nations organs because the Charter is so binding. For this purpose, presumably, this substantial identity would have to be accepted by those concerned. Beyond this point the Definition could not bind anyone, except perhaps the Secretary-General and his staff *vis-à-vis* the General Assembly.

(6) *Reimportation of Uncertainties of the Charter, even if the Constituent Terms of the Definition are Sufficiently Precise.* It could conceivably be argued that a General Assembly definition could legally go beyond the obligations imposed by the Charter, so long as the additional obligations remained within the limits of any ambiguities, gaps or self-contradictions within the Charter text. The Definition might then, within these ambits of doubt, give a precision to obligations not found in the Charter, and *in this sense* add to or diminish what was in the Charter *per se* while remaining "consistent" in one sense with it.

However this be, all concerned in the 1974 Definition made clear that no addition or diminution was to be permitted even on this basis. As has been seen, not only do Preamble, Paragraphs 2 and 4, preserve the exclusiveness of Security Council authority, but Article 6 is also peremptory that the Definition cannot "enlarge or diminish the scope of the Charter, including its provisions concerning cases in which the use of force is lawful". The effect seems to be to leave *any question concerning aggression which is controversial under the Charter, also controversial under the Definition.*

Moreover, even were this not so, the critical Article 2 of the Definition produces a similar effect by other means. For it stipulates, as to the whole range of conduct caught by the Definition, that the conduct, in addition to being of the nature specified, shall also be "in contravention of the Charter". So that whatever conduct can be argued to be stigmatisable or justifiable under the Charter, continues so notwithstanding any terms of the Definition. This would be so even if we assume that the terms of the Definition as they apply to the impugned conduct had maximum precision (which, of course, they do not), even if they were peremptory (which we shall see they were not), and even if the General Assembly had the requisite power of legally binding decision over Members and over Security Council (which it does not).

IV

In submitting Resolution 3314(XXIX) to these various criteria of its binding force, it may be of incidental interest to see how far the delegations active in the Special Committee and the Sixth Committee were aware of the complex issues involved. Were the preambular recitals that the resolution ought to "deter aggressors", "simplify the determination of acts of aggression and the implementation of measures to suppress them", and provide "basic principles as guidance for such determination", based on consideration of or inadvertence to these issues of binding force?

It was as to Issue (4) above that minds were clearest. Chinese representative An Chih-Yuan[18] went directly to that issue, and there was no square dissent. Whatever its force, he said, the Consensus Definition could not legally prevent Permanent Members of the Security Council from using the veto to prevent determination that a State is an aggressor. This alone, M. An Chih-Yuan thought, was enough to render the above recitals baseless, especially the one about deterring aggressors. And he was referring, no doubt, not only to deterrence of the Permanent Members, but also of the many other States on whose behalf a Permanent Member is prepared to vote. The Soviet delegate, M. Kolesnik,[19] replied only rather transparently, by advocating that the General Assembly should "appeal to the Security Council", to give the Definition binding force by Security Council decision. This very proposal implied at least that unless so adopted by the Security Council, Resolution 3314(XXIX) would not bind that body at all. It also implied that (in accordance with its voting rules) any Permanent Member could by its veto block such adoption. But what above all made the Soviet position transparent, was that even after a veto-free adoption any Permanent Member could still block by veto any future determination of an alleged aggression. Only a Charter amendment under Articles 108 or 109 (itself subject to veto) could change that situation. And this, presumably, is the basis on which both the United Kingdom and United States representatives pointed out that even the Security Council could not make the Consensus Definition binding on itself.[20]

The implications thus visible through M. Kolesnik's transparent rhetoric, were made quite explicit in the views of Soviet bloc countries. East Germany's M. Goerner[21] made no effort to conceal them.[21a] The definition, he said, "was a strict application of the basic provisions of the Charter . . . , according to which the Security Council was the only United Nations organ empowered to determine the existence of acts of aggression." For the Ukrainian delegate, M. Reshetnyak,[22] only the Security Council could decide aggression issues taking into account all circumstances in each case, including the purposes and intentions of the States concerned. Otherwise, actions consistent with the Charter might be qualified as aggression. So M. Nyamdo of Mongolia[23] thought that the Security Council's discretion under Articles 2 and 3 of the Definition was an application of that body's exclusive authority under the Charter.

Western States stated the point as almost self-evident. M. Wehry (Netherlands)[24] observed that there "could be no act of aggression unless its existence had been explicitly determined by a positive pronouncement on the part of the Security Council." Article 39 of the Charter "left no room for doubt . . .". The International Court would so hold if consulted. Nothing in the Definition, said the Australian representative should be interpreted as affecting "the discretionary powers of the Security Council in relation to the maintenance of international peace and security."[25] M. Eustathiades of Greece[26] noted that the Consensus Definition itself, in particular Articles 2 and 3, reaffirmed this full discretion.

The United States representative, M. Rosenstock, joined this particular issue of lack of General Assembly power to bind the Security Council (Issue 4 above), with the separate Issues (1 and 2 above) that the terms of the Consensus Definition were not in any case in the precise and peremptory terms capable of binding. Paragraphs 2, 4 and 10 of the Preamble, and Articles 2 and 4 of the text, he pointed out, acknowledged the Security Council's final discretion under the Charter. "There was nothing that the General Assembly *or the Security Council* could do under the Charter, as currently drafted, to alter the discretion of the Council."[27] (Italics supplied.) Even the words "*prima facie*" in Article 2 (he thought) respected Article 39 of the Charter "which required that the determination of an act of aggression *must result from a positive decision* of the Security Council." The Definition merely provided guidance to the Security Council.[28] Such views were not limited to Communist and Western States. M. Orrego of Chile flatly observed that a State is not to be considered an aggressor "as long as the Security Council has not reached a specific determination on the matter".[29] Anything else would be inconsistent with the Charter. And for M. Dabiri of Iran[30] the Definition could only guide, not restrict, the Security Council. The General Assembly's resolution would have "*moral* force", implying in the context a *lack* of legal force.

As to Issue (2) above, namely whether the terms transmitting the Consensus Definition to Members and the Security Council went beyond mere exhortation or recommendation, the views expressed were almost as clear. M. Kolesnik pointed out that in paragraph 4 of Resolution 3314(XXIX) to which it was annexed, the General Assembly only "called attention" of the Security Council to the Definition and "recommends" that it should, as appropriate, take account of it "as guidance in determining, in accordance with the Charter, the existence of an act of aggression".[31] M. Migliuolo of Italy[32] saw the Definition as having "the same recommendatory status as any other General Assembly resolution", implying that, whatever its terms, its effect could not be more than recommendatory. Its legal consequences "were and remained those provided for in existing international law".[33] The Israel representative, M. Rosenne,[34] focusing particularly on this point, cited the view of the United Nations Office of Legal Affairs[35] that a "declaration" or "recommendation" could not be made binding upon Member States, in the sense of a treaty or convention, by the device of terming it a "declaration" rather than a "recommendation". This truth also held, he pointed out, for the term "Definition".[36] The resolution, said M. Villagren-Kramer, would have a "declaratory" and not a "law-making" effect.[37] For M. Bracklo, the definition was to be recommended by the General Assembly for use, hence it has to be "in conformity with the Charter while avoiding the impression of complementing it."[38]

We have already observed on the important point supplementing the fact that Paragraph 4 of the transmitting Resolution 3314(XXIX) merely "recommended" the Definition as guidance to the Security Council. (So far as Member States were concerned it did not even do this.) It is that Paragraph 3 called upon States "to refrain from acts of aggression and other uses of force" *not as specified in the Definition,* but as "contrary to the Charter ... and the Declaration ... Concerning Friendly Relations between States in Accordance with the Charter ..." (*sic*).

V

It will be seen throughout this work how, on critical substantive points, opposed positions constantly confronted and succeeded in neutralising each other, leaving the final text in the Consensus Definition ambivalent or vacuous for concrete situations. It is at first sight eerie in such a context to observe how wide was the agreement that the Definition could not legally bind the Security Council and its Permanent Members. A second look reveals, however, that this unusual area of agreement is really only an exception which proves the general rule of ambivalence or vacuity springing from opposed and mutually neutralising positions.[39] In this area the failure of the Definition to make any difference follows from *the agreement* that the Charter with all its own ambivalences and other doubts prevails, as surely as it follows from the *opposed* positions on critical substantive points.

A number of delegations, indeed, thought that the Definition *should* legally bind the Security Council, but even they (as will emerge) reluctantly agreed that finally it did not. With the minor qualifications shortly to be mentioned, none of them framed an argument asserting that it *was* so binding. M. Hassouna of Egypt was emphatic that Article 2 *ought to* have removed any discretion of the Security Council to determine whether or not an aggression had been committed. The designated acts *should have* been made not merely *prima facie* but conclusive evidence of aggression. The Security Council's determination *should* have been "declaratory and not constitutive".[40] Obviously, in his view, it did not (as it stood) so bind, nor was it such conclusive evidence, presumably because of lack of precision and peremptoriness in its terms. (Issues (1) and (2) above.) The same orator later criticised the failure of the Resolution as finally submitted to include a "request to the Security Council to apply the Definition when discharging its responsibilities under the Charter."[41] (Issue 2, above.) M. Booh of the United Republic of Cameroon[42] complained of the likely continuance of abuse of the veto, and thought it *should have been* restricted. (Issue 4.) But this was precisely because, as he observed, the Security Council's discretionary powers under Article 39 were left legally intact by the Definition. Miss Mpagi of Uganda was of similar mind,[43] and M. Ikouebe of Congo added the explanation that the Security Council's performance was hampered by "the fact that the Council counted among its members some of the greatest perpetrators of aggression, and States which supported the aggressor countries."[44] Yet the only remedy he could see was by amendment of the Charter, which presumably was also what M. Booh had in mind in proposing restrictions on the veto.

VI

We come now to the respect in which a few delegations did suggest that the Definition might affect discretional power of the Security Council or the legal position of the alleged aggressor under the Charter. The bolder thesis is that Article 39 of the Charter read with Articles 2 and 3 of the Definition obliges the Security Council to find either that an act of aggression has occurred, or that it has not occurred, and does not permit a mere non-determination. The less bold thesis is that even if the Consensus Definition does not affect the Security Council's liberty to refrain from determining either way, it does change the effect of the refrainer on the legal position of the alleged aggressor.

According to the former, bolder, thesis, Article 39, before the Consensus Definition, was taken to mean that until and unless the Council determines that there is an act of aggression, no aggression legally exists. Yet the words of Article 39 were that the Council "*shall* determine the existence of any ... act of aggression." (Italics supplied.) And now, by virtue of the Consensus Definition, the Council's duty to decide one way or another thus implied is inescapable. For Articles 2 and 3 of this (the difficult argument runs) now make the first commission of the designated act "*prima facie* evidence of an act of aggression". The presumption thus created continues until rebutted by a determination that no aggression was committed.

The difficulty on the face of this thesis, so far as it seeks legally to compel a determination by the Security Council, is that the same Article 2 expressly provides that, despite such *prima facie* evidence, "the Security Council may, in conformity with the Charter, conclude that a determination that an act of aggression has been committed would not be justified". The most coherent argument seeking to overcome these express terms of Article 2 is that of the Spanish delegate Elias.[45] He insisted that the Security Council's liberty under Article 2 to find that a determination of aggression would not be justified must still, by the same words of Article 2, be exercised "in conformity with the Charter". It was not open to the Security Council merely *to abstain from determining* that an aggression had taken place, *as distinct from determining that no aggression had taken place*. For to abstain would be tantamount to an agreement among its members "not to declare that in a given case an act of aggression had existed." This would be at odds with the words of Article 39 of the Charter—"The Security Council *shall* determine . . ." —which *require* the Security Council to determine that question. It would thus not be in conformity with Article 39 of the Charter to interpret Article 2 of the Definition so as to allow the Security Council *to abstain* from determining it.[46] It would also change the functions of the Security Council contrary to paragraph 4 of the Preamble of the Consensual Definition itself, and the range of lawful use of force under the Charter, contrarily to Article 4 of it.

Among the many mansions of United Nations theology, few have ever been as strangely empty as this. M. Elias sought to exclude any meaning of Article 2 of the Consensual Definition which would permit the Security Council merely to refrain from determining that an aggression had taken place, as opposed to determining either that there had or had not been an act of aggression. For this purpose, he argued that on principle and by virtue of the words of Article 2 itself, that article must be held within the limits of the Charter. And since Article 39 opens with the words "The Security Council shall determine . . .", the Charter must be taken to require a determination and to exclude a mere refraining from such. Unfortunately the argument breaks down at this very crucial point. For Article 39 goes on to read: "*any* threat to the peace, or act of aggression". The word "*any*" implies (as common sense also dictates) that the duty is one to determine the act of aggression if any—that is, if it deems there to be any. More important, however, than this point of mere exegesis is that Mr. Elias' thesis would require us to ignore the factual and legal reality of thirty years of practice of the Security Council. Not only had that body repeatedly exercised its liberty to refrain from making a determination, it had never in face of alleged aggression, done anything else but refrain. It has never yet made such a determination, though clearly among the more than a hundred resorts to major armed hostilities since 1945 quite a number, if not more, must have involved "aggression", however we define this. Even if the Definition could legally override the Charter (which M. Elias categorically denied it could), the meaning of Article 2 of the Definition which he laboured to show was inconsistent with the Charter, turns out to be precisely what the Charter in terms both of exegesis and practice must mean.

VII

The less bold claim that the Consensus Definition has affected the operation of Article 39 of the Charter, does not assert a change in the Security Council's powers, but only in the effect on the legal position of the alleged aggressor of that body's failure to determine whether or not an act of aggression has occurred.

The Egyptian delegate, M. Hassouna, as already seen,[47] criticised Article 2 for making the first designated act merely *prima facie* rather than conclusive evidence of aggression. This very criticism presupposes that, as Article 2 stands, it is *not* conclusive. Other delegations, however, attempted (though without much sustained argument) to read a degree of conclusiveness even into Article 2 as it stands. M. Mai'ga of Mali[48] argued that the Security Council's discretion under Article 2 did not give it power to determine aggression otherwise than in conformity with the Definition. He seemed inadvertent, as M. Elias had been, to the Security Council's discretion under the text of Article 39 of the Charter itself. Nor did he refer to the question how, if the definitional text was not "in conformity with the Charter", that text could, either on principle, or in view of Articles 2 and 4 of the Consensual Definition itself, amend the Charter. M. Obadi of Democratic Yemen[49] pronounced, rather oracularly, that under Article 2, first use of armed force was an act of aggression which *not even the Security Council could justify*. He meant, presumably, that the Council must decide either that there was or was not an act of aggression, and that a mere refrainer from determination cannot determine that aggression has *not* been committed. M. Mahmud[50] came more directly to the point, with the thesis that if "the Security Council did not specifically determine otherwise, the presumption of aggression would remain" under Articles 2 and 3; and M. Njenga of Kenya[51] spelled out the same thought:

> The presumption of aggression provided for in article 2 should continue to operate until the State which first used force . . . was exonerated by the Security Council. If the Council was prevented from taking a decision . . . [the victim] was entitled to take measures to eliminate the effects of the aggression. That was the only interpretation . . . which was rational.

It was to this kind of argument that M. Wehry replied when he said that the Security Council might still properly under the Consensus Definition continue its wise practice of not determining the question of aggression if it so thought fit. The reference to *"prima facie* evidence" in Article 2 did not, even in combination with Article 3, allow "implicit determination of the existence of ... aggression" merely because the Security Council does not reach a decision to exculpate.[52]

This particular line of argument was given a nice collateral twist by M. Bessou of France.[53] He thought the words "in contravention of the Charter" qualifying "the first use of armed force" in the opening line of Article 2, were regrettable, "since an aggressor might claim that he was acting in accordance with his own interpretation of the Charter." M. Bessou had no objection to the words as addressed solely to the Security Council, so that he would not have agreed with suggestions like those of MM. Mai'ga, Obadi or Mahmud that the Definition could inhibit the Security Council's freedom to refrain from determining whether or not an aggression had taken place. What he objected to was the possible meaning that where no such determination was made, each State at variance could unilaterally determine that the other had first resorted to force "in contravention of the Charter".

This, of course, is a real problem, but it is not a problem newly arising under the Consensus Definition. It already existed under the Charter, where armed attack gave and still gives rise to the overriding liberty of self-defence under Article 51, until the Security Council takes action, whether this be the "action necessary to maintain ... international peace and security" under Article 51, or a determination of "threat to the peace, etc." and consequential action under Article 39, and following articles. Necessarily, if the requisite majority for such action is not available, the arena is left free for what M. Njenga called the putative victim's measures to meet the "aggression", and what M. Bessou regards as its "unilateral determination". But all this was so under the Charter, and is in no way a new legal result of the Consensual Definition.[54] And it would have continued to exist after the Consensus Definition, even if the probably redundant words "in contravention of the Charter" had not appeared in Article 2.

VIII

It is probably such *non*-differences made by the Consensual Definition which M. Migliuolo had in mind when he said that the legal consequences of the Definition "were and remained those provided for in existing international law".[55] It is only in the light of the above careful analysis that puzzles like those set by Belgium's M. Van Brusselen are to be resolved. He declared that "if the General Assembly adopted the draft definition, it would then be regarded as part of positive law" and contained principles to which the Security Council could refer. He then added, almost in the same breath, that "it in no way limited its powers and prerogative, and the Council alone could determine whether an act of aggression had been committed."[56]

No less paradoxically, the most ambitious bid to show that the Definition is "binding on all States and even on the Security Council", resolves itself on full analysis into an assertion that whatever was the legal position before adoption of the Consensus Definition is also the position after it. In a *tour de force* as impressive as its circularity, M. Yasseen of Iraq, proceeded as follows:[57]

(1) The Consensus Definition could not be more important than the Charter;

(2) Adoption of it by the General Assembly would mean acceptance of its terms as "explaining the exact meaning of the Charter";

(3) It would follow that the Definition "must be binding on all States and even on the Security Council, which derived its authority from the Charter and could not fail to be bound by it".

Pausing here, it is to be noted that (3) would be a *non sequitur* unless, indeed, the terms accepted by the General Assembly (under (2) above) as "explaining the exact meaning of the Charter" *correctly state that exact meaning.* For the General Assembly has no legal authority to settle the meaning of the Charter except for the purposes and within the limits of its own domestic proceedings; and this exception certainly does not include the determination of aggression.

(4) Setting this problem aside, we proceed to M. Yasseen's next step. This was to admit that "legally, the definition . . . would take the form of a General Assembly resolution and would therefore only have the force of a recommendation"; yet simultaneously to insist that its substance would be the very stuff of the Charter, which States are bound to respect, and that it is not liable to the same conflicts of interpretation as the Charter.[58]

Here, again, the present writer has to point out the persistent *non sequitur.* Unless in fact (and not merely in the opinion of the General Assembly) the terms of the Definition are "the very stuff of the Charter", the conclusion that Members are bound by them does not follow. Moreover, even if they were (on this assumption) binding, they would be "binding" only within the leeways of the conflicts and indeterminacies of meaning embodied—sometimes deliberately—in the Charter itself.[59] This valiant demonstration thus disappears finally into a tautology. Insofar as the General Assembly adopts as its Consensus Definition the law concerning the powers and obligations of Members of the Security Council under the Charter and international law existing prior to the Consensus Definition, that Definition will be binding because *ex hypothesi* the pre-existing Charter and international law are binding.

Once the circularity is recognised, there is little difficulty (and also little significance) in agreeing with M. Yasseen that *within the above most severe limits* the definition would bind the United Nations and its organs and its Members. That learned orator himself may have come near to seeing how little distance his circular argument had taken him. For he finally added the hope that application in practice of the Consensus Definition would "*in the long term*" give the force of "custom" to the Definition.[60] Binding law does not require to become custom to make it binding, though it may require observance to make it effective.

IX

A curious feature of this part of the recent aggression debates is the sparsity and low-key of references to either the standing of the Consensus Definition in the General Assembly, or generally to the actual role of the General Assembly in peace-keeping. This is despite the notable record of that body under the Uniting for Peace Resolutions, and despite the apparent value of an agreed definition of aggression for promoting voluntary cooperation of members in peace-keeping operations.[61]

It is, of course, natural that the Western Powers and those aligned with them, fearing hostile majorities on many matters in an expanded General Assembly, may have wished to check any nascent expansions of its role. Of course, too, the Soviet Union has steadily opposed, since the Korean Affair, what it regards as usurpation by the General Assembly of the Security Council's exclusive powers of peace enforcement under Chapter 7 of the Charter. While the Soviet bloc now often finds itself aligned with anti-Western majorities in that body, it is still jealous of admitting these majorities to peace-enforcing prerogatives. The power to determine an aggressor, is thus a power which Moscow shows little sign of conceding to General Assembly majorities *which it cannot be sure of controlling* in every conceivable circumstance.

What remains somewhat mysterious is the apparent low key of concern or even disinterest of non-aligned States, in promoting the General Assembly's role. Among the few explicit references from any quarter was that of M. Petrella of the Argentine, who pointed out that the Security Council's powers "did not prejudice the subsidiary powers which had in practice been developed for other United Nations bodies".[62] There was, as we shall later see, a strong bid by many non-aligned States to establish the "inherent right of self-determination" alongside that of self-defence under Article 51 of the Charter, as a basis for licensing use of force under Article 7 of the Definition. And against that background, it is significant that M. Petrella supported his championship of other United Nations bodies by pointing out that it was the General Assembly which had "established" the right of self-determination.

Yet perhaps the mystery is not so great when we remember the constant unmistakable pressure of non-aligned States to read down the Security Council's powers, and the frequent insistence that its determinations are "declaratory" and not "constitutive" so that a *prima facie* "aggressor" under Article 2 of the Consensus Definition may be legally treated as an aggressor even if the Security Council "concludes" (as Article 2 permits) that a determination of aggression would not, in all the relevant circumstances, be justified.[63] Such positions, insofar as sustained, would leave to the so-called "automatic majorities" in the General Assembly a residual legacy of *de facto* power to determine aggression. The bid for a transfer of power to that body was perhaps sufficiently strong on that implied and unspoken level, to make it neither necessary nor prudent to voice expressly ambitions which might meet the adamant resistance of both Western and Soviet blocs.

Professor Schwebel has, if anything, added to this mystery in his attempted explanation. He points out[64] that both the (non-aligned) Thirteen Power Draft, paragraph 2 and Soviet Draft, paragraph 6, seem to provide that only action under authority of the Security Council (*not* also the General Assembly) qualifies as action under authority of the "United Nations". Only the (Western) Six Power Draft (Art. III) he observes, referred *simpliciter* to "authorisation by competent United Nations organs" without exclusively specifying the Security Council.

He finds it surprising, referring back to the earlier history of this matter, that so many small States ("third world" States?) sided with the Soviet Union in its 1964 and 1965 refusal to act in accordance with the International Court's holding that the General Assembly was sufficiently competent to recommend and take peace-keeping measures, so as to make the expenses of these measures apportionable against Members as United Nations expenses under Article 17(2) of the Charter. He finds it still more "puzzling and remarkable" that the Thirteen Powers in 1972, by not admitting General Assembly authorisation as a basis for use of force, should now seek to cut back General Assembly powers, from what the International Court had recognised, rather than agreeing with the Six Powers (including the United States and United Kingdom as Permanent Members) in acknowledging such General Assembly powers. And it is clear in this and most other contexts that the Thirteen Power Draft bears a close relation to the views of the so-called non-aligned States and "Group of 77" in the General Assembly.[65]

On the other hand, Professor Schwebel found it *not* surprising that the Soviet Union maintained its traditional position of resisting an extension or recognition of extension of General Assembly powers. And he wondered how long the United States and the United Kingdom will continue to champion wider powers of the General Assembly in this regard, if the smaller States are not willing to support this wider view of its powers. And in this complex of puzzles he thought, as at 1972, that at any rate in the definition of aggression context, differences about the authority of the General Assembly were insoluble, so that the question would have to be avoided by the use of language which did not specify which organ was authorised to use force.

What remains of this analysis in the light of the post-1972 history? Superficially, a good deal. First, the above provisions of the Soviet and Thirteen Power Drafts, apparently omitting General Assembly competence, do not appear in the Consensus Definition. Second, there is left standing the recital in paragraph 5 of the Soviet Draft that Article 39 confers the powers of determining aggression, etc. and of peace enforcement on the Security Council. Third, there is included in paragraph 4 of the Preamble of the Definition a recital that "nothing in this Definition shall be interpreted as in any way affecting the scope of the provisions of the Charter with respect to the functions and powers of the organs of the United Nations". It would thus appear that the issue as to the *legal authority* of the General Assembly in relation to peace enforcement (including determination of aggression, etc.) or even to mere use of force in peacekeeping operations is left, without further clarification, as it was before the Consensus Definition. To this extent the Schwebel analysis was correct.

This analysis, however, darkens rather than illuminates the more important question as to the *political authority* of the General Assembly, that is the facilities and instruments by which the General Assembly can assume, without serious challenge, competence to deal even with questions which may legally be exclusively within Security Council competence. And it is important to correct, in this respect, the insights afforded by Professor Schwebel's analysis of Great Power and Small Power attitudes with regard to force authorised by the General Assembly.

This is especially necessary in view of the starkly opposed positions as to the meaning of Article 3(f) and (g) and Article 7 of the Consensus Definition in their bearing on the question whether Article 7 expressed the liberty of any people struggling for self-determination *to use armed force* against the parent State, and the liberty of third States to aid them *in this*. This substantial issue itself will be examined at length in Chapter 6. But it is also the most important context for gauging State attitudes towards the authority of the General Assembly. As we have seen, and will further see in Chapter 6, the Western States denied that force could lawfully be used in such struggles, while a wide range of Asian, African, Communist and non-aligned States were emphatic, to use the eloquent words of Cuban delegate Alvarez Tabio,[66] that Article 7 made it legitimate to use armed force "to defend the inalienable right of peoples to self-determination". Even if, as the present writer believes, a correct legal interpretation negates any such claim, recognition that this point remained thus debatable even after the Consensus Definition gives quite another dimension to Professor Schwebel's discussion about whether the General Assembly is an organ which can authorise legitimate use of force under the Charter.

Clearly, under the rule that each principal organ of the United Nations is in control of its own proceedings, nothing could prevent the General Assembly from declaring that a given conflict was one in which a people was struggling for self-determination and was therefore entitled to use armed force, and entitled to receive armed support from third States in this by way of collective self-defence. Thus, a resolution like that on the Palestine Liberation Organisation of November 22, 1974[67] has already laid ground for this, by expressly approving in Paragraph 5 the use of "all means" by the Palestine Liberation Organisation for achieving its ends. The very gross illegalities, and even floutings of the General Assembly's own positions by that Resolution[68] gave an advance display, prior to the adoption of the Consensus Definition on December 14, 1974, of the irresponsible licence that can be expected in the "Group

of 77" in the General Assembly (now moving beyond 100). If a resolution so reckless of legalities could be passed without the aid and comfort
of the built-in contradictions of the Consensus Definition, how much
more easily will this occur now that that aid and comfort are available.

In this new dimension, we must expose two other puzzles for ponder-
ing, somewhat at odds with those offered by Schwebel. The first puzzle
is as to how Western States and their advisers can have so failed to
perceive the dangers looming for them from steady "automatic"
majorities of a certain orientation in the General Assembly, that they
offered even ambiguous support in the Six Power draft to pretensions
of the General Assembly to competence to authorise the use of force.
Noblesse oblige is not a principle of the Charter, nor even of international politics, and even less of that momentous part of international
politics concerned with the imputation of aggression. It is rather an
understatement for Professor Schwebel to refer to "certain dangers"
for the security interests of Western States from their own draft, when
he has characterised as "puzzling and remarkable"[69] the apparent failure
of the small and middle States to support the enlargement of General
Assembly powers which would be so advantageous to them. Of course,
we share his surprise as regards the small and middle Powers to a degree.
Yet we would add even there that the need for surprise is perhaps
reduced when we recognise the room for manoeuvre afforded to General
Assembly majorities by the conflicting views as to the legitimation of
force for ostensibly "liberation" struggles under Article 7.

The other ground of surprise neglected by Professor Schwebel concerns the Soviet position. He thinks that that State's maintenance of its
traditional view as to the exclusive Security Council competence over
the use of armed force is "no cause for surprise".[70] The present writer
begs respectfully to differ. The traditional Soviet position was, as seen
in Chapter 1 above, first fully formulated when the Western Powers
in 1950, after the Soviet return to the Security Council, shifted the
Korean Affair into the General Assembly, and secured the passing of the
Uniting for Peace Resolutions. Its opposition to the role of the General
Assembly, in which the Western States could at that time usually (though
even then not automatically) marshal majorities, was understandable.
It perhaps continued so as the number of Third World Members began
to multiply with the process of decolonisation, in the late 'fifties and
early 'sixties. For the legal and financial implications of the Korean
Affair and Middle East 1956 crisis were still working themselves out,
through the Advisory Opinion on Certain Expenses of the United
Nations,[71] and the struggle in the General Assembly in 1964-1965 concerning budget contributions due from the Soviet Union.

It must have become plain to Soviet leaders, however, long before
1974, that a General Assembly in which Soviet and satellite votes, added
to the expanding Group of 77, could usually produce even a two-thirds
majority, was a far more effective instrument of its own policies than the
General Assembly of the 'forties and 'fifties had been of Western

policies. Soviet persistence in asserting into 1974 that "only the Security Council has the right to use force on behalf of the United Nations to maintain or restore international peace",[72] seems therefore also on its face surprising. One explanation may perhaps be that Soviet spokesmen recognised the wide power *de facto* falling to the General Assembly, in any case, by dint of the equivocations of the Consensus Definition, and the paralysis of the Security Council by vetoes. In these circumstances, they might well calculate, the Soviet Union might even have its cake (reserve the right to challenge the legality of General Assembly authority to use force in the unlikely contingency of itself facing a hostile majority), and also eat its cake (enjoy the political advantages of association with and manipulation of the present anti-western orientated majority blocs in the General Assembly).

A related difficulty affects another stimulating comment of Professor Schwebel,[73] as regards the possibility of clarifying the legal meaning of aggression through "case-by-case" definition by the Security Council and the General Assembly. He thinks that serious progress cannot be expected along this path since rulings on aggression by these bodies have been so rare. He adds that "in view of the manner in which the Security Council and the General Assembly have for the most part functioned in recent years", this state of affairs is "just as well".[74] When, however, we consider the potential use of the Consensus Definition by General Assembly majorities in political warfare rather than for legal determinations in peace enforcement, there is little comfort in this conclusion. Here again the learned writer's analysis stops just short of manifest political realities. These realities involve the many critical conflicts between State interests now covered under the cloak of verbal consensus of the Consensus Definition, which will be explored in the succeeding Chapters, and the role of the General Assembly in handling them to which the final Chapter will return.

CHAPTER 4

Priority of Act and Aggressive Intent

I

How far the *intention* of the putative aggressor is a constituent element of what is stigmatised as aggression has been perhaps the most continuously central issue throughout the fifty-year debate about the definition of aggression. It is not difficult to see why it was so controverted. Insofar as definition is sought for the purpose of deterring aggressors (and thus reassuring their prospective victims), and for guiding States and United Nations organs, as well as inspiring Members to quick cooperative action in a crisis, precise, objectively recognisable criteria seem strongly indicated. To require reference to the alleged aggressor's intentions would, it is argued, work against such precision and objectivity. "The devil himself", in the common law adage, "knoweth not the mind of man!". If this is so even for individuals, how much less knowable is the "mind" or "intention" or "purpose" which is to be imputed to the complex and often diffuse process of decision-making within the apparatus of a State! And even when particular national leaders openly launch what history shows to be calculated aggressions, they often cloak this carefully in language of self-defence, legitimate defence of rights, *Lebensraum, liberation,* and the rest. So that, it is concluded, to make intent of the impugned actor-State an element of definition, invites defeat for all the purposes of definition.

The value of such arguments, as the present writer pointed out in 1958, may vary according to the kind of operation in which a definition is proposed to be used. If the operation envisaged is international action to restore peace in a crisis, that is one situation. If the operation envisaged is criminal prosecution of individuals for the crime of aggressive warmaking, which can be a process well after the event, that (at least in some respects) is another.[1] Thus, one might say, the aggression symbol has special value for triggering quick voluntary cooperation of Members precisely because of its emotive value components. Also since precision and objective import are vital for quick decisive action for peace-keeping in an emergency, this operation cannot brook the delays involved in inquiries about intention, and this element should be excluded from the definition. On the other hand, since trials of individuals for war crimes can be more leisurely, the delays involved by including intent and purpose as a factor are not serious. Moreover, on the contrary, the traditions of western countries dictate that in general criminality requires not only that the act be a guilty one (*actus reus*), but also that it be done with a guilty mind (*mens rea*).

So that the main desiderata for an efficient definition conflict as between the two functions of peace enforcement in a crisis, and criminal punishment of individuals. But the matter is rendered still more difficult by the fact that subordinate desiderata may conflict with the main ones, even *within each function*. This is clearest as to peace enforcement. The emotive components of the aggression symbol which offer hope of triggering quick voluntary cooperation of Members also, because of these very emotive-value references, invite subjective reactions of each State in a crisis, thus permitting differences and delays of judgment. When it is sought to forestall such conflicts or delays, precise, objective criteria are offered to guide States and organs, and inspire common cooperative reactions of third States. Yet simplification of criteria usually, by omitting emotive-value elements, also dampens the desired trigger-effect. And, moreover, as Austen Chamberlain long ago observed, such simplified criteria can serve as a signpost for the aggressor and a trap for the unwary State. Insofar as the ill-intentioned can with impunity thus manipulate them, the objective of deterring the aggressor is defeated. When States are sensitive (as they usually are) to these ambivalences, cynicism at the pretence of precision and objectivity of criteria will impair rather than enhance swift cooperation in peace enforcement. And such conflicts may be found also within the judicial-criminal function. For there, while precise objective criteria are not needed for inspiring swift cooperation of States, they may still be called for because we should avoid imposing *ex post facto* punishment, especially when we are trying men for their lives.

The question, then, whether aggression should imply the *animus aggressionis* is necessarily plagued by these ambivalences within each function. But the greatest source of confusion remains the historical failure to distinguish between the functions of peace enforcement on the one hand, and punishment of individual crimes on the other. The first United Nations impulse towards defining aggression arose precisely in the area of criminal punishment of individuals rather than peace enforcement. The mandate given to the Committee on Progressive Development of International Law and its Codification, by the resolution of December 11, 1946, opened the effort to formulate the principles of the Charter and Judgment of the Nuremberg Tribunal, and to draft a code of offences against the peace and security of mankind impinging on the present matters. This, then, was directed to criminal punishment of individuals. It was (as already seen) only after 1950 that definition in aid of peace enforcement came to dominate and (partly by reason of failure to distinguish the problems involved)[2] to confuse the debates.

After 1950, in this context of efforts to build up the General Assembly peace-making functions to replace those of the Security Council paralysed by Great Power vetoes, the question of defining aggression became a major diplomatic political, rather than merely legal, issue. And this impetus increased when the International Law Commission abandoned the search for full definition in the criminal law context, and fell back by way of compromise (in Article 2 of its Draft Code of Offences against Peace and Security of Mankind) on listing mere non-exhaustive illustrations of acts which were and acts which were not "acts of aggression".[3] General Assembly efforts proceeded (as was seen in Chapter 2) through its Sixth Committee and the series of Special Committees of which the Fourth produced the Consensus Definition of 1974.

The "aggression" notion thus moved towards the centre of the post-World War II stage in two distinct roles—the judicial-criminal and the political-military. The gist of the former, symbolised by "the Nuremberg Principles" was the punishment of individuals for "the planning, preparation, initiation and waging of a war of aggression, or a war in violation of international treaties". Simultaneously, as seen in Chapter 1, the "aggression" notion had also figured in Article 39 of the Charter as one trigger, along with "any threat to the peace [or] breach of the peace", for the Security Council's peace enforcement powers.[4] The draftsmen of both the Nuremberg and San Francisco Charters deliberately refrained from defining "aggression".[5] The latter, by conferring full peace-enforcing powers on the Security Council as to any mere threat to the peace or breach of the peace, whether or not there was also aggression, probably intended to avoid any *need* for the Security Council to resort to the notion at all.

This duality of history made it, perhaps, the more important to distinguish the problems of definition as they affect these distinct functions. In broad terms, as already seen, this seems easy to state. In relation to punishment of individuals, effectiveness as a deterrent and the policy against *ex post facto* punishment may seem to demand precise and objective criteria in advance definition. Yet basic traditions of criminal law demand a requirement of *mens rea,* and the more leisurely judicial enquiry after the event is also tolerant of more refined and complex criteria, including such questions of purpose and intent. On the other hand, in relation to peace-enforcing or peace-keeping action of the Security Council or General Assembly, precision and objectivity are also called for, but here the military crisis situation involved is not tolerant, in terms of time for deliberation, of the addition of complex or subjective elements, such as the intentions or purposes of the alleged aggressor. Yet, insofar as General Assembly peace-keeping depends on inspiring Members to swift voluntary cooperation, there is a strong temptation also to intrude into the precise objective criteria, an emotive symbolism capable of stirring States to voluntary assumption of heavy risks and burdens. It is clear therefore that there is a certain inconsistency of the desiderata with each function: and it is no less clear that some differences between the two functions remain important. Even as early as the 1956 Special Committee, delegates became concerned that differences arising from the different addressees of the norms, and the different sanctions, might lead to contradiction between separate definitions directed to the respective functions.[6]

II

As an element which tends, if embodied in a definition, both to complicate and subjectivise the process of judgment, the role of the intention element in defining aggression is caught in the centre of these confusions. Further perplexities also spring from the difficulty of saying what precisely would be the *mens rea* involved if intention were to be admitted as an element in definition of aggression.

In relation to criminal punishment, it certainly seems unthinkable that some *mens rea* should not be required for so grave an individual crime.[7] While, in relation to politico-military tasks of peace-keeping, it is difficult also to see how any *mens rea* apt for punishment of individuals could be apt also for the purpose of the peace-enforcement and peace-keeping purposes. Even thinkers deeply convinced that the aggression notion is absolutely necessary for peace enforcement admit that a requirement of proof of *mens rea* might impede this function.[8] Definers of aggression, therefore, unless they sharply separate the two functions, face the awkwardness that it may be necessary ethically and in terms of the concept of "crime" to require and define the *mens rea* in "aggression", and yet also conceptually impossible and practically unwise to do this for purposes of peace enforcement and peace-keeping.[9]

The perplexity, however, runs deeper still. For this "necessity" which is also an "impossibility" may (as seen in Section I) sometimes exist even *within the peace enforcement and peace-keeping function itself.* There are cases where, except by reference to the mental element accompanying the warlike action, we cannot distinguish "aggression" from innocent action. Was the impugned action honestly taken in legitimate "self-defence"? For example, was it a mere accidental projection of a missile into foreign territory?[10] Corresponding problems have, of course, arisen as to *mens rea* of corporations in municipal law.[11] Yet, however it be as to the solutions there adopted, it is clear that the complexity of the policy-making process in many modern States, especially democratic States, makes it doubtful whether we can *always* identify the mind or minds whose content in relation to the impugned action we impute to the State as *mens rea.* The bridge between "necessity" and "impossibility" would have to be a constructive or imputed *mens rea,* drawn as best we may from the chronology of external events and our notions of what was "reasonable" in face of them.

III

It is a symptom, perhaps, of intellectual regression, that such problems surrounding the question of *animus aggressionis,* already recognisable in 1958, stirred little thought in the debates leading to the 1974 Consensus Definition. The issue starkly divided the participants; but it did so on the crude level of yes or no, and it remains on this level even under the 1974 Definition, with a final text arguably saying both yes and no.

In the draft of Article 2 immediately preceding that final text, it was expressly provided that the circumstances to be taken into account in determining whether a first resort to force in violation of the Charter justifies a determination of aggression, included "purposes of the States involved".[12] One of the changes which emerged in the course of the informal proceedings leading up to "the consensus" was the substitution of the present formula in Article 2. In this present formula any express reference to purposes or intention has been eliminated, but the reference to "the relevant circumstances" to be taken into account is so broad that it is difficult to see how it can exclude an element so important as the intent with which the *"prima facie"* stigmatised act is done.

This difficulty is increased when we recall the emphatic importance attached to intention by many States right into the consensus stage. The Draft Proposal of the Six Powers (Australia, Canada, Italy, Japan, U.K. and U.S.A.) stipulated as essential elements a list of acts which *might* constitute aggression, *but would only do so if they were committed for any of certain enumerated purposes* listed in the very next Paragraph. These purposes were: (1) to diminish the territory or alter the boundaries of another State; (2) to alter international agreed lines of demarcation; (3) to disrupt or interfere with the conduct of the affairs of another State; (4) to secure changes in the Government of another State; or (5) to inflict harm or obtain concessions of any sort. This critical role of purpose or intention was further underlined by the provision in Paragraph III of the Six Power Draft that "the use of force in the exercise of the inherent right of individual or collective self-defence, or pursuant to decisions of or authorisations by competent United Nations organs . . . consistent with the Charter of the United Nations, does not constitute aggression".[13]

IV

The role of the intention element was thus still a main bone of contention right into the final stages of the Consensus Definition. It was presented, indeed, both before and after consensus was achieved almost as a rival to, and certainly as a delimitation of, the so-called "priority principle". A "priority principle" which can be displaced by the Security Council's judgment concerning "other relevant circumstances" and concerning whether the Charter has been "contravened" remains today a focus of conflicting interpretations of the key Article 2 of the Definition. Even commentators partial to the definitional enterprise depict this matter as one on which the negotiators were only concerned "to reach a consensus *regarding the phrases* in the text", not about their *"meaning"*.[13a]

"The priority principle" had been the keystone of Soviet proposals ever since M. Litvinov first offered it to the League of Nations Disarmament Conference in 1933. In the classical explanation by Greek statesman Nicolai Politis at that Conference, the principle fixes culpability for aggression by the chronology of events. That State which first *commits* any act designated by the definition is the aggressor. Conversely, once that moment and that culpable State are thus fixed, the opponent's response, even by acts of the designated kind, is to be seen as legitimate defence and not as aggression.

Stephen M. Schwebel[14] has acutely pinpointed the "profound dangers", exposed in the last four decades, of too facile a resort to this Litvinov-Politis principle.[15] One danger is of assuming that the question, who did what to whom first, can always or even usually be simply established. Recent history abounds in cases of profound obscuration of the course of events, for instance by concealed operations, and by the forging of confused chains of events, quite apart from the well-known problems of frontier incidents and disputes, and (of course) of guarding against surprise nuclear attack.[16] Another danger is that "the specification"—we would rather say specific descriptions—of the designated acts in the definition will lead to undue weighting of *them,* and undue neglect of *non-listed acts,* in judging future situations. The need to avoid these dangers imbues the demands preceding the 1974 Consensus Definition that the priority principle be qualified by reference to the purposes or intentions of the States concerned.

The intent requirement of the Six Power Draft, quoted in the last section, distinguished it starkly from both the Soviet Draft, and the (non-aligned) Thirteen Power Draft. The requirement was criticised as placing on the victim of an armed attack the burden of showing with what intent the attack is made. This, it was said, would be especially unjust since intention is a subjective fact often difficult or even impossible to prove. Such objections assume that if intention is relevant, it must be shown by separate proof. This, of course, is not so. The more common situation, for instance, in criminal proceedings, is that intent is sufficiently inferable from the very circumstances in which the *actus reus* (here the designated act) is shown to have been committed. Intent need then only become a matter for separate proof by virtue of unusual pleas such as mistake or lack of mental capacity; and no undue burden of proof on the alleged victim would be involved. On the other hand, where intention is not inferable from the external facts, as where a war missile sent by one state lands on the territory of another and friendly State, only a showing of intention can distinguish between an external fact which is a mere accident and an act of first commission which constitutes aggression.

This leads to the more cogent objection to admission of intent as an element. This is that the external act designated as constituting aggression by the State first committing it, *may* be so designated *precisely in order to make it condemnable regardless of motive and intent,* however innocent or even benign. In short, motive and intent may be made irrelevant by the terms of the definition itself. This argument could be conclusive, provided that the designation of the external acts in question *did* indeed *refer only to external facts*, such as the entry of a missile on to the victim's territory. It breaks down, however, insofar as the designation itself contains a reference, express or implied, to motive or intention as well as external facts. If the designation were "entry of a missile on to the victim's territory from that of the putative aggressor", intent would be irrelevant. But if it were the "sending" of such a missile, intent would be as relevant as the fact of entry.

Suppose, for example, the Six Power proposal had been adopted designating as aggression "a use of force" resorted to "in order to diminish the territory or alter the boundaries of another State, etc." *The specified intent element would then clearly have been part of the designated facts* which, if first committed by a State, constitute aggression. It would have been, strictly speaking, one of the very facts in issue. But the mere fact that the *explicit* reference to intent or purpose was omitted, does not foreclose the question whether the intent element is a part of the designated facts by reason that they fall within "other relevant circumstances".

This position is sometimes sought to be met head-on by urging that to insist on designating intention as part of the facts charged would sabotage the whole definitional enterprise.[17] But does this not beg the question? By its very terms, Article 39 of the Charter concerns determination of "breach of the peace" as well as "act of aggression"; and if these notions are ever to be distinguished from each other, as they must, intent or purpose must be a decisive criterion. Again, how could there be an "armed attack" under Article 51 without intent? The Six Powers could also support this answer by reference to the phrase "*against* the territorial integrity or political independence of another State" in Article 2(4) of the Charter, which is now pivotally embodied in Article 1 of the Consensus Definition, as it was in Paragraph II of the Six Power Draft.[18] I have recently examined in the opening Chapter of *Of Law and Nations* (1974, especially S.VI) the reasons why the word "against" must there import an *intention to impair* territorial integrity or political independence similar to that made explicit in the Six Power Draft. They will again be referred to in Section IX of the present Chapter.

In the complex give-and-take among the delegations leading to the Consensus, the Six Powers' express statement of intent or purpose, side by side with an external fact (being one of the designated acts) was replaced, in Article 2 of the Consensus Definition, by a qualification on the priority principle. In its initial form, this qualification required due regard to be had, in concluding whether a finding of aggression is justified, to "other relevant circumstances including, as evidence, the purposes of the States involved". In the final text this wording was again changed to "other relevant circumstances, including the fact that the acts concerned or their consequences are not of sufficient gravity". Can one infer from this history of the text that the Six Power view was reversed and the priority principle left quite unqualified by intention?

Certainly, as will shortly appear, this was not the understanding of States which pressed for express reference to intention or purpose. Nor does it automatically follow from the mere dropping of such express references. They may have been dropped as redundant, on the basis that intention and purpose are necessarily embraced in "relevant circumstances" of acts. So that intention and purpose would still be impliedly referred to, unless it can be cogently shown that these elements *cannot be relevant* in identifying the acts designated in the Consensus Definition. In addition, of course, since Article 6 of that Definition explicitly saves whatever limits on lawful use of force were set by the Charter, that designation must include the distinction between mere "breach of the peace" and "aggression" in Article 39 of the Charter, as well as the more likely meaning of the word "against" in Article 2(4) of it (which in any case is, as already seen, substantially reproduced in Article 1 of the Consensus Definition itself).

V

On the one hand, the plea of self-defence rests on the principle of priority as virtually self-evident; the State *first* resorting to stigmatised acts is the aggressor, and the response to that *prior* force is exculpated. This exculpation could, indeed, also be grounded on the lack of "aggressive intention" of the self-defending State, and in the standard case this concurrence of priority and intention criteria presents no problems. In *anticipatory* self-defence the priority criterion points *ex hypothesi* one way (regarding the response as aggressive) while, assuming the plea to be in good faith, the criterion of intention points the other (regarding the response as non-culpable).

The interplay of the dubieties of the Charter with those of the Consensus Definition is admirably exemplified in relation to the chronic controversy whether there can be circumstances in which a threatened State may resort to "anticipatory self-defence" (sometimes loosely termed "preemptive strike").

The arguments for excluding such resort rest mainly on renderings of Article 2(4) and Article 51 of the Charter. First is the view of Article 2(4) which reads its prohibition of "threat or use of force" as if the qualification following that phrase ("against the territorial integrity etc.") were not a substantial one. Some objections to this will be discussed in Section IX. Another objection is that this rendering assumes that "threat or use of force" refers only to *armed* force, which is far from self-evident. If the prohibited "force" is not so limited, then the question would remain open what range of force is lawful by way of response to the various kinds of "force" which the Paragraph prohibits.

Second, it is argued that anticipatory self-defence is always prohibited because Article 51 of the Charter provides that "nothing in the present Charter shall impair the inherent right of individual or collective self-defence if an armed attack occurs against a Member . . .". It is said that by these very terms the licitness of self-defence is limited to the situation *after an armed attack has occurred*. Two considerations make this conclusion rather problematic. First, this view assumes that the words "if an armed attack occurs" qualify the words "nothing in the present Charter shall impair". So that the phrase is an adverbial phrase of time, indicating the moment as from which the non-impairment arises. But this is a strained interpretation. In the standing text the words in question are more apt to be an adjectival phrase describing *the kind of self-defence which is not impaired, namely, self-defence against armed attack*. Second, this view assumes that Article 51 became the only legal basis for self-defence under international law after the Charter came into effect. By its terms, however, Article 51 does not purport to state the exhaustive range of self-defence under international law, but *only to protect the self-defence which it describes from being impaired by any restriction contained in the Charter*. Insofar as acts of self-defence may be within the wider range of self-defence permitted by international law, *and these acts are not prohibited by the Charter*, Article 51 would not affect them either way. Being thus lawful, and not prohibited by the Charter, they remain lawful without any aid from the "saving" clause of Article 51.

Those who interpret Article 2(4) in the sense restrictive of self-defensive action by States, tend also to interpret Article 51 in a similar sense. And these interpretations of the two Articles then support each other, and produce usually the wishful conclusions that all use of armed force by Members is prohibited except (1) self-defensive force in response to "armed attack" and (2) "collective measures" authorised by United Nations organs. Unfortunately, the mere fact that a dubious interpretation of one Article of the Charter is supported by a dubious interpretation of another Article, does not remove the dubiety of either interpretation. Nor does it remove the dubiety of the conclusion drawn from both together. We have elsewhere argued at length both the technical questions of interpretation and the issues of policy involved. They lead this writer to conclude that the limits of lawful resort to force are far wider after the Charter than the above restrictivist view rather confidently asserts.[19]

At the present point, we are only concerned to show the persistence of these doubts on the vital question of anticipatory self-defence, despite the advent of the Consensus Definition. After that Definition, as before it, those who take the restrictivist view can still deny the legitimacy of *anticipatory military initiatives* even in cases of the severest imminence of armed attack by the adversary. They can also invoke the priority principle of Article 2 of the Definition as confirming that whoever attacks first is the aggressor.

Those who reject the restrictivist positions, however, may not only continue to deny that Article 2(4) and Article 51 lead to any such conclusion. They may also point out that Article 2 of the Consensual Definition itself does not make first use of armed force a conclusive, but only a *prima facie,* test of aggression. Moreover, they may point out that Article 2 itself goes on to authorise the Security Council to conclude "in the light of other relevant circumstances" that such first use in the particular case should not be characterised as aggression. And they could properly point out that relevant circumstances negativing aggression must include the fact that the complainant State or States had by concentration of forces or other measures faced the alleged aggressor with the choice of either armed response or submitting like a "sitting duck" to its own destruction.

What is clear in conventional warfare terms is even clearer in terms of nuclear warfare. As Professor D. P. O'Connell has observed,[20] to rule out anticipatory self-defence here would require that the victim of a nuclear attack submit to the risk of destruction by a "first strike". For "to await the launching of a controlled projectile ... may well be to lose the capacity of self-defence, for whoever employs his weapon first may have a pre-emptive advantage which can prove decisive." Thus, the Article 51 "inherent right of ... self-defence" may prove to be illusory if the phrase "if an armed attack occurs" is interpreted restrictively. In order to avoid denuding the concept of "self-defence", these words should be interpreted broadly and liberally and should include any increased tension or pressure which leaves the victim State with virtually no alternative save military response.[21] Thus, if the priority principle breaks down in conventional cases of anticipatory self-defence, its application is even more dangerous in "a nuclear age, when the victim of an attack can ... suffer unbearable casualties, at the first strike".[22]

Yet, even as to nuclear warfare, arguments have been offered for the absolute exclusion of anticipatory self-defence. Tom Farer has offered a thoughtful, if not wholly convincing response, to the "creative and inquisitive" minds who have pressed the continued legal importance of anticipatory self-defence.[23] In his view they have failed to "examine with wonted care the consequences of a ban on preemptive strikes in the nuclear age". He argues that "analysis would identify far more ambiguous consequences flowing from the availability of nuclear weapons". The use of nuclear weapons in an anticipatory strike would result "in the murder of a substantial proportion of the inhabitants of the country erroneously perceived to have been preparing an attack". A pre-emptive nuclear strike would also "catalyze retaliation", and would end in the "massive hemorrhage and devastation of both societies". In both situations, the use of an anticipatory attack, therefore, seems to him never to be justified. He further challenges the thesis that a pre-emptive advantage (in a nuclear context) is decisive and would result in "victory" and "destruction of the enemy's forces". Tom Farer does not contend "that a pre-emptive strike is necessarily and invariably irrational", but that the challenged thesis, at least, is hardly self-evident as a general proposition.[24]

In the end, and this is what is important for the present study, even Mr. Farer recognises that, in relation to anticipatory defence, both interpretations of Article 2(4) and Article 51 are exegetically available to the minds he is addressing, and that the different conclusions reflect different policy preferences and different "calculations of the efficacy of alternative strategies" for promoting policies.[25] I entirely agree. This, of course, left the legal position as to anticipatory self-defence under the Charter in debate before the Consensus Definition. We have seen that the priority principle and its qualification within Article 2 of the Definition itself carefully preserve this debatability. And, in any case, as has been several times observed, other provisions of the Definition scrupulously save the Charter provisions as to limits of lawful use of force from any change by the Definition. So that on the anticipatory self-defence issue, as on so many others, the Consensual Definition does not advance the search for clarity in the meaning of aggression.

VI

How did the States joining in the Consensus interpret the outcome of this sharply divisive drafting history, and in particular the final omission of any express reference to intent or purpose, and the substitution of a wide reference to the "relevant circumstances"? The answer is an intriguing example of how opposed standpoints can both be embodied in a *verbal* "consensus", invocable *by each side* as embodying its own view and excluding the view which it opposed.

We may sample first the position that intention may and must be taken into account in determining whether a first resort even to armed force constitutes aggression. Soviet representative Kolesnik, after noting the omission of any express reference to intention, was clear that the Security Council "would of course attach importance to the question of aims".[26] Verosta of Austria noted that the omission was by way of compromise, and recognised that it would be rare for a State first using armed force to be exculpated for lack of intent. But he stressed the importance of precisely such cases. Where one State's "aggressive intent" was manifest by troop concentrations against a target State, that State could under the Charter, as under general law, exercise its inherent right of individual and collective self-defence. If a State so menaced fired the first shot, the Security Council could "in the light of other relevant circumstances" (Article 2) *qualify the menacing State, and not the target State, as the aggressor,* and recognise the latter's right of self-defence, even though the first resort to a designated act was by this latter State.[27] And United Kingdom representative Steel observed flatly that the "relevant circumstances" under Article 2 included but were not limited to the presence or absence of aggressive intent.[28] Like M. Verosta's view, this refers to the intents of both putative aggressor and putatively reacting victim.

Mr. Lee of Canada interpreted Article 2 to mean that the use of armed force raised a rebuttable presumption of aggression: it was an important but not the only element. Aggressive intent could still be one of the "relevant circumstances" to rebut or support that presumption. His delegation was therefore pleased that the concept of aggressive intent *had been retained in the wording of Article 2*.[29] M. Godoy of Paraguay added to Mr. Lee's reference to rebuttable presumption, the point that "objective presumption" from first use of force might not be completable without the subjective criterion.[30] M. Chaila of Zambia ranked the aggressive intent factor as of importance comparable to the military character of the action, the use of force, the seriousness of the situation, and the priority principle itself.[31] Greek representative Eustathiades was sure that Article 2 allowed for reference to the notion of intent. It was a compromise of the priority principle and intent and "it was unfortunate that that subjective element was not mentioned in it."[32]

M. Wehry of the Netherlands saw the point as applicable to both putative victim and putative aggressor. As to Articles 2 and 3, he said that it could rightly be inferred that those acts did not constitute acts of aggression *per se*. Rather, the Security Council must weigh them in the light of all relevant circumstances *including* the intent of the perpetrator. "In the view of his delegation", indeed, "[A]rticles 2 and 3 . . . did *not* mean that there could be *no* aggression . . . without the first use of force being established."[33] (Italics supplied.)

VII

At the opposite pole, M. Petric of Yugoslavia[34] was emphatic that "Article 2 could therefore not be interpreted as meaning that intent should be included among the relevant circumstances". He inferred this from what he asserted as the view of the majority, that the intention test was liable to abuse and should be rejected. Somewhat more cogent, but far from conclusive, was Algeria's argument through M. Boulbina,[35] that the omission of the express reference to intention "had constituted the necessary counterpart to the many concessions made by the majority of delegations". He thought that interpretative statements reintroducing that element virtually destroyed the compromise, and brought "the real scope of the text" into question. But, of course, it was not correct (as already seen in Section III) to equivalate the dropping of *express* reference to intention, with agreement that it was *not relevant*.

M. Boulbina, indeed, provided the answer to his own position when he observed that his delegation had wished to make "intention" irrelevant, for reasons similar to those which made it deplore the inclusion of the words "in contravention of the Charter" in Article 2. His delegation, he said, had wanted the first "use of armed force" to be conclusive and not merely *prima facie* evidence of aggression. His admission that they had finally agreed to the existing compromise in which first use of armed force was *not* conclusive, is at odds with his dogmatic insistence that "other relevant circumstances" could not be interpreted to include evidence of intent. Nor is his further argument persuasive that to admit the relevance of intention was to deprive the definition of any substance and mark a return to *before the consensus*. The result of the present examination is precisely to show, on this and other vital matters, that the definition is vacuous, precisely in the sense that consensus was only reached by dint of leaving issues in conflict in their *status quo ante*.

Other delegations, without supporting arguments even as plausible as M. Boulbina's, were just as peremptory. For Alvarez Tabio of Cuba it was simply "inadmissible" that the question of intent should bear on the existence of "armed aggression".[36] For M. Njenga of Kenya, "[h]owever noble the motives of the State which first used armed force . . . it had committed aggression and was to be condemned."[37] And M. Hassouna of Egypt was so sure, despite the preceding contrary assertions of so many other delegations, that intent could not be relevant to Article 2, that he applauded the Special Committee for having excluded it.[38]

VIII

Between these continuing head-on conflicts as to what the Consensus Definition meant on this vital matter, some delegations retreated into the oracular. For M. Rydbeck of Sweden[39] the main virtue of the draft is that there is no need to prove *subjective* intent. For M. Rossides of Cyprus[40] "there was no room for differences of opinion on the interpretation of either the meaning of the expression '*prima facie*' evidence or the importance to be attached to intent." For him, "[i]ntent was inherent in the armed attack itself, unless it was conclusively shown that it was due to a mistake" or not grave enough. For M. Güney of Turkey, "Article 2 struck a delicate balance between priority and aggressive intent."[41] M. Jaipal of India thought that intention should not be regarded in determining aggression. First use of force should be conclusive, not *prima facie*. Yet he also argued that indirect and economic aggression should have been covered and stressed that by virtue of Article 4 of the Definition, the Security Council had power under the Charter, Article 39, to take into account *all forms of coercive action* which might be described as aggression.[42]

Since, on this view, the "first use" of force might be a justifiable response to preceding indirect and economic aggression, the Jaipal position presents an interesting contradiction *in se* creating a vacuity of meaning not only for inter-State conflicts, but for conflict within a single State's own foreign policy. And confounding all positions by making intent the most decisive factor in a finding of aggression, Fuentes Ibañez of Bolivia asserted that "[c]lear intent would obviate in part the need for *prima facie* evidence, which would be difficult to establish after the event."[43] The fact that Article 6 of the Definition reserved the liberty and limits of lawful use of force under the Charter, and that this excluded from the reach of the Consensus Definition all cases where use of force was lawful in order to defend the inviolability, territorial integrity, sovereignty, or political independence of a State under Article 2(4) of the Charter, or in other cases under Articles 51, 52 and 53, was highlighted by M. Zuleta of Colombia.[44] Bearing in mind the possible meaning of Article 2 (4) discussed in Section III above, similar contradictions flow from this point for any view which denies the relevance of intention to the determination of aggression under the Consensus Definition.[45]

A final delicate flavouring of *je ne sais quoi* on this issue was added by Iraq's M. Yasseen. He thought that the effect of the provision of Article 5(1) of the Definition saying that "[n]o consideration of whatever nature, whether political, economic, military or otherwise" could justify aggression meant that motives for the alleged act of aggression (as distinct from actual commission of it) *could not be* taken into consideration.[46] Article 5(1) had its immediate origin in the last paragraph of the Preamble of the 13-Nation Draft which, however, expressly excepted Article 51 self-defence from its ambit.[47] It has, however, a longer history back into the elaborate Article 2 of the early Soviet proposal of February 6, 1933.[48] In the form it finally took in Article 5(1), if this be taken as literally as the Iraqi delegate proposed, it would provide that even self-defence against armed attack (surely a "military" consideration if ever there was one) could not justify armed response. In terms of the Definition, Article 51 of the Charter would be rendered nugatory. If to avoid absurdity and conflict with the Charter *in this respect,* Article 5(1) cannot be read to mean what it appears literally to say, this may also be so for the political, economic and other considerations mentioned. And whatever be the final outcome of this verbal gambol (also perhaps a verbal gamble), it is not likely to leave much force to M. Yasseen's confident inference.

IX

The Iraqi delegate's argument does have the value of reminding us that the issue as to the relevance of the intent with which a designated act is resorted to is deeply entangled, not only with the priority of commission principle (examined in this Chapter), but also with issues as to "economic" and "indirect aggression" (to be examined in Chapter 7).

Some transitional remarks are here in point in preparation for the later discussion of those other issues in that Chapter.

Insofar as aggression is given a meaning of which one component is the putative aggressor's resort to armed force, the diverse activities rather vaguely indicated by "economic" or "indirect" aggression would not be within it. They might, of course, be tainted with some other gradation of illegality, but not (assuming a definition based solely on resort to armed force) with "aggression". Article 1 of the Consensus Definition does appear to set such a limit. "Aggression is the use of armed force by a State against the sovereignty, territorial integrity or political independence of another State . . .". Yet Article 5, para. 2, may put a cloud over the clarity of this limit by making a distinction between "a war of aggression" which is designated "a crime against international peace", and "aggression" which is said to "give rise to international responsibility." On one meaning of this enigmatic paragraph, the cloud need not arise.[49] "War of aggression" and "aggression" may be taken as synonymous, both giving rise, on the penal side, to liability to criminal punishment of individuals for a crime against the peace, and on the side of inter-State relations to "civil" international responsibility for a State delinquency. And some delegations were concerned to make this identification.[50]

On another interpretation, however, "war of aggression" in this paragraph would refer to one kind of aggression, namely the aggression by armed force dealt with in the above Article 1, and in the Consensus Definition generally. While "aggression" would refer to a range of aggression *other than by armed force, not so dealt with,* yet nonetheless constituting a delinquency giving rise to "international responsibility" (and presumably to remedial liberties of self-help and possibly even self-defence, against such delinquency). This last interpretation might perhaps have importance for the kind of crisis referred to by President Ford and Dr. Kissinger in 1975, of the use of measures of coercion like the 1973 OAPEC oil boycott, which produce "an economic stranglehold" upon the victim State. Self-defence, if need be by the use of armed force by that target State to secure the conditions of its economic survival, might then be argued to be lawful, even under the Definition. For it could be said that such economic coercion of the extreme severity proposed constituted "aggression" which under Article 5(2) gives rise to "international responsibility". It would follow from such an argument that such "a first use" of armed force *by way of response to this coercion* would fall outside the *"prima facie"* ambit of the words of Articles 1, 2 and even 3. This possibility is underlined by other important provisions of the Consensus Definition.

One is that under Article 2 itself, "the first use of armed force" is only *"prima facie* evidence of an act of aggression", leaving it open to the Security Council "in conformity with the Charter" to conclude "in the light of other relevant circumstances" that no finding of aggression is "justified". Another is that Article 6 of the Definition spells out that "[n]othing in this Definition shall be construed as in any way *enlarging* or *diminishing* the scope of the Charter, including its provisions concerning cases in which the use of force is lawful". Even, indeed, without the explicit provision of Article 6, the same saving of existing residual liberties of States under international law to use of force for legitimate defence in situations not expressly forbidden by the Charter,[51] seems to arise from the words "in contravention of the Charter" within Article 2 itself. Only a "first use of armed force" which contravenes the Charter is even *prima facie* evidence of an act of aggression within the Definition. And we saw in Chapter 3 that even without these savings of the Charter in Articles 2 and 6 of the Consensus Definition, the latter would have to be read subject to the Charter provisions, which do not (for example, in Article 2(4)) limit the culpability of force to *armed* force.[52]

Insofar as the scope of Articles 1, 2 and 3 of the Definition is thus qualified, the fact that the intention with which a State first resorted to force was to ward off grave dangers created by extreme coercion wielded by the opposed State, must obviously be a deeply relevant if not indispensable consideration. And this is so, as will be further discussed in Chapter 7, after all reserves have been registered about questions of proportionality of response, and about the degree of severity of the economic coercion which may produce this relevance. The level of coercion justifying particular forceful responses is probably different from that rendering a treaty void under Article 52 of the Vienna Convention on Treaties, 1970. The two cases are likely to share, for a long time, chronic uncertainty as to the operative level required.[53]

Yet, of course, the consequences of the uncertainty may be different in the different contexts. We are here concerned only to indicate that at some level of severity there is an important linkage between the question of the relevance of the *animus aggressionis* to the commission of the crime of international aggression, and the question whether there may be forms of aggression of which the use of armed force is not an essential element.

The same organic linkage is also reached by a more direct route. This turns on the meaning of the word "against" as it appears in Article 2(4) of the Charter, prohibiting "the threat or use of force *against* the territorial integrity or political independence of any State". A similar phrase is now incorporated into Article 1 of the Consensus Definition, declaring aggression to be "the use of armed force . . . *against* the sovereignty, territorial integrity, etc." For example (focusing on territorial integrity) we can take the word "against" to refer to the mere fact of physical impact of the armed force on the territory, regardless of whether or not the actor's aim was to diminish the victim State's territorial integrity. Such an interpretation would, of course, forbid one State's use of armed force to attack the territory of another, for the purpose of divesting that State of its territory; but (and this is the point) it would also forbid the target State, defending itself against this attack, to drive back the attacking State's forces *into that State's own territory.* The self-defending State would be required peremptorily to stop its pursuit and its military operations at the frontier, as some thought that in the Korean Affair the United Nations Forces should have remained below the 38th parallel.

Such an interpretation seems at odds with military and common sense. Both of these require that the self-defending State ought to be free to pursue the attacker at any rate to a line which gives the former State some assurance against resumption of the attack. The doctrine of "hot pursuit" in other parts of international law observes these precepts even when no such grave perils are involved as are involved in the aggression situation. For these reasons, another meaning must probably be given to the word "against", by which it refers not merely to physical impact of military force against the territory, but to the *intention* of the State concerned to apply such force *in order to diminish the territorial integrity of the target State.* And what thus applies to use of force *against territorial integrity,* would apply also to its use *against* "*sovereignty*" or "*political independence*".

On this basis, just as the phrase "in contravention of the Charter" in Article 2 of the Definition, and the explicit saving in Article 6 thereof, preserve after the Consensus Definition the legality of any use of force which would be lawful under the Charter, so also the precise meaning of the term "against" in Article 1 would constrict the reach of the term "aggression" throughout the Consensus Definition. So that the "intention" or the *animus aggressionis* of the resort to force by a State, far from being irrelevant to the legal existence of aggression, would be an essential element to be established in each case. And this would be so even though, in the facts of a particular crisis, very little beyond the simple chronology of events may be required to establish it.

CHAPTER 5

Aggression, Military Occupation and Acquisition of Territory

I

Indeterminacies or self-contradictions within State positions about defining aggression may be inspired by a mere general identification of interest with a particular bloc or ideology. They are, as it were, attractive marshalling grounds within which General Assembly majorities will be assembled against particular target States or kinds of States. They may also, however, be targeted in an even more *ad hoc* manner against a particular aspect of a particular conflict with a particular State. Nowhere is this more dramatically seen than in the debates concerning references to be made in the Consensus Definition to military occupation and territorial acquisitions. The *ad hoc* preoccupations of the interested States are rather unconcealed throughout discussions of them preceding the final draft, as well as in the interpretations of the final text thereafter. In the history of the drafting the issue as to occupied territories was raised in the Thirteen Power Draft as a part of the self-determination question. But these Powers did not succeed in having it included in the final Article 7 dealing with that matter. For this reason, but also because the issue is legally a different one, I have preferred to devote this separate short Chapter to it.

If war is the conduct of policy by other means, one could also say that defining aggression is conducting political warfare by other means. The Special Committee's exchanges concerning military occupation can only be fully understood as a phase in the continuing debate concerning certain words sandwiched into the Preamble of the Security Council's famous Middle East Resolution 242 of November 22, 1967. The words in question were there interposed between recitals of "continuing concern with the grave situation in the Middle East" and of the "need to work for a just and lasting peace".[1] The interposed words were: "emphasising the inadmissibility of the acquisition of territory by war". Their insertion was by way of consolation to the Arab States for the refusal of the mover, Lord Caradon, to amend the present words "withdrawal of Israel forces from territories occupied in the recent conflict" in Paragraph 1 (i) of the operative part of the Resolution, by changing the word "territories" to "all the territories". Lord Caradon's refusal to yield to strong Arab State pressure for automatic return of all territories occupied by Israel in the 1967 War, which this amendment would have implied, was endorsed by the Security Council when it adopted unanimously the *un*amended resolution, including the above compensatory recital in the Preamble.[2]

Resolution 242 consisted finally of certain expressed "principles", "necessities" and "provisions" (including the above as to withdrawal, and those as to peace for all States in the area "within secure and recognised boundaries") which were to serve as directives to the Special Representative. On their basis he was instructed to "establish and maintain contacts with States concerned in order to promote agreement and to assist efforts to achieve a peaceful and accepted settlement". All this obviously presented great difficulties for the Arab States' demand that withdrawal of Israel forces was to be total, and not a subject of negotiation; a demand, indeed, that total withdrawal by Israel was itself a preliminary condition for negotiation. This demand persisted into and throughout the maturation of the Consensus Definition.

II

A duty of unconditional total withdrawal under international law could conceivably have arisen in the 1967 war if it were assumed that the hostilities from which the occupation ensued were illegally resorted to by Israel. This would have been, of course, by virtue of the principle *ex iniuria non oritur ius*. But, of course, the actual facts of the June war were not as so assumed, but precisely the contrary. Even according to the criteria of aggression adopted by the Soviet Union herself at that time and since, as well as according to the later terms of the Consensus Definition itself, acts of aggression were committed by the Arab States in the 1967 conflict, before any Israel move across their frontiers. These warlike acts included the naval blockade of the Straits of Tiran, shelling from the Gaza Strip by Egypt, the air-runs over Israel and bombardment from the Golan Heights by Syria, and (*vis-à-vis* Jordan) the bombardment of West Jerusalem by Jordan. This is even apart from questions of the Israeli right of anticipatory self-defence in view of the massive mobilisation of armies, armour and aircraft on all her frontiers which, in the view of a wide range of publicists at the time, left her no choice but to act in self-defence.[3] Insofar as such acts entitle the target State to respond in lawful self-defence, the principle *ex iniuria non oritur ius* is simply not applicable to such response. As between the unsuccessful aggressor who loses control of territory to the prospective victim, and that prospective victim, the rule of international law clearly applicable pending a peace settlement is that of *uti possidetis*. This leaves the final outcome of the occupation to the peace negotiations. Lacking this, the parties remain *in statu quo*, no principle requiring or even justifying any particular change. Moreover, the acceptance by both sides of a Cease-Fire also bars renewal of hostilities by the aggressor as a way of ending the occupation.

In this condition of international and Charter law, the Arab States' demand for total and automatic withdrawal had therefore to depend on whatever could be made of the preambulatory recital in the November Resolution of the "inadmissibility of the acquisition of territory by war". For it to assist their cause, it would be necessary to show that this recital had made a legislative change in the existing rule, *ex iniuria non oritur ius*. Indeed, the change would have to be almost a flat reversal, requiring the Occupant to withdraw even if his entry was, as in the case of Israel, perfectly lawful. Such a reversal by a mere preambular recital would be rare, even if Resolution 242, even in its operative part, could be said to be legally binding as such (which is difficult), and even if it purported by its terms to impose obligations other than the obligation to negotiate in good faith on the basis of its terms, which it clearly does not.

In view of the impossibility of giving this phrase in the Preamble a meaning so much at odds with long established principles of international law, common sense requires us to ask whether any other meanings are available. There are two at least, neither requiring a reversal of existing law by so frail a side-wind. The first is that the recital was merely recalling, in the eloquently ambiguous and conciliatory style apt for a preamble, the *ex iniuria* principle as this applies to war. Second, it may be a restatement of the rather technical but commonplace principle of customary international law, that mere military occupation does not transfer title, this requiring some further act in the law, such as formal annexation or cession under a negotiated treaty of peace.

III

It may perhaps be added that the very idea that international law would be improved by changing from the present rule to one requiring automatic withdrawal by a military occupant who lawfully entered in course of self-defence, seems undesirable to the point of absurdity. Such a changed rule would assure every prospective aggressor that, even if his aggression fails, he can immediately regain any territory lost in the attempt. It would do this even if he intended to renew his aggressive design, and even if (as with Egypt in Gaza), the territory in question was formerly seized unlawfully by him and had since been consistently used as a base for his aggressive activity against the present Occupant. In short, for any State planning an aggression, such a change would underwrite unconditionally that State's risks of territorial loss arising from defeat in course of aggression. By such a rule, an international law which at present sets out by the *ex iniuria* principle to discourage aggressors, would be amended into a rule *encouraging aggressors* by insuring them in advance against the main risks involved in case of defeat.

A meaning thus unsustainable in terms of policy, would also be at odds with the operative clauses of the resolution, its interpretation as a whole, and its drafting history. As has been seen, the unanimous Security Council did not make the change demanded which would have required withdrawal from *all the* occupied territories. Lord Caradon himself firmly withstood pressures from Arab and other States to employ in his draft their alternative formulation, namely, "*all the* territories." He also resisted the Indian delegate's argument (supported at one stage by the threat of a Russian veto) that the Indian understanding of the Resolution as in effect embodying the definite article, which India threatened to enounce as its basis of voting, would create an understanding as to the meaning of the Resolution binding on the Security Council and its Members.

The Indian delegate later agreed to vote for the British Draft without such an enunciation, Lord Caradon in turn agreeing not to include in *his* remarks, his own otherwise projected retort: "But the Indian interpretation is not binding on the Council." Lord Caradon said instead that—"it will be recognized that it is only the resolution that will bind us, and we regard its wording as clear." It was on this note that the unanimous adoption took place.

The footnote should perhaps here be added as to Egypt in Gaza and as to Jordan on the West Bank, that their own presences there were certainly based on their earlier warlike entries of 1948. So that even if the rule of automatic withdrawal regardless of illegality *had* been newly legislated with retrospective effect, it could not have improved *their* present legal positions *vis-à-vis* Israel. Except by an unprincipled discriminatory application of the new rule to one side and not the other,[4] it would negative any right of theirs to be in those territories either. In historical fact, of course, their entries were in course of military invasions which many States, including the Soviet Union, at that time regarded as aggression, and unlawful, and subject to the *ex iniuria* principle.

IV

None of the parties changed their positions on this issue as to the occupied territories during the fruitless mission of Special Representative Jarring. Nor did the Arab States succeed in changing either the legal position or the basic political position by their surprise armed attack on Israel in 1973. Indeed, the rejection of their thesis was, if anything, reinforced by the express call in Security Council Resolution 334 of 1973 for immediate negotiation between the Parties on the basis of Resolution 242 of 1967 without any such pre-condition of total withdrawal as had been demanded by Arab States. Meanwhile, these demands had been pressed elsewhere, and perhaps lay behind the paragraphs quoted below in the Declaration on Principles of International Law concerning Friendly Relations ... among States, 1970.[5] That Declaration does not, of course, purport to change the pre-existing rules of international law, and (for the present context) it is significant that its reaffirmation in Paragraph 8 of the Preamble to the Consensus Definition immediately follows after Paragraph 7 concerning military occupations and acquisition of territory.[6] That Paragraph 7, as well as other parts of the Consensus Definition itself, as we have seen, carefully preserves the pre-existing legal position as to the scope and effects of the Charter.[7]

The relevant paragraphs of the Declaration of 1970 were:

Every state has the duty to refrain in its international relations from the threat or use of force against the territorial integrity or political independence of any state, or in any other manner inconsistent with the purposes of the United Nations . . . Such a threat or use of force constitutes a violation of international law and the Charter of the United Nations and shall never be employed as a means of settling international issues . . .

The territory of a state shall not be the object of military occupation *resulting from the use of force in contravention of the provisions of the Charter.* The territory of a state shall not be the object of acquisition by another state resulting from the threat or use of force. No territorial acquisition resulting from the threat or use of force shall be recognized as legal. *Nothing in the foregoing shall be construed as affecting*:

(a) *Provisions of the Charter* or any international agreement prior to the Charter régime and valid under international law;[8] or

(b) The powers of the Security Council under the Charter.

(Italics supplied.)

The whole paragraph referring to military occupation in the 1970 Declaration seems controlled by the opening specification that what is being spoken of is the use of force *in contravention of the Charter.* Though this qualification is not expressly repeated in each of the two consequential sentences concerning "acquisition" of territory resulting from "threat or use of force", it certainly seems implied, not only by this context in the Declaration, but also by the overriding saving which immediately follows of the provisions of the Charter and of the powers of the Security Council. Yet the failure to refer back to the specification in the opening sentence does indicate either poor drafting, or a deliberate injection of ambiguity in these two sentences. Subject to this, the two sentences merely restate the established rule of international law based on the *ex iniuria* principle discussed above. And it is to be noted, in confirmation of this, that the preceding paragraph of the Declaration (also quoted above) incorporates *verbatim* at its heading the provisions of the Charter, especially Article 2(4). So that the "threat or use of force" in the second quoted paragraph which is said to bar acquisition of territory must be read to incorporate the fuller terms of the first, namely, "threat or use of force against the territorial integrity or political independence of any State, or in any other manner inconsistent with the purposes of the United Nations", as also required by Article 2(4) of the Charter.

V

When we now turn to the proposals concerning occupied territory after the above Declaration and *preceding* the Consensus Definition, there is first to be noted the stark division between the principal drafts presented to the Fourth Special Committee.

The Thirteen Power Draft proposed, *without qualification as to lawfulness,* that territory of a State "may not be the object, even temporarily, of military occupation or of other measures of force taken by another State on any grounds whatever, and that such territorial acquisitions obtained by force shall not be recognised" (Paragraph 8).[9] Such an unqualified rule would obviously involve the drastic, and in policy incomprehensible, departure from existing international law discussed in Section III.

The Soviet proposal was in this respect flatly opposed to the Thirteen Power Draft. Paragraph 4 forbade territorial gains or special advantages not from use of force as such, but only from "armed *aggression*". (Italics supplied.) And Paragraph 2B also carefully stipulated that it was only a *first* resort to certain weapons, to bombardment or attack on land, sea or air forces, or to invasion or attack against a State's territory or to military occupation or blockade, which constituted acts of "aggression". Clearly, an occupation arising in the course of self-defence against any of these acts would not be "armed aggression" and would not activate the rule in Paragraph 4. As opposed to both the above drafts, the Six Power Draft made no express reference to occupation or acquisition of territory, but what it implies is near to the Soviet rather than to the Thirteen Power position. For a use of force to qualify as aggression, the Six Power Draft required a showing of one of a number of specific intents—for instance, to diminish territory of the target State, change its Government, or impose demands on it. (Paragraph IVA.) This draft, moreover, explicitly provided *ex majore cautela* that use of force in self-defence could not be aggression. (Paragraph III.)

The Consensus Definition clearly rejects the above Thirteen Power proposal on this matter. First, its only separate operative provision forbidding acquisition by force (namely, Article 5, paragraph 3) refers, not to mere threat or use of force, but to "aggression". Second, like the Soviet Draft, it declares the designated acts to be aggression *only if first committed,* thus excluding acts done in self-defence (Articles 2 and 3). Third, even then such acts only constitute aggression if "in contravention of the Charter".[10] Fourth, the Consensus Definition made clear in its Preamble, Paragraph 7, that it was merely "reaffirming" an existing rule, and in case any doubt might still remain it states that the rule recited against acquisition or military occupation of territory or other measures of force applied when these were "in contravention of the Charter". On all these points the Soviet and the Six Power proposals marched together to yield the same clear result, that military occupation in the course of lawful self-defence by the occupant is in no way impugned. On one further point it differed from the Soviet draft. It did not even include military occupation in the list of acts in Article 3 which, if first committed, constitute aggression. Presumably this was because it is difficult to conceive a military occupation not preceded by some other designated act (such as armed attack or invasion) of one side or the other.

The *ad hoc* purpose, for which the Arab States pressed for the inclusion of a provision about military occupation, was therefore again defeated. The Definition on this point conformed to and did not go beyond the customary law principle *ex iniuria*.

VI

The States concerned, however, made still another effort, even after the Special Committee's adoption of what became the final text of the Consensus Definition, to use the definitional exercise as a step in their *ad hoc* political warfare on Middle East issues. At its 112th Meeting, on April 12, 1974, the Special Committee was persuaded, on recommendation of its Working Group, to incorporate a number of notes to Articles 3 and 5, of which the relevant Note 4 was as follows:

> 4. With reference to the third paragraph of Article 5 ... this paragraph should not be construed so as to prejudice the established principles of international law relating to the inadmissibility of territorial acquisition resulting from the threat or use of force.[11]

Since the "established principles" on this matter were precisely those based on the *ex iniuria non oritur ius* principle already (as we have just seen) embodied in the Consensus Definition, it is intriguing to ask what might have been thought to have been achieved by Note 4. The answer would appear to lie in the virtually literal repetition in it of the same phrase "inadmissibility of the acquisition of territory by war", first found in the preamble to Resolution 242 on the Middle East, of November 22, 1967. It may be recalled that this phrase was there inserted by way of compensation for the Security Council's *refusal* to accept Arab demands for automatic and total Israel withdrawal from occupied territories.

The net outcome in terms of legal analysis, therefore, is that the Consensus Definition is left with one of its rare moments of unambiguous clarity as to the legal position of a military occupant who entered lawfully. It merely restated, even after the desperate *arrière-pensée* of Note 4, the long-accepted position under the Charter and international law. As M. Lee for one of the Six Powers observed, Article 5, paragraph 3 above was but a necessary corollary to the *illegality* of aggression.[12] M. Goerner of the German Democratic Republic saw the paragraph in the same way, and stated the point in precise Soviet terms, as referring to acquisition *by aggression*, not by force as such.[13] Perhaps because the language was so plain, few other Western or Communist State delegates troubled to express interpretations of it. Some delegates, however, mentioned refinements. M. Godoy of Paraguay thought that it should be made clear, as to the principle applied in Article 5, paragraph 3, that force might be unlawful on grounds other than that it constituted aggression, and that if it was so unlawful, the rule against acquisition by it should apply.[14] Somewhat similarly, M. Obadi thought that threat to use force might be unlawful (presumably under the conditions of Article 2(4) of the Charter) even if it did not fall within the definition of aggression, and that the non-acquisition rule should then also apply.[15] As seen in the Chapter on economic and indirect aggression, the point is an important one. For instance, the 1973 Arab State oil boycott might well violate Article 2(4) of the Charter, even if the Consensus Definition of Aggression did not reach it.

VII

In this state of the matter, not even M. Hassouna of Egypt was prepared to assert frontally that Article 5, paragraph 3, forbade acquisition by force lawfully exercised, as in the case of self-defence. He did say, somewhat ambiguously, that acquisition should be denied not only because of aggression, but also in case of "threat or use of force". This, of course, might mean unlawful threat or use of force *insofar as contrary to Article 2(4) or other provisions of the Charter*. The fact that he seemed careful not so to specify is perhaps understandable. At a certain point, as seen in Chapter 4, Sections V and IX, and will further be seen in Chapter 7, the argument that force may be unlawful under Article 2(4), even if it is not "(armed) aggression", leads to the possible illegality of the Arab State oil boycott. It then becomes rather counterproductive in terms of the Arab side of Middle East political warfare.

What M. Hassouna preferred was to seek to revive the debate concerning the effect of the Security Council's Middle East resolution of November 22, 1967, by quoting verbatim the language of the above Explanatory Note 4, re-echoing (as just seen) the recital in the Preamble to that Resolution.[16] No other delegate was prepared squarely to accept the interpretations thus rather gingerly offered by the Egyptian delegate. M. Mahmud of Pakistan, indeed, was concerned to object to Article 5, paragraph 3, precisely because it *did* limit the non-acquisition rule to *aggression* or *unlawful* use of force, whereas he thought it should apply to *any* use of force.[17] M. Jaipal of India straddled the fence—perhaps inadvertently. He approved of Article 5, paragraph 3 in its reference to aggression. But he also welcomed Paragraph 7 of the Preamble, which however he paraphrased in terms which omitted its qualification "in contravention of the Charter" discussed above.[18] Romanian delegate Ceasu was blandly ambivalent. Without referring to the Egyptian position, or to any controversy, he seemed roundly to assert that Article 5(3) makes territorial acquisitions from the threat or use of force "inadmissible", and he made no qualification as to whether the force must be illegal or not. He also asserted, however, that this derives from "the general principles of international law" which, in the light of what these principles are, would rule out the possible inference that he thought the inadmissibility applied even to force used in lawful self-defence.[19]

VIII

It is clear from the preceding Sections that on the point whether military occupation and territorial acquisition are forbidden even to a State acting in self-defence here under consideration, the non-aligned States did not succeed in embodying their thesis into the Consensual Definition. The failure was clearer on this point, spearheaded to the end by the Egyptian delegate, than it was on the question central to Chapter 6, immediately following. This is as to whether Article 7 on self-determination struggles allows armed force to be used by the peoples concerned and third States supporting them, in derogation from Articles 3(f) and 3(g).

Yet, even from the clear failure as to military occupation and territorial acquisition, the Egyptian delegate, and States sympathetic with him, could draw some comfort in terms of the Political Warfare Drive and the role of the General Assembly. It has already been observed that, in relation to the future outcome on issues left indeterminate or in self-contradiction in it, the Consensual Definition could in any case rarely lead to decisions in the Security Council on matters seriously in dispute. Either that body would simply not even try to pass on the issue of aggression, or the attempt to pass on it would be blocked by the veto. It would therefore usually be in the General Assembly that the issue of aggression or not would be canvassed, in connection with some resolution which, though not legally binding, would be politically important. For that forum, the addition to the Consensus Definition of the above Note 4 in terms closely paralleling the superficially ambiguous recital in the preamble to the Middle East Resolution 242, was a definite asset which could be useful to marshal anti-Israel majorities in other ways. And these other ways were exemplified even after the text of the Consensus Definition was settled, by the General Assembly's adoption of Resolution 3246(XXIX). Paragraph 3 of that resolution reaffirms "the legitimacy of the peoples' struggle for liberation from colonial and foreign domination and alien subjugation by all available means including armed struggle".[20] The orchestration of these actions in the General Assembly again suggests the operation of merely *ad hoc* and spurious objectives of various proposals as to occupied territory, and their lack of principled relevance to the main definitional task of the Special Committee.

CHAPTER 6

Aggression and Struggles for Self-Determination

I

The legal position of non-State entities, such as insurgent groups or peoples, struggling to break away from the State under whose sovereignty they live, was not a major issue for the General Assembly's first two Special Committees on defining aggression in the 'fifties. Whether such entities could commit or be victims of aggression became an issue as decolonisation multiplied the number of new African and Asian States. That background, and the struggles of the 1960's in Indo-China and in Southern Africa, frame the present doctrine of "wars of liberation".

This is, even today, a frankly political rather than legal doctrine. A General Assembly increasingly dominated by the newer States and their political allies, however, has attempted (for example, by the Declaration on Principles of International Law Concerning Friendly Relations and Co-operation Among States, 1970 (Resol. 2625(XXV)) to invest it with some kind of *legal* standing.[1] In relation to defining aggression, the main rationale for legitimating use of force by peoples struggling for independence, and by third States supporting them, might rest on an ingenious reading of Article 51 of the Charter. The "target" State, insofar as it resists the self-determination demand, is said not to be a "target" State at all, but an "aggressor" in a continuing state of "armed attack" against the people concerned. That people, and third States giving armed support to such a people, may thus be said to be acting lawfully in individual and collective self-defence under Article 51.

This basis for legitimating use of force in struggles for self-determination has been stated as "a right of self-defence of peoples and nations against colonial domination".[1a] Even those publicists sympathetic to wars of liberation have doubted whether self-defence in the international legal sense is involved, preferring two other bases. One is that since the Charter restraints on the use of force are applicable only to States, the right of a people to fight Governments of "foreign" domination, such as colonialist regimes, "is not to be deduced from the law on the use of force, but rather from the principle of self-determination and the political right of revolution."[1b] The other possible ground rests, of course, on various cumulative declarations of the General Assembly onwards from the 1960 Resolution 1514(XV) on the Granting of Independence to Colonial Countries and declaring in para. 4 that "all armed action . . . against dependent peoples" should cease. Resolution 2131(XX) of 1965 declared in para. 3 that "the use of force to deprive peoples of their national identity constitutes a violation of their inalienable rights and of the principles of non-intervention."

And Resolution 2625(XXV) of 1970 on Principles ... Concerning Friendly Relations ... Among States affirmed the applicability of such self-determination within existing States (paras. 7, 5 and 3 read together).

The "self-defence against colonial domination" ground seems, indeed, inconsistent at points even with the above Friendly Relations Declaration. The equal rights and self-determination principle there states in its second paragraph that States should "bring a speedy end to colonialism, having due regard to the freely expressed will of the peoples concerned." This clearly stops short of declaring colonialism illegal *per se,* and very far short of declaring it to constitute standing aggression. And para. 4 of the same principle reinforces this point by indicating modes of peaceful emergence of new political status.[1c] Moreover, even if the contents of these resolutions were more supportive, this would not have removed the widely felt difficulties affecting the incapacity of the General Assembly to change international law, nor those arising from Article 2(7) of the Charter concerning matters falling essentially within the domestic jurisdiction of States.[1d]

The claim (correct or not) that this doctrine might represent existing international law and/or Charter law is essential background for some central issues of this Chapter. Paragraphs 6 and 8 of the Preamble to the Consensus Definition invoke the above Declaration on Friendly Relations of States and the right of self-determination; and Article 7 of the Definition saves the legality of self-determination "struggles", without explicitly providing that such "struggles" may include armed force of the kinds stigmatised in the Definition as aggression, for example, the sending of "armed bands" under Article 3(g). The cogency, however, of the rationale for exempting "wars of liberation" from the ambit of the Consensus Definition also depends on the soundness of certain preliminary legal arguments equivalating an insurgent people to a State, and for subjecting the sovereignty of the existing States to the insurgent people's resort to armed force.

One conceivable argument flows from the above assumption that the State's authority over the particular people must at some past time have been imposed by armed force, in suppression of that people's Sovereign Statehood, and must now be deemed to be a standing armed attack against that people's former Sovereign State. The people now struggling for independence is then, as it were, irrebuttably presumed to stand *in loco* of the former State, now also irrebuttably presumed to have been unlawfully suppressed by armed force. In this way the people is deemed vested with an Article 51 right of self-defence, the "war of liberation" being but an exercise of it. Another argument might invoke some principle like *omnia praesumuntur rite esse acta,* or related natural law principle. Its gist would be that under the assumed "right" of self-determination, the people concerned *ought to be* freed and restored to Statehood. What ought to be done is then deemed to have been done, so that its *legal* position and that of the State dominating it, are *deemed* to be *as they would have been if the initial unlawful suppression of sovereignty had not occurred or had been reversed.* Both arguments then proceed by constructing a *notional* legal right of self-defence against a *notionally continuing* armed attack on the insurgent people's *notional* political independence. Correspondingly, one learned writer has suggested, if the struggle for independence succeeds, the "liberated people" should be seen not as a *new* State acquiring sovereignty, but as an old State reverting to former sovereignty, after unlawful interruption of it.[2]

In a particular case, of course, some or all of the above notional attributions may be simply not so. An insurgent people in 1976 may never have enjoyed sovereign statehood, the present State may never have used armed force to suppress it, so that there was no ground for imputing a standing armed attack, or invoking Article 51 of the Charter, or "reversion" to notionally continuing sovereignty. My purpose, however, has been to present these positions with maximum cogency in order better to understand the debates which so often presuppose them, not to suggest (as is clearly not the case) that they are endorsed by existing international law. As a question *de lege ferenda*, of whether such a condition of the law would be desirable, the matter was not before the Fourth Special Committee or the Sixth Committee, their terms of reference proceeding on the basis of existing international and Charter law.

II

How far does the Consensus Definition commit the participating States in some way to any of the above theses treating a "people" engaged in armed struggle for self-determination against the State, under the sovereignty of which it lives, as a State defending itself from armed attack by that State? This is the main topic of the present Chapter. The arguments involved are often tenuous and tedious, resting on a plurality of textual points in the Definition. We proceed first to collect these points of textual attachment in the present Section, before submitting them to analysis thereafter. The points of the Definition to which such a commitment might thus conceivably, but with often tenuous and tedious looseness, be attached are as follows:

(1) Paragraph 6 of the Preamble refers to the duty of States not to use armed force to deprive peoples of their right of self-determination, freedom and independence, or to disrupt "territorial integrity". (The last phrase, as will be seen, seems directed less to advancing struggles for independence, than to protecting existing sovereign States against them.)

(2) Paragraph 7 of the Preamble "reaffirms" that territory should not be occupied or "the object of acquisition" by force, etc. "in contravention of the Charter".[3]

(3) Paragraph 8 of the Preamble "reaffirms" in general terms the Declaration on Principles of International Law Concerning Friendly

Relations and Co-operation among States, 1970.[3a] This Declaration may be seen on perusal to contain the following possibly relevant though sometimes mutually neutralising paragraphs:

(a) The Preamble recited the obligation of States not to intervene in the internal or external affairs of any other State.

(b) It expressed conviction that alien subjugation, domination and exploitation of peoples are a major obstacle to international peace and security, and that the equal rights and self-determination principles are a significant contribution to contemporary international law.

(c) It expressed the conviction that any attempt aimed at partial or total disruption of the national unity, territorial integrity or independence of a State or country is incompatible with the purposes and principles of the Charter, and that these principles are worthy of progressive development.

(d) The body of the 1970 Declaration condemned as unlawful armed intervention and all other interference or threats against the personality of the State or against its political, economic and cultural elements.

(e) It similarly forbade States to "use or encourage the use of economic, political or any other type of measures to coerce another State in order to obtain from it the subordination of the exercise of its sovereign rights and to secure from it advantages of any kind. Also, no State shall organize, assist, foment, finance, incite or tolerate subversive, terrorist or armed activities directed towards the violent overthrow of the régime of another State, or interfere in civil strife in another State".

(f) The Declaration then, with Olympian ambivalence, forbade the use of force to deprive peoples of their national identity, thus violating their "inalienable rights and ... *the principle of non-intervention.*" (Italics supplied.)

(g) A section of the Declaration headed "The Principle of Equal Rights and Self-Determination of Peoples" then proceeded as follows:

By virtue of the principle of equal rights and self-determination of peoples enshrined in the Charter of the United Nations, all peoples have the right freely to determine without external interference, their political status and to pursue their economic, social and cultural development, and every state has the duty to respect this right in accordance with the provisions of the Charter . . . .

Every state has the duty to promote, through joint and separate action, realization of the principle of equal rights and self-determination of peoples . . . .

Every state has the duty to refrain from any forcible action which deprives peoples referred to above ... of their right to self-determination and freedom and independence. In their actions against, and resistance to, such forcible action in pursuit of the exercise of their right to self-determination, such peoples are entitled to seek and to receive support *in accordance with the purposes and principles of the Charter.* (Italics supplied.)

The territory of a colony or other non-self-governing territory has, under the Charter, a status separate and distinct from the territory of the state administering it; and such separate and distinct status under the Charter shall exist until the people of the colony or non-self-governing territory have exercised their right of self-determination in accordance with the Charter, and particularly its purposes and principles.

Nothing in the foregoing paragraphs shall be construed as authorizing or encouraging any action which would dismember or impair, totally or in part, the territorial integrity or political unity of sovereign and independent states conducting themselves in compliance with the principle of equal rights and self-determination of peoples as described above and thus possessed of a government representing the whole people belonging to the territory without distinction as to race, creed or colour.

Every state shall refrain from any action aimed at *the partial or total disruption of the national unity and territorial integrity of any other state or country.* (Italics supplied.)

(h) Each of the above and all other principles of this 1970 Declaration were (according to its terms) to be construed in the context of the others. None of them could prejudice the provisions of the Charter or the rights and duties of Members thereunder *or the rights of peoples under the Charter, taking into account the elaboration of these rights in this Declaration,* and that the Charter principles embodied in the Declaration were basic principles of international law.

(4) The Declaration on the Strengthening of International Security (1970),[3b] reciting *inter alia* the above 1970 Declaration, reaffirmed the principle that States "desist from any forcible or other action which deprives peoples, in particular those still under colonial or any other form of external domination, of their inalienable right to self-determination, freedom and independence and to refrain from measures aimed at preventing the attainment of independence of all dependent peoples, . . . and render assistance . . . to the oppressed peoples in their legitimate struggle in order to bring about the speedy elimination of colonialism or any other form of external domination."[4]

(5) Explanatory Note (a) attached to Article 1 of the Consensus Definition stipulates: "In this Definition the term State(a) is used without prejudice to questions of recognition or to whether a State is a Member of the United Nations . . . ."

(6) Article 7 of the Definition provides:

Nothing in this Definition, and in particular Article 3, could in any way prejudice the right to self-determination, freedom and independence, as derived from the Charter, of peoples forcibly deprived of that right and referred to in the Declaration on Principles of International Law concerning Friendly Relations and Co-operation among States in accordance with the Charter of the United Nations, particularly peoples under colonial and racist régimes or other forms of alien domination; nor the right of these peoples to struggle to that end and to seek and receive support, in accordance with the principles of the Charter and in conformity with the above-mentioned Declaration.

(7) The "armed bands" head of the acts of aggression, as stigmatised by Article 3(g) of the Consensus Definition, covers: "The sending by or on behalf of a State of armed bands, groups, irregulars or mercenaries, which carry out acts of armed force against another State of such gravity as to amount to the acts listed above, or its substantial involvement therein."

Under the preceding Article 3(f) there is also stigmatised the action of a State "in allowing its territory, which it has placed at the disposal of another State, to be used by that other State for perpetrating an act of aggression against a third State."

*   *   *   *   *

The answer to the question what is the legal status of armed force used by or in support of a people "struggling" for self-determination must be some net result of interaction of all these provisions. This is a *legal* question, however, and it therefore depends not only on the textual contents of the above items, but also on *the extent to which the text concerned, and any resolution into which it is incorporated, have legal binding force.* Starkly opposed positions on all this were apparent right up to the emergence of the Consensus Definition. They remained virtually unchanged after its adoption, in corresponding conflicting interpretations of its terms. The tangled interrelations between the provisions, the ambiguities, indeterminacies, and conflicts among their terms, and the doubts as to what legal force some of them had, present an exquisite example of how conflict can be consummated in consensus. Nor, in view of the central place of abusive exploitation of the right of self-determination by third States as part of the techniques of indirect aggression since World War II, should this occasion any surprise.

III

Is aggression only a State-to-State relation? United Kingdom delegate Steel pointed to one focus of the complexly interrelated issues touching armed force and self-determination when he asserted that the aggression to be defined was concerned with the acts *of one State against another State.* On this basis, he insisted that the saving of self-determination struggles in Article 7 was not strictly relevant to the Definition; so that the clause, if included, did no more than preserve the legitimacy of struggles *by means other than use of force.*[5] Surprisingly, at first sight, M. Ustor of Hungary[6] also asserted that Article 1 deals only with State-to-State armed force. But he removed the cause of surprise by explaining (with obvious Soviet *bloc* overtones about internal dissent and the Brezhnev Doctrine) that "ordinary police action" of a State to suppress disorder within it could not possibly be caught by the Definition. With no sign of felt inconsistency, he then went on, in flat contrast with M. Steel, to say that neither the State-to-State context, nor even the armed bands provision of Article 3(g), could bring into doubt the legitimacy of *armed* struggles by national liberation movements, since these were "not included in the notion of aggression but [were] considered a lawful form of the use of force".[7] To reach this latter point, M. Khan of Bangla Desh had to proceed from a denial of the State-to-State limitation, and a claim that the acts of aggression enumerated in Article 3 are such *whether committed against peoples or against States*.[8] This would, of course, if consistently followed, make serious inroads on the Soviet reservation of liberty to take "police action" against peoples, e.g., Lithuanians, Estonians, Latvians, Ukrainians, or Jews (not to speak of Hungarians and Czechs), held in subjection to its sovereignty. So also M. Elias,[9] carrying the point to explicit extremes, thought that Article 7 not only allowed a people struggling for self-determination to invade the "territorial integrity" of a State, but meant that such a people also had its own right of "territorial integrity". He thus cut through the ambivalence of the final phrase of Paragraph 6 of the Preamble about "disruption of territorial integrity", simply equivalating "people" with "State".

If there is any basis for this last extreme view, it might conceivably be found (though only with great strain) in the Explanatory Note (a) to Article 1, quoted in paragraph 5 of the preceding Section, but mentioned by neither of these orators. This provides that the term "State" is used in the Definition "without prejudice to questions of recognition or to whether a State is a member of the United Nations". This Note, as B. B. Ferencz points out, is closely related to the provision in Paragraph II of the Six Power Draft that if the territory of a State is delimited by international boundaries, or internationally agreed lines of demarcation, it could be an aggressor or a victim of aggression within the Definition, despite non-recognition of it as a State (or of its Government) by other States.[10] The Note says that despite such non-recognition, and without changing it, the Definition embraces such cases.

This, which is perhaps the most plausible meaning of Explanatory Note (a), would not support extreme views like that of M. Elias here under discussion. It would be directed to such well-known situations as that between Israel and the Arab States, in which a central controversy was whether the Charter obligations of the Arab States not to resort to armed force bound them *vis-à-vis* Israel, in view of their refusal to recognise Israel's statehood. In this context, the Note would mean, on the one hand, that despite their non-recognition of Israel, their first use of armed force against her would constitute aggression; and, on the other, that if they did respect their Charter obligations, this would not in itself constitute recognition of Israel by them.

Another plausible meaning of Note (a) was offered by the New Zealand delegate, M. Quentin Baxter.[11] He referred to the case of hostilities across disputed boundaries, which by their very nature are intractable to criteria of aggression turning on the armed crossing *of boundaries*. He thought that the effect of Explanatory Note (a) was that the Consensus Definition would not be applicable to such cases. Since the Explanatory Note, as it were, bars any prejudice to "questions of recognition" of either State's boundaries, to apply the Definition to such cases would violate this by prerequiring recognition of some particular boundary.

Neither of these more obvious meanings of Note (a) would support the view of M. Elias, wholly assimilating "people" to "State". To base such views, the reference to "recognition" in Note (a) would have to be understood as requiring us to assume that every aspiration to self-determination of a "people" living under sovereignty of an existing State be deemed, as soon as it is expressed, to have matured into a separate new Statehood displacing or breaking away from the old State. None of the protagonists of this equivalation of "people" with "State" ventured to rest it on such an interpretation of Explanatory Note (a).

Oddly enough, the delegation which (according to the Summary Record) came nearest to giving Explanatory Note (a) a meaning which could accommodate the equivalation, did not accept this equivalation. Canadian delegate Lee said roundly that the above-quoted words of Explanatory Note (a) meant that "the concept of Statehood was not an essential element of the definition of aggression".[12] This raised a formidably wide range of inconsistent possibilities. It would support (as we have seen the more obvious meanings to do) the view that the Arab States were in Charter violation in resorting to armed force against Israel, even if they did not recognise her as a State; and that, conversely, their respecting the obligations not to resort to armed force against her did not imply recognition. M. Lee's too oracular words, however, would also support the claims (which, as will be seen in Section IV below, he firmly opposed) that a State is forbidden to respond by armed force to the armed insurgency of one of its peoples (since "a people" is still equivalent to a State even if the parent State does not recognise it). Examples might be secessionist islands of the Philippines, or of Indonesia, or secessionist States of India, or the secessionist Papuans or Bougainvillians in newly-independent Papua-New Guinea. And the oracular words would also, contrarily, support the claim of the parent-State in such situations that its resort to full-scale hostilities in order to suppress such a movement could not be construed as such a recognition as to raise other than internal police questions.[13]

IV

Article 3 of the Consensus Definition includes among acts qualifying as acts of aggression, "(g) The sending by or on behalf of a State of armed bands, groups, irregulars or mercenaries, which carry out acts of armed force against another State of such gravity as to amount to the acts listed above, or its substantial involvement therein". Among other matters debated before adoption of this provision was an Indonesian view[14] that it should cover "supporting and organising" as well as "sending" and (in the final phrase) "active participation" even without "substantial involvement".

This element of aggression definition first appeared as a significant addition to the Soviet proposals of February 6, 1933 on the definition of aggression to the League of Nations Committee on Security Questions. It ran:

> Provision of support to armed bands formed in its territory which have invaded the territory of another State, or refusal, notwithstanding the request of the invaded State to take in its own territory all the measures in its power to deprive those bands of all assistance or protection.

This exact text appeared in later Soviet proposals to the United Nations, for instance, the drafts of 1953, presented to the first Special Committee on the Definition of Aggression on October 23, 1956 (para. 1(f)).[15]

The crucial point for the present Chapter is the relation between Article 3(g) and the self-determination reservation of Article 7. The preliminary matter of the degree of involvement of the host State required for culpability within Article 3 (g) must, however, first be considered in the present section. The omission in Article 3(g) of any express reference to mere "support" or "organisation" suggests a narrowing of the range of culpability as compared with many earlier proposals. Yet this omission was balanced by adding the final phrase (following a comma)—"or its substantial involvement therein" (that is, involvement in the sending of armed bands by or on behalf of a State). It was implicit in the Indonesian comments quoted above, that support or organisation of forces to be sent into the target State may amount to such "involvement", even if it is not the culprit State itself which actually "sends" the bands against the target State. Indeed, this might well, in appropriate cases, inculpate not merely the State playing host to the armed bands, but even third States, for instance, a Syria supporting or organising P.L.O. military arm units to operate from Lebanon or Jordan against Israel.

The *travaux préparatoires* are indeed consistent with this interpretation. In the drafts immediately preceding the Consolidated Text of 1973[16] there were still stark divisions on the matter of armed bands. The Soviet draft listed as "an act of indirect aggression", the "use by a State of armed force by sending armed bands", etc. and "engagement in other forms of subversive activity involving the use of armed force". The Thirteen State Draft of Asian, African, Latin American and other States did not designate such acts as aggression by the host State, but declared in Paragraph 7 that the target State "may take all reasonable and adequate steps to safeguard its existence . . . without having recourse . . . to . . . self-defence against the other State under Article 51 . . .". This would have been an extraordinary grant of immunity to States promoting attacks by armed bands or other terrorist organisations.[17] At the other extreme, the Six State Draft (Australia, Canada, Italy, Japan, U.K. and U.S.)[18] listed among the means, use of which constitutes aggression if used for the wide range of purposes there enumerated, the following: "(6) Organizing, supporting or directing armed bands or irregular or volunteer forces that make incursions or infiltrate into another State, or (7) Organizing, supporting or directing violent civil strife or acts of terrorism in another State"; or (8) such activities aimed at violent overthrow of another State's government.

In the Consolidated Text which emerged from the Contact Groups and Drafting Group, Article 3(g) was already virtually in final form, save that the final phrase ("or its substantial involvement therein") read "or its open and active participation therein". Neither the Soviet view that the activity in question is only "indirect aggression" nor the view of the Thirteen that it is not aggression at all and does not even give rise to a right of self-defence, was accepted. Rather it was the view of the Six which prevailed. This is that such activity is a case of aggression *simpliciter*, giving rise like other direct aggression to response by self-defence under general international law and under Article 51 of the Charter. It was possible to imply from the Soviet Draft, and it was expressed in the Thirteen State Draft, that guilt of aggression is limited to a host State which *actually sends*. Quite clearly, under the Six Nation Draft, aggression would also embrace organising, supporting or directing armed bands which are sent into the target State, and even organising, supporting or directing violent civil strife merely within the target State aimed at violent overthrow of its government. As between these positions the final Article 3(g) is a compromise.

Article 3(g) (as well as the preceding Article 3(f) concerning a State allowing its territory to be used for committing aggression) derives (as already seen) from "old benchmarks" of international law.[19] What the Definition adds are clouds of doubt as to how much knowledge of such use, and capacity to control it, will thus implicate the host State. As the operations of armed bands against Greece from Albania, and against Israel from various Arab States, have shown in the post-World War II period, these were questions which did not need the further obfuscation they received. Even apart from the matter of "struggle" for self-determination (just examined), the end-product of Article 3(g) compares unfavourably with the pre-existing legal position. And it does not much remedy this fault that the Security Council might in theory close any loopholes by resorting to its discretion under Article 2 to regard "other relevant circumstances", in judging the response of a victim State to such indirect aggression.[20]

M. Rossides, of Cyprus, who said his State had proposed the final compromise in Article 3(g), thought it covered a form of indirect aggression which amounted in practice to armed attack. While it requires there to have been a "sending" into the target State, it inculpates the host State not merely when that State did the sending, but also when it has a "substantial involvement therein".[21] The critical point, said M. Bessou of France, is that mere organising or preparing armed bands is not of itself aggression "[u]ntil they have crossed the frontier of another State".[22] M. Lee of Canada applauded Article 3(g) as "acceptance of the thesis that the distinction between direct and indirect aggression was artificial . . . terroristic acts might be of such magnitude as to be as harmful as the acts of aggression."[23] On this basis, a Government of Lebanon, which has an agreement to play host to P.L.O. armed bands in southern Lebanon, explicitly for armed operations across the border in Israel, could scarcely deny that it is "substantially involved" in the sending of such bands into Israel. (This, of course, could not in fact prevent the Arab-Opec Members from marshalling a majority in the General Assembly to support the denial.)

V

As late as 1972, when Mr. Ferencz[24] and Professor Schwebel[25] discussed the deliberations about "indirect aggression", the full antimony between the self-determination saving clause (Soviet Draft, Paragraph 6, Thirteen Power Draft, Paragraph 10) and the indirect aggression armed bands provision (Article 3(g) of the Consolidated Text) had not emerged. The Soviet Draft, Paragraph 6, did not ambiguously save merely "struggle" for self-determination in vague terms but unambiguously specified "the use of armed force in accordance with the Charter" *including* exercise of the inherent right of self-determination. The Thirteen Power Draft, Paragraph 10, contrarily saved the Charter's provisions as to "the right of peoples to self-determination, sovereignty and territorial integrity", but did not make express whether armed force could be used by them. And the Six Power Draft was careful in Paragraph II to make an exception to its treatment of a non-recognised "political entity" with internationally demarcated boundaries as a State which can be the victim of aggression, precisely for cases where the political entity concerned is "subject to the authority" of the State alleged to be committing aggression against it. Some Committee Members resisted even this degree of concession for non-State political entities, and thought the Definition should be limited to aggression between States.

At this stage Dr. Schwebel was able to speculate about the problem of non-State entities in virtual abstraction from the political issues burning fiercely in the background. He wrote, by way of example, of "an entity which sought to break away from an African State", and "in the course of its rebellion attacks a neighbouring State sympathetic to the cause of the Central Government", being an aggressor. And, conversely, of a European State attacking a neighbouring entity which (because of its supposed revanchism) is not recognised as a State. Would not the entity be a victim of aggression? Except for the hypothetical breakaway from an African State, Schwebel is obviously thinking of an entity of stable governmental authority over defined territory such as was contemplated in Paragraph II of the Six Power Draft above referred to.

He thought that the whole problem was solved by the formula "without prejudice to questions of recognition" in Explanatory Note (a). And he even found it "difficult to see why use of the concept of non-State entities would be confusing". Such words from so perceptive a scholar as late as 1972 provide an intriguing measure of the treacherous layerings of the *arrière-pensées* of political warfare surrounding these matters. They are oblivious to the complex and often dangerous possibilities of proposals to licence "peoples", who might have neither ostensible control of territory nor any stable government, and third States who choose from whatever motive to support them, to use armed force against any selected target State. It is no less intriguing, in view of the problems which the following Sections will reveal, that Professor Schwebel thought that the question of non-State entities "may be readily solved".

It was in the context of this failure of the Thirteen State Draft to free the use of armed bands and other modes of indirect aggression from the stigma of aggression, that there appeared in draft Article 5 of the Consolidated Text the saving clause about self-determination which, with notable changes, later became Article 7. In draft Article 5 (as to which the Contact Group was careful to say that there was at that stage "no general agreement") the bid to legitimise *use of force* by non-State groups and by States assisting them is quite explicit, following in this respect the above Paragraph of the Soviet Draft. Nothing in the definition (it ran) was to prevent "peoples . . . from using force and seeking or receiving support and assistance" in exercise of "their inherent right to self-determination in accordance with the principles of the Charter . . .".

It is clear that *if the above quoted words in draft Article 5 had survived through to the final Article 7,* this would have compensated the proponents of wars of liberation for the failure (seen in the last Section) of their bid to free the sending, etc. of armed bands from the stigma of aggression.

The quoted words, however, did not survive. In the final Article 7, the range of conduct saved from inculpation was narrowed in various respects. The special inclusion of "peoples under military occupation" disappeared. Not "foreign domination" as such, but only "forcible deprivation" of the Charter right of self-determination was the basis of the right to "struggle". *Above all, it was stripped of any express reference to a right to use force* in the "struggle", and to third States to use force in assisting them. What remains in Article 7 is the blander formula of "the right of these peoples to struggle to that end."[26] As between the States utterly opposed to extending the freedom to use armed bands or other indirect aggression under the banner of "wars of self-determination" or "liberation", and those resolved to extend this freedom and legalise (as it were) "such wars", the latter again (and finally) failed to embody their view in the Consensual Definition.

It, nevertheless, nicely exemplifies the vacuity of the Consensus Definition on a number of critical points that sufficient vagueness of language was left in the final Article 7 to ground plausible arguments (plausible, that is, in terms of political warfare rather than of law), for neutralising the rather clear words stigmatising the sending of armed bands as aggression. As will be seen in the next Section, the champions of the opposed positions prior to the adoption of the Consensus Definition, continued to maintain virtually the same positions as representing correct interpretations of Articles 3(g) and 7 as adopted.

The corresponding point as to Article 3(f) did not have as much attention, but it is no less real.[27] That paragraph qualifies as aggression a host State's allowing forces of a foreign State to use its territory for committing an act of aggression against a third State. Suppose, however, the action of these guest forces is by way of assistance to a "national liberation movement" against the third State? M. Omar of Libya was critical of Article 3(f), apparently because he thought it *should* have explicitly made an exception for such a case.[28] If, however, such an exception were necessary to subject Article 3(f) to the qualification of the legality of armed "struggle" for self-determination, it would also be necessary for so qualifying Article 3(g). (For the saving clause in Article 7 refers without distinction to the whole of Article 3.) None such, of course, is found.

Moreover, on the view (very dubious as already indicated) that the provision of Explanatory Note (a) to Article 1 that the term "State" is used "without prejudice to questions of recognition", means that "State" includes a people which has not yet achieved Statehood, Article 3(f) would be an even more serious obstacle. It would stigmatise as aggression not only a host State's allowing *another State* to use its territory for perpetrating aggression against a third State, but also a similar facility accorded to insurgent forces, for instance by Lebanon to Palestinian forces. This would be a more severe rule than that under customary international law which only requires the host State to abate the depredations, and on its default authorises the victim State after due notice to enter the host territory and itself abate it. Explanatory Note (a) could not have been intended to produce the more extreme result.

It was urged by the Italian delegate, in relation to Article 3(f), that the conduct of the host State could not be stimatised as aggression unless the aggressive hostilities against the third State[29] were carried on with its consent. If "allowing" in Article 3(f) refers to grant of consent, this would be self-evidently correct: but, of course, that word may mean merely "not preventing", which would make this view incorrect. This remains one of the many questions not settled by the Definition. So probably is the question whether the host State is an aggressor if it lacked the means to prevent the guest forces from committing their aggression. (Presumably, if it had the means of prevention and refused to use them, this would be a tacit consent incriminating it.) Whatever be the correct answers to these questions, it seems clear as to forces both of a guest State or of a guest insurgent force, that the customary rules mentioned above impose on the host State the duty to abate the activities, and confer on the victim State the liberty of taking measures of abatement after notice to the host State defaulting in its obligation.[30]

As with self-defence against armed bands under Article 3(g), discussed in Section IV above, so with Article 3(f), it would appear that the efforts of the Thirteen Power Draft to deny to the victim State the usual right of self-defence against aggression were (in one of the rare moments of clarity of drafting) rejected by the Consensus Definition. Where the impugned conduct of the host State does *not* fall within the terms of Article 3(g) and Article 3(f), so that the position depends on customary international law, important questions have been recently raised as to the limits of the right of lawful response accorded to the victim State. It has been argued, for example, that forceful retaliation may further weaken the host State's control over its own territory, may strengthen the insurgents, and even lead the host State to overt support of them. Such prudential considerations cannot, of course, dispose of the undoubted legal rights of States to respond to organised violence directed against them, whether from other States or from private or insurgent groups organised, supported or tolerated by these, and to seek to put an end to such activities. Nor can they bring into question the long-accepted rule that such measures may have to be taken across the frontiers of the host State which wilfully or by other default fails, after due notice, to abate them.[31] Certainly, there is much to be said for the development of adequate standards of proportionality of responsive force, both for self-defence situations and those at present under discussion.

To say that standards of proportionality ought to be worked out for both self-defence and other measures taken by a State for what customary law termed its self-preservation is, however, only to state the problem, not to solve it, nor, indeed, to imply that it *can* be solved. Some delegations saw the need to require proportionality in the Definition as flowing from the principle that force in self-defence is only legitimated insofar as defensive action must be immediate, from the danger that otherwise self-defence would be used to justify wars of "revenge", and from the need to centralise the control of force in the United Nations. At the other extreme, the Soviet view was that such a requirement would unreasonably hamper the victim of aggression and favour the aggressor, who in the nature of things already had the advantage of surprise as to timing, weapons and the like. The effect of such a requirement in shifting the *ex post facto* burden of proof as to justification from the aggressor to his victim, was also resisted. And it was argued that the drafting history of Article 51, and its designation of self-defence as an "inherent right" excluded such a requirement. Most delegations, for one reason or another, thought that a proportionality requirement was irrelevant to or unnecessary for the definition of aggression, or that its meaning was too uncertain and required further study, or must so vary with the circumstances that it could not be spelled out and the whole matter should be left to the Security Council. The British and American views seemed to go with the Soviet, unless the definition of aggression stigmatised acts of indirect aggression going beyond "the most serious cases of direct armed aggression." Only so far as such indirect aggression was included, and the right of self-defence against it acknowledged, were they disposed to favour a requirement of proportionality.[32]

The de Brouckère Report of League days mooted, as long ago as 1926, the idea that the principle of proportionality might even be an *indicator* of aggression. A victim of aggression might, he thought, even become the aggressor unless the defence was "proportionate to the seriousness of the attack and justified by the imminence of the danger."[33] Clearly, no such view was accepted in the Consensus Definition, which otherwise might have been expected to include use of disproportionate armed force in self-defence in the list of acts of aggression in Article 3, or at least to make some provision about proportionality. Neither these nor any other references to proportionality were made. And the omission is especially significant since the Thirteen Power Draft did propose that even States acting in self-defence be limited to measures reasonably proportionate to the armed attack,[34] and, at one point in the Fourth Special Committee's work, 20 of the 35 Member States seemed to favour some reference to proportionality.[35]

VI

We turn now to the post-Consensus interpretations of the relation of Article 3(g) (Armed Bands) and Article 7 (Self-Determination), and, first, to the views opposing the expansive interpretation of Article 7. The positions as to armed bands in the Six State Draft were reasserted by these and other States as the meaning of the final Article 3(g), and as in no way qualified by the additional Article 7 on self-determination.

Neither Article 7 nor the Preamble, said M. Migliuolo,[36] could legitimate actions disrupting the territorial integrity of States complying with the Charter and thus "ruled by a Government representing the people inhabiting the territory." The Belgian Government, said M. van Brusselen,[37] "had always maintained that the use of violence as a means of settling . . . conflicts . . . was inadmissible . . .", and Article 7 could not sanction resort to force beyond the limits set by the Charter. M. Wehry of the Netherlands[38] thought "it was important to guard against interpreting the affirmation of the right of the peoples concerned to receive support as a legitimation of armed support". The Charter allowed no such exception. "[P]eoples which did not enjoy democratic government deserved support, but not . . . armed support."

For the United Kingdom, indeed, as already seen, M. Steel thought it was not merely that Article 7 did not endorse any use of force even in pursuit of self-determination.[39] Article 7 was really not relevant to the Consensus Definition of aggression at all, this latter being limited to State-to-State relations.[40] And M. Lee of Canada[41] was more specific. "Struggle" of peoples meant struggle by peaceful means. His delegation denied that Article 7 could be interpreted to license the use of force, or to condone assault contrary to the Charter on the territorial integrity or dismemberment of any State by violent means. M. Bracklo extended the point as against supporting third States. The right to receive support could not legitimise armed support, and this could also not be justified as either the "self-defence" or the "collective" measures licensed under the Charter.[42]

M. Martins of Portugal added two points on the text. First, to read Article 7 as sanctioning the use of force would contradict Article 5, paragraph 1, of the Definition providing that "no consideration of whatever nature, whether political, economic, military or otherwise, may serve as a justification of aggression". Second, Article 7 could not be read as derogating only from paragraph (g) of Article 3, and negating simply that use of armed *bands* in struggles for self-determination is aggression. For, by its terms, Article 7 derogated from all the paragraphs of Article 3, all of which designated various acts as acts of aggression. If, as against Article 3 as a whole, Article 7 were given the meaning claimed by way of derogation from paragraph (g) sanctioning armed force for self-determination, this would involve also similar derogations from all the other stigmatised acts. This would produce the absurd result of legalising "for the solution of certain disputes, those very means which the definition defined as constituting illicit aggression".[43]

From the above standpoints, Article 7 could be read only as a general precautionary saving of the self-determination principle. United States Representative Rosenstock added that, in view of the careful negation by the immediately preceding Article 6 of any construction enlarging the scope of lawful force under the Charter, Article 7 could not, in any case, be read as legitimising any acts of force which would otherwise be illegal under the Charter.[44] M. Rosenne of Israel, who found Article 3 too weak as to aggression even without any further derogation by Article 7, was concerned to point out that the fact that such derogation was not warranted, meant that target States of armed interventions inspired by unwarranted interpretations of Article 7, would be legally entitled to react to such aggression.[45]

VII

Those who championed use of armed force for self-determination were, if anything, even more categorical than those who denied its permissibility under the Consensus Definition. For M. Obadi,[46] Article

7 was closely related to Article 3(g), and confirmed the view that peoples oppressed could use armed force for the stated end. M. Nyamdo of Mongolia flatly associated Article 7 with Article 51 of the Charter on self-defence against armed attack.[47] For M. Boulbina of Algeria[48] the only possible effect of Article 3(g) read with Article 7, was that self-determination struggles can be pressed and supported by third States *despite Article 3(g),* by any appropriate means, "including armed force".[49] He saw this as *the chief merit of the Consensus Definition,* and while he spoke of different interpretations of the Definition, did not mention any differing interpretations *on this.*

The internal incongruities in the positions of some delegations make it impossible not to see the primacy of the Political Warfare Drive in much of these discussions. M. Siage of Syria emphatically agreed that armed force could be used, despite Article 3(g),[50] in self-determination struggles, *even though he would have wanted Article 2 to provide* that use of armed force was "automatically . . . aggression, not *prima facie* evidence of aggression"![51] Miss Mpagi of Uganda, taking a similar position as to armed force, was even able to think that Article 3(g) "gave full support to the right of peoples to struggle for their liberation . . . ; that right was reiterated in Article 7."[52] M. Maniang of Sudan simply asserted that the word "struggle" in Article 7 should be interpreted to refer to all forms of struggle, "including armed struggle".[53] M. Kumi of Ghana, in like spirit, simply "did not accept any interpretation of Article 7 which might eliminate the use of force in the struggle for independence".[54] So did M. Essy,[55] though (he said) his own country's experience was that peoples struggling did not necessarily have to resort to armed conflict.[56]

M. Rassolko (Byelorussia) repeated the general Soviet bloc view both that aggression is only State-to-State, so that it does not affect police action within a Sovereign State, and that Article 3(g) "could not be interpreted as calling into question the legitimacy of the national liberation struggle of peoples, *partisan* war, etc."[57] This second limb was obviously too loosely stated. M. Kolesnik of the U.S.S.R. prudently tightened it up in asserting that Article 7 recognised that "armed struggle, etc." was lawful for both the peoples concerned and third States supporting them. For he was careful to specify that he was talking about armed struggle against "colonial oppression".[58]

The Angola Affair of 1976, the first and rather problematic case in which the Security Council formally stigmatised a State as an aggressor, illustrates well the self-serving contradictions invited by these aspects of the 1974 Definition, and of the 1970 Declaration . . . Concerning . . . Friendly Relations . . . among States. As a basis for stigmatising South African conduct, the resolution (S.C. Resol. 387 (1976)) recited, significantly, not Article 7 of the Definition, but the paragraph of the Declaration forbidding intervention in the internal or external affairs of another State. In order at the same time to excuse Cuban and Soviet conduct not really distinguishable from South Africa's, the resolution then recited "the inherent right" of every State in exercise of its sovereignty, to request assistance from any other State or group of States.[58a] The resolution passed by a bare majority of 9, France, the U.K. and U.S. abstaining, and China not participating in the vote. The U.K. delegate complained that the effect of the latter recital was to make an unwarranted exception to the legal duty not to intervene. But this underrates the Soviet position. The objection is rather that when interventions by third States are requested by more than one insurgent faction, each claiming to speak for the Government of a still emergent new State, it cannot be said in advance of the outcome which request is the request of the new State. Prior interventions of third States, therefore, would seem, on principle, to be either all lawful or unlawful.

VIII

There is some purpose in separating off, as far as we can, those positions favouring the licence to use armed force in "liberation struggles" *which are argued for rather than merely asserted.* There is, indeed, a fascinating spectrum between those who show awareness that the force-for-liberation claim has somehow to be legitimated under international and Charter law, and those who seem confident that the making of a legal place for this new-fangled licence *has apparently ceased to be a problem altogether.* This confidence is associated no doubt with the phenomenon sometimes described as "automatic majorities" in the General Assembly.

Those who argue rather than merely assert begin, of course, with the general Charter references to self-determination. Their apparent awareness of how tenuous these are, in relation to legal obligations, is manifest in the far more frequent and emphatic invocations of General Assembly pronouncements, especially the Declaration on Principles Concerning the Friendly Relations of States . . . 1970, which is quoted at length in Section II above.[58b] The law-making character of such General Assembly acts is, of course, at best controverted. But the richness of their rhetoric is used to attempt to elbow out a place in the Charter for this novel privilege of using armed force.

The more persuasive arguments follow the directions we have already outlined in Section I.

M. Goerner of the German Democratic Republic saw Article 7 as authorising the use of armed force in self-determination struggles, because colonialist and racist domination was "permanent aggression" against the people concerned, and the people's response to it by use of armed force is lawful as self-defence.[59] Without this elaboration, M. Obadi (Democratic Yemen)[60] observed that Article 51 confers rights on peoples as well as States. M. Petric of Yugoslavia was concerned to ensure that this rationale should not be reduced in its ambit by the reference in Article 7 to "peoples forcibly deprived, etc.". This, he seemed to say, does *not* mean that the people's right to use armed force only arises when *present* forcible deprivation can be shown.[61]

At the other end of third world arguments, the legal problem is met by flat assertion that the new "law" is already set. M. Alvarez Tabio declared that it was legitimate to use armed force "to defend the inalienable right of peoples to self-determination".[62] For M. Mahmud of Pakistan, Articles 2 and 3 of the Consensus Definition mean that the first use of armed force is presumed to be aggression unless it is justified as either (1) self-defence under Charter Article 51; or (2) *in exercise of the self-determination envisaged in Article 7 of the Definition*.[63] M. Reshetnyak of the Ukraine declared that the right of "armed struggle" for self-determination is not only already provided by the Charter, but the Charter has somehow precisely limited it to "colonial oppression, racism and occupation".[64] M. Asaduzzaman Khan was so sure that "State" within the Definition includes any people struggling for self-determination against colonialism and racism, that he regarded the "acts of aggression" designated by Article 3 of the Definition to be such when committed against "a people" as well as against States.[65] He did not advert to difficulties of making either grammatical, or politico-strategic sense, of a number of them on such a basis. Nor did M. Elias refer to them, when he read Article 7 (combined with the reference in Paragraph 6 of the Preamble to the duty not to deprive people by armed force of their self-determination) as giving *each people* protection of its own right of *territorial integrity*, as well as legitimating invasion of the territorial integrity *of States* by peoples struggling for self-determination, etc.[66] M. Obadi found the outcome of Article 51 of the Charter, as preserved by Article 6 of the Definition no less clear. They "should be interpreted as meaning that peoples who were victims of alien domination had the right to use force" in order to win self-determination, freedom and independence.[67]

Of course, this is only so if we import into Article 51 the postulate discussed above that every such people concerned is the victim of standing armed attack by the State of which it is a part. The universal truth of that postulate is problematic. It begs the central question of what should be, today, the effect in international law of armed attacks of centuries ago. It also leaves unexplained the right of States such as the Soviet Union to invoke prerogatives like that of "police action" to suppress by force, as at the present time, movements of secession among its constituent peoples.

Between these two extremes are many other third world positions already summarised. These have in common a varying mixture of legal hesitancy and bloc-political commitment. M. Ikouebe of the Congo admitted that the terms of Article 7 were confused, *but was still surprised that anyone could interpret Article 7 as not justifying the use of armed force by oppressed peoples*. He did not allay his own surprise when he himself criticised Article 7 as failing to provide "unequivocally" that it was not aggression for a third State to furnish armed support to a national liberation movement.[68]

IX

The bandwagon surge of efforts to read down the armed bands prohibition by reference to self-determination of peoples—even when they
failed—had embarrassing side-effects for some State positions. These
effects perhaps explain some curious samples of reasoning. M. Baroody
of Saudi Arabia was contemptuous of notions that extreme coercion
other than by arms—such as the oil boycott which his country pioneered
in 1973—could be aggression; but he was clear that the Definition
"should contain at least one paragraph informing the world community
of the scope of neo-aggression" and neo-colonialism. "All States suffered
from that and all States practised it; all were to blame."[69] M. An Chih-
yuan of China[70] was concerned to have it clear that Article 7 sanctioned
use of force against "imperialist" and "Zionist", as well as the "colonial"
and "racist" "domination". Presumably "imperialist" could be turned to
catch Soviet practices, but not (on the Chinese interpretation) Chinese
policy in Tibet. And, of course, "Zionist" ranged China neatly in her
contest with the Soviet Union for influence with the Arab States.

Most Soviet bloc States were careful (as we have seen) to stress
"*colonial* oppression" as the target, so as presumably to protect the
right to take "police" or "Brezhnev doctrine" measures within the Soviet
sphere.[71] M. Ustor of Hungary afforded the neatest sample of the
double talk involved. On the one hand, he discounted fears that mere
"police actions" within a State might be regarded as aggression, Article
1 of the Definition having made it clear that only State-to-State
aggression was covered. On the other, with no effort to explain the
inconsistency, he asserted that, despite Article 3(g), armed struggles for
national liberation are legitimate since "not included in the notion of
aggression, but . . . a lawful form of the use of force."[72]

M. Mahmud of Pakistan,[73] (as already observed), sanctified self-
determination struggles, alongside Article 51 of the Charter, as a chief
basis of lawful use of force of the Charter. Then, perhaps recalling his
country's dismemberment, he added that the right of self-determination
must be exercised in accordance with the Charter "in those cases which
were covered by relevant decisions of the United Nations". *Article 7
should not (he said) be construed as calling into question "the territorial
integrity of sovereign States"*. And he maintained a perhaps prudent
silence on the relation of Article 7 to the armed bands provision of
Article 3(g).

Here no doubt, as elsewhere, we must see as two-forked the strategy
of protagonists for the "inalienable right" of a people to "struggle" by
armed force for "self-determination", and for the immunity of third
States which use armed force to assist them. One fork was to prevent
such activities being qualified as aggression, as the actual text of Article
3(f) and (g) of the Consensus Definition, despite their best efforts,
finally did qualify them. The other fork aimed to leave room for one-
sided interpretations in areas of definitional indeterminacy or self-
contradiction, in the confidence that these will be resolved favourably

in a particular conflict by the highly predictable third world majorities in the General Assembly.

This strategy did, indeed, have some articulation. Pakistan said that the right of self-determination "must be exercised in accordance with the Charter . . . in those cases which were covered by relevant decisions of the United Nations",[74] these latter decisions being pointed presumably at General Assembly pronouncements. M. Petrella of the Argentine frankly based the rights which he claimed Article 7 embodied, on their supposed "establishment" by the General Assembly.[75] M. Hassouna of Egypt based the meaning which he gave to "struggle" in Article 7 as including "armed struggle", on the phrase "all methods" used in General Assembly resolutions (unspecified) on "acceptance by the international community" and on "historical reality".[76] And as to loopholes which (he thought) still worried third world countries, he insisted that interpretations would be guided by decisions "of the United Nations". This was in the context a demand that even the Security Council should be guided by the views of General Assembly majorities.

CHAPTER 7

"Indirect" and "Economic" Aggression

I

Even in an area where elementary notions have been so long disputed, and terminology correspondingly shifting and confused, the term "indirect aggression" stands preeminent in its chaos of references.

For those who think that "aggression" properly embraces only large-scale armed hostilities *between States*, hostilities between insurgents and their own government would not be aggression. For, first, they are not hostilities *between* States, even if third States provide the arms or the training or otherwise support the insurgents. And, second, quite often, at any rate, such hostilities may also not qualify as aggression because not of a sufficient scale. Others, however, while regarding State-to-State hostilities as an essential element in aggression, would say that third States promoting such hostilities against a target State, even though they act through the instrumentality of the insurgents, are guilty of "aggression". But they will usually add, to betoken the special mode by which the hostilities are pressed, the adjective "indirect". "Indirect aggression" will for them mean the promotion or support by the aggressor State of resort to armed force by insurgent or other forces of sufficient scale, *though not actually carried out by the "indirect aggressor"*.

Those who do regard the "force" which States are forbidden to exercise against another State as *wider than* armed hostilities, may equally be found to say that the third State, in the supposed circumstances, is guilty of aggression, since its use of the insurgents as an instrument against the target State is an application of "force" within the prohibition of the Charter. For even though the putative aggressor is not himself resorting to armed hostilities, he is still using force in the Charter sense of extreme coercion. For them, too, this is a case of "aggression", to which they will often attach the adjective "indirect"; but now the adjective will indicate forbidden activity of the aggressor State not involving his own actual use *of "armed force", but only extreme coercion*.

In the above instance of uses of the term "indirect", armed hostilities are still being used against the victim, though it may not be the putative aggressor (the third State) who uses them. Insofar, however, as the prohibited "force" referred to by the term "indirect aggression" is given the wider meaning of "extreme coercion" *simpliciter* ("extreme", that is in its impact on the "sovereignty, territorial integrity or political independence" of the target State) that term may also be found to be applied to operations in which no armed hostilities *from any quarter* at all are involved. The commonest examples of this usage of the term have been as a kind of generic term for aggression not involving armed hostilities, including "economic aggression", "ideological aggression", and other "indirect aggression", alongside "armed aggression".

We have to be aware of these diverse uses of the term "indirect aggression", varying with context, as opposed to "armed aggression", between States. Once neither the State-to-State element, nor the element of use of armed force is seen as indispensable to aggression, but only extreme coercion in the above sense, then other non-armed activities of sufficient intensity may also fall within "aggression". To distinguish them, the proponents may use the term "indirect" to refer to all non-State-to-State, or non-armed State-to-State extreme coercion. Unless we are alerted to this plurality of possible references the confusions of the debates and the literature will be even greater than they need be.

While it is important to be thus aware of this historical jungle of verbal usage, the important contrast in the Fourth Special Committee was between "indirect" aggression, on the one hand, and *State-to-State armed* aggression, on the other. This contrast became central as a facet of the sharp conflict of views as to whether "the inherent right of self-determination of peoples" grounded a licence of the people concerned for use of armed force in struggling for this right, and of any third State to assist in this armed struggle, against the target sovereign State concerned. Where a third State openly participates in such an armed struggle, the opposed positions were, on the one hand, that its action was "armed aggression", or, on the other, that it was lawfully using armed force, justifiable under some notion such as "collective self-defence" with the struggling people. On neither view was there strictly any need for a category of "indirect aggression".

Where, however, the third State assists the struggling people without openly participating in the use of armed force against the target State, the disapproving view described this conduct as "indirect aggression"; the approving view again regarded it as a lawful use under the above notion of whatever measures are taken. The opposed standpoints were starkly illustrated, as Chapter 6 has shown, in the 1974 polemics as to the interrelations between Article 3(g) (on acts of aggression through armed bands) and Article 7 (on self-determination) of the Consensus Definition.

II

While both the Soviet and Six Power Drafts treated "indirect" aggression in some of the above senses (including the sending of armed bands) as aggression, the Thirteen Power Draft did not.[1] It made only the mild provision in Paragraph 7 that a State victim of "subversive and/or terrorist acts by irregular, volunteer or armed bands organized or supported by another State" may take reasonable steps to protect itself "without having recourse" to self-defence under Article 51 of the

Charter. The Soviet Draft (Paragraph 20), on the other hand, was explicit that a State sending such armed bands, "terrorists or saboteurs" to the victim State's territory, or engaging in other forms of "subversive activity" involving the use of armed force aimed to promote "internal upheaval" or "reversal of policy", was guilty of "indirect aggression". So also the Six Power Draft included as uses of force qualifying as "aggression" (if resorted to with appropriate intent) "[o]rganizing, supporting or directing" armed bands, irregulars or volunteer forces, or violent civil strife or acts of terrorism, into or in another State, or organizing, supporting or directing subversive activities aimed at the violent overthrow of its Government.[2]

It will be noted that the Six Power Draft termed such acts "aggression" *simpliciter*; and though the Soviet Draft termed them "indirect aggression", it did not specify any difference in legal consequences flowing from the different name. To produce such different legal consequences (and in particular to take away the right of individual and collective self-defence) was, of course, the precise purpose of the Thirteen Power provision above described. It sought to achieve this purpose, both by withholding the stigma of aggression, and by express statement. Acceptance of such a provision would have been at odds with the Charter and general international law as hitherto accepted in a number of respects.

First, as seen in Chapter 6, international law imputed responsibility to a State knowingly serving as a base for such para-military activities, and gave the victim State rather wide liberties of self-defence against them.

Second, none of the Charter provisions dealing with unlawful use of force, whether armed or not, offers any basis for distinguishing between force applied by the putative aggressor, or indirectly applied by him through armed bands, irregulars and the like. As a United States spokesman on an earlier Special Committee observed: "There is simply no provision . . . which suggests that a State can in any way escape or ameliorate the Charter's condemnation of illegal acts of force against another State by a judicious selection of means to its illegal ends."[3]

Third, as Professor Schwebel also observes, the General Assembly has more than once included at least some species of "indirect" aggression within its description of "aggression". For example, the Declaration . . . on . . . Friendly Relations . . . among States . . . (Resol. 2625 (XXV)) provides, by way of elaboration of Article 2(4) of the Charter, that "[e]very state has the duty to refrain from organizing or encouraging the organization of irregular forces or armed bands, including mercenaries, for incursion into the territory of another State," and from organising, assisting or participating in acts of civil strife or terrorism in another State involving a threat or use of force, or acquiescing in organised activities within its own territory directed to commission of such acts.[4] Moreover, Resolution 2131(XX)) entitled "Declaration of the Inadmissibility of Intervention . . ." adopted 109 to 0 on December 21, 1965, condemns armed and all other forms of intervention against the personality or political, economic or cultural elements of a State; and it also forbids "economic, political or any other type of measures to coerce another State in order . . . to secure from it advantages of any kind".[5] Armed intervention of these kinds is declared to be "aggression"; all other forms, direct or indirect, are declared to be violations of the Charter.

Fourth, it may be added that from at least the Spanish Civil War onwards, the most endemic and persistent forms of resorts to armed force in both Europe and Asia have been in contexts caught as "aggression" by the Soviet and Six Power drafts, but condoned more or less fully by the Thirteen Power Draft.

III

Descriptions of "indirect aggression", "economic aggression" and "ideological aggression" had figured in classical (and abortive) Soviet proposals of the 'fifties, the tenor of which needs now to be recalled.

Within "indirect aggression", Paragraph 2 of the Soviet 1956 draft included encouragement of subversive activity, such as acts of terrorism or diversionary acts, against another State, promotion of civil war, internal upheaval or a change of policy favouring an aggressor, in that State. Significantly, at that stage, the case of "indirect aggression" by sending (etc.) of armed bands (later to be expressly included in the Consensus Definition) figures in the 1956 draft not in the paragraph on "indirect" aggression, but as a final subparagraph to paragraph 1 on "aggression" *simpliciter*.[6]

Within "economic aggression", paragraph 3 of the 1956 Soviet proposal included measures by a State—(a) of economic pressure "violating [the] sovereignty and economic indepedence" of another State and "threatening the bases of its economic life"; (b) preventing another State "from exploiting or nationalizing its own natural riches"; (c) imposing an economic blockade on another State.

What this category of "economic aggression" really amounted to was rendered enigmatic by the continued Soviet inclusion in paragraph 6 of the 1956 proposal of the substance of paragraph 2 from its earlier proposal of 1933,[7] directed at that time to the paradigm case of *State-to-State armed aggression*. This declared that

> No considerations whatsoever of a political, strategical, or *economic nature*, including the desire to exploit natural riches or to obtain any sort of advantages or privileges on the territory of another State, no references to considerable capital investments or other special interests in a given State . . . shall be accepted as justification of aggression as defined in Clause 1." (Italics supplied.)

These "non-justifications" for "aggression" are then particularised as including the following conditions or acts in the putatively victim State—

> political, economic or cultural backwardness, or alleged maladministration (paragraph 2A(a) and (b));

danger to life or property of foreign residents (paragraph 2A(c));
  the revolution or counter-revolutionary movements, civil war, or the
    political, economic or social order (paragraph 2A(d) and (e));
  infringement of the commercial, concessional or other economic
    interests of a given State or its citizens (paragraph 2B(b));
  rupture of diplomatic or economic relations (paragraph 2B(c));
  economic or financial boycott (paragraph 2B(d));
  repudiation of debts (paragraph 2B(e));
  non-admission or limitation of immigration, or restriction of rights
    or privileges of foreign residents (paragraph 2B(f) and (g));
  frontier incidents (paragraph 2B(j)).

A central problem of this sweep of negative assertions is how a State
imposing the measures of economic pressure described on another State
can be guilty of "economic aggression", when it is also provided that
no economic consideration whatsoever, not even "economic and financial
boycott" *by* the putative victim against the putative aggressor, can
justify "aggression". If, for example, in reply to the Arab State oil
boycott of 1973, the United States, Japan or other industrialised countries had declared a blockade of all movement of their manufactures
to the oil boycotting States, which side would have been guilty of
"economic aggression" in terms of the Soviet definition? Was the sudden
oil boycott any less a measure "violating [the] sovereignty and economic
independence" and "threatening the bases of [the] economic life" of ·
the industrialised States, than would have been the latters' ban on
manufactured exports in relation to that of the oil boycotting States?
Insofar as the oil boycott was such a measure, must it not have constituted "economic aggression", and the ban on manufactured exports a
legitimate response?

One possible answer is that these Soviet proposals of 1956 were
aimed at having it both ways. Because of the self-contradictions as to
economic aggression, it provided a basis (albeit a specious one) for
stigmatising extreme economic pressures *by disfavoured States* as
economic aggression, while immunising extreme economic pressures *by
favoured States* as mere expressions of its internal situation or laws
and regulations, immune on that account from external interference.
This kind of design, as will be observed in this and other respects, continues to haunt the definitional exercise up to the present.

As to "ideological aggression", the Soviet 1956 proposal declared
it committed when a State—"(a) encourages war propaganda; (b)
encourages propaganda in favour of using atomic, bacterial, chemical
and other weapons of mass destruction; (c) promotes the propagation
of fascist-nazi views, of racial and national exclusiveness and contempt
for other peoples."

While the category of "ideological aggression" had no prominence in
the Fourth Special Committee, the notions of "economic aggression"
and "indirect aggression" did (as already observed) play roles important
in the debates leading to the Consensus Definition. "Economic

aggression" will be dealt with in the present Chapter, and "indirect aggression" has been dealt with along with the supposed liberty to use force in struggles for self-determination of peoples in the last Chapter. Both topics, and their outcomes, led to great obscurities. The economic aggression category has, however, no *explicit* base in the actual words of the Consensus Definition; while, as to "indirect aggression", there is at any rate the "armed bands" provision of Article 3(g). Despite this, the debates show a legal importance of extreme economic coercion, at least as a factor exculpating armed aggression, which makes the absence of express provision about it rather deceptive. Partly, this paradox reflects vicissitudes of international politics after the Cold War and decolonisation periods. Partly, it results from the fact that, by the terms of the Consensus Definition itself, its text is to be interpreted within the legal framework of the Charter, which of course includes the framework of international law of which the Charter is a part.

IV

The prominence of the question, what acts (if any) not involving State-to-State armed force are to be legally qualified as aggression, is a by-product of modern movements of psychological warfare, fifth columnism, liberation, decolonisation and terrorism. As just seen, Soviet espousal of Latin-American proposals as to "economic", "cultural" and "ideological" aggression dates only from the 1950's. Until 1953, with perhaps the notable but quickly aborted exception of the proposed Three Power Pact with Britain and France in 1939,[8] the Soviet Union had *not* espoused the notion of "indirect aggression" .

Assuming that the earlier Soviet position is to be explained by the importance at *that* time of subversive techniques in the Soviet Union's own strategy, the change of front in 1953 calls for explanation. One may, for example, speculate that Soviet tactics here were a belated catching-up with changes in Great Power relations. The disintegration of the colonial empires was, by 1953, leaving Western interests increasingly exposed within the territories of newly emergent States. Definition forbidding even non-armed pressure would thus increasingly cripple Western means of protecting them. Conversely, the vast extension of Soviet domains, and of her own hegemony over the buffer zones of satellite States in Europe, may have persuaded her to the importance of checking "indirect aggression", a persuasion, indeed, which later led to the extreme invention of "the Brezhnev doctrine".

There was also, of course, a natural Soviet interest in winning diplomatic goodwill from the Latin-American sponsoring States, and thus penetrating their normal solidarity at that time with the United States. With present hindsight, indeed, it may even be speculated that Soviet policy planners foresaw that this espousal would favour Soviet influence with the emerging African States and even (at a stage long before soaring oil prices and oil boycotts) with Arab States also. The year

1953 was also, of course, be it noted, the date of Stalin's death, which was a signal for a number of major reviews of Soviet policy.

It is a fact, at any rate, that the first major entry into United Nations debates of the problems of the status and meanings of "indirect" and "economic" aggression was on this Soviet endorsement of Latin American proposals.[9] And it was the Sixth Committee's deliberations on these matters which preceded the General Assembly's establishment of its first Special Committee on the "Question of Defining Aggression".[10]

V

It was, indeed, pressure for a definition embracing "economic" and other kinds of non-armed or non-State-to-State aggression, which thrust to the fore the question of the relation of definition to existing international law and especially Charter law. While, as we have seen,[11] this question is perplexing as to the conventional "armed aggression", the difficulties are still more dramatic with these other proposed heads of aggression.

The 1956 Committee's discussions illuminated the objections to the "indirect", "economic" and "ideological" heads of aggression, voiced on their introduction in 1953.[12] They also exposed the relation of these proposals to some of the deepest obstacles to the definitional drive. Insofar, for example, as such non-armed or non-State-to-State invasions of the interests of other States were now to be characterised as "aggression", logic as well as the emotive and value components in that symbol seemed to require that the State suffering them be allowed to defend itself, if necessary by arms, against such "aggression" without itself being branded as an "aggressor".[13]

Here delegation standpoints splintered off still further. Opinions which objected to extending the meaning of aggression argued precisely that the extension "might suggest the right to go to war in self-defence against acts of economic and ideological aggression",[14] and thus extend the legitimacy of the use of force under the Charter.[15] (Of course, this begs the questions whether the prohibition of use of "force" in Article 2(4) of the Charter is limited to "*armed* force", and what responses to the prohibited use are permitted by the Charter.) But even some delegates who wished to widen the aggression notion also resisted the corresponding extension of the self-defence notion, asserting that "economic or ideological aggression did not entitle individual States to the same defensive action as did armed attack".

These exchanges made patent that the emotive and value components of the symbol "aggression" do not permit any clean-cut demarcation between armed and other aggression.[16] In the minds of many delegations the degree of "unjustifiable" invasion of another State's "legitimate" interests or rights was as central to the current notion of aggression as the element of physical force. But as soon as this is asserted against the alleged "aggressor", the very notions "justifiable" and "legitimate" require consideration to be given not only to what was "justifiable" against the alleged victim's "legitimate" interests or rights, but also what was justifiable to protect any "legitimate" interests and rights of the alleged "aggressor".

This confrontation of claims of legitimacy directs attention to the elements of legislative demarcation of a just international legal order which are hidden within the aggression debate.[17] If a distinction is to be made between "armed aggression" on the one hand, and what is referred to as "indirect" or "economic" aggression on the other,[18] for instance by stigmatising one and not the other, or as to whether armed reaction to the former and not the latter is permitted,[19] it would have to turn on something other than the *mere gravity* of the invaded legitimate interests of the victim.[20] For so far as the interests, or even the "legitimate" interests of States are concerned, there may obviously be an "armed attack", the effects of which on the victim's legitimate interests are negligible as compared with some forms of "indirect" and "economic" aggression.[21] This raises the question whether the special treatment of resort to armed force is not really a matter distinct from the problem of defining "aggression", and is not better seen and handled as a function of the special dangers of a chain reaction leading to general or even thermo-nuclear war. It is likely, as I ventured to say in an earlier work, that more progress might come if these questions were separated.[22]

The valuable service of the 1956 Committee in raising these and other problems[23] did not include any solutions. No State, for example, was really asserting that *every* degree of economic pressure should constitute aggression: but little light was cast on *the degree which would*. Clarification was indeed rather blocked (as already suggested) by the bland Soviet assertion (on the one hand) that economic blockade against another State constitutes "economic aggression", and (on the other) that such "economic aggression" may not be justified by "any consideration whatsoever of a political, strategical or *economic nature*". So that (the Soviet draft spelled out) it could not be justified as a defensive response to the victim's violation of "the rights and interests" of the "aggressor" in the sphere of "trade, concessions, or any other kind of economic activity acquired by another State or its citizens", or to "rupture" by the "victim" of "economic relations" with the "aggressor", or to violation of treaties by the "victim", *or to economic or financial boycott imposed by the victim*. Even if we assumed that these assertions are mutually consistent, it would be necessary, in recognising economic coercion as a category of aggression, to draw some legislative lines between permissible and impermissible actions and responses.

The mutual confrontations of claims to legitimacy of their respective interests which are at stake thus involve complex questions of value and degree. This is one factor which has aborted attempts at definition in terms *merely* of simple, isolated, objectively identifiable, external facts. For exceptions and modalities are necessary to meet these complex questions. And as soon as exceptions and modalities are admitted, for instance, for "self-defence" against armed attack, we are beyond definition in simplistic terms, and (in particular) *in terms of acts merely of the putative aggressor*. The "legitimacies" of one side confront those of the other *a fortiori* as the qualification moves out to notions of "legitimate self-defence", "defence of rights", "just cause of war", response to "economic aggression" and the like. In terms of socio-juristic theory, the armed coercion is only one form of coercion.

Unless this is recognised, attempts to define aggression are doomed to fail. If it is recognised, the task of definition can no longer be seen in terms of isolated and simple external acts of putative aggressors, or even of such acts of both putative aggressors and victims. It would also have to take account of the conflicting demands of States. It must be preceded by establishment of basic norms acceptably adjusting these conflicts. And it must leave room for enormous variation of the circumstances and environments in which the particular acts and responses will in future occur, and will have to be judged. In a world of sovereign States, at any rate, an adequate definition of aggression has to be framed in a theory of the "rights" of States *de lege ferenda* as well as *lata*; that is, in terms of present law, as well as future justice. By the same token, no definition of it can prove operable save one which is based on a minimum of mutual acceptance of such "rights". This, at any rate, is recognised (if rather crudely) in Article 2 of the Consensus Definition, when it provides for the "relevant circumstances" of the future *prima facie* act of aggression to be taken into account.

We do not escape this legislative aspect—of minimal justice in unforeseen future situations—by offering the *animus aggressionis* along with some simple external conduct as the touchstone. This notion, after all, only refers us back to "aggression", as if we knew what aggression was.[24] In relation to any situation on which there can be a division of opinion as to whether aggression has taken place,[25] the test of *animus aggressionis* is likely to be circular. If a State declared on invading another that the latter had no right to exist, that its purpose was to destroy or annex that other, *and made no claim of provocation or other claim of right*, this would probably manifest a clear *animus aggressionis*. Yet such an example is trivial. For when destructive or rapacious purpose and all lack of claim of right are so manifest, no dispute will occur as to whether it is a case of "aggression". Of course, there are such core cases where no debate is possible. But what inspires the search for definition is rather the far more numerous and usual cases where the purpose is not so manifest and claims of right are not merely one-sided. It is for these cases, too, that the search has proved so endlessly frustrating.

In these usual cases neither the undefined concept of aggression itself nor any definitions offered, can exclude the need for application by human agents, individual and collective. The freedom of appreciation necessarily left to such agents, on the above analysis, goes beyond matching a set of facts to the terms of a rule. The organ concerned cannot avoid, in the course of its *ad hoc* determinations, a quasi-legislative drawing or redrawing of the boundaries of the *meum* and *tuum*, of aggression and self-defence or defence of rights (or similar complementary notions). And such activity must involve considerations of "ethical" or "justice" or other "value" elements built into the notion of aggression. For that notion in what it predicates is not like a simple precept concerning theft, or parking a motor vehicle. It is, as I have shown, a quite elaborate "fact-value complex".[26]

Even in municipal systems, this kind of power given to mere human beings is the subject of suspicion and even challenge. Stable municipal societies with strong legal traditions must finally still rely, in many critical questions, on the creative choices made by "right-minded men of the community",[27] guided to some degree (but not wholly controlled) by the duty of rationalizing the decision within the body of traditionally received authorities and the received ideals of the legal system. Despite restlessness and occasional crises, and with beneficent relief from moderating and corrective legislative and constitutional amending power when judicial *Rechtsgefuehl* strays too far from what is tolerable, the men and women of municipal societies learn to live with and even respect such decision-making authorities.

In the relations of States, however, not only is the frame of existing law settling the bounds of the *meum* and *tuum* meagre and patchy, but enforcement of that law is weak and at best sporadic, and the relief of adjustment by legislative power is almost wholly lacking. In such a context the difficulty of finding men who can be said to be "right-minded men" of the international community to play an analogous role is an outright impossibility. And if we could find them, we would still have grave difficulties in securing their appointment to the arbiter's role. Nor, in an area such as that of determining aggression, is there any stock of traditional authorities or ideas to guide and check them in judgment.

VI

The failure of the Consensus Definition to name "indirect" or "economic" aggression, and the focus of its opening articles on *armed* force, do not necessarily rule out the legal relevance of these other modalities of aggression. Such elements would, as already suggested, be circumstances which could be "relevant" for judging that determination of aggression would not be justified, under Article 2. Insofar, moreover, as Article 6 expressly saves the Charter limits on the use of "force", and as the "force" prohibited by Article 2(4) of the Charter is not deemed to be limited to *physical* force, indirect and economic aggression might be caught within it. They would thus be forbidden by the Charter, even if not otherwise mentioned in whatever the Consensus Definition said. In fact, of course, Article 4 of the Consensus Definition expressly provides that the Security Council may determine that *other acts than those mentioned in the Definition* "constitute aggression under the provisions of the Charter".[28]

It is common ground that the Consensus Definition (in the words of Soviet representative Kolesnik) "concentrates on" or "deals only with" armed aggression as "the most dangerous form of the illegal use of force".[29] Does this exclude the above possibilities that non-armed "aggression" is still caught by the prohibitions of the Charter, even after and under Definition?

A substantial number of delegations certainly attacked the Consensus Definition in terms which might imply the negative answer. They thought that once it was adopted, "indirect", and in particular "economic", aggression would not be forbidden. Perez de Cuellar of Peru[30] charged that the Definition did not, as required by Resolution 2330(XXII) cover all aspects of aggression, that it ignored "economic" aggression and should be revised for the protection of developing, and not only developing, countries.[31] M. Njenga of Kenya complained that the Definition ignored "systematic sabotage of a country's economy" which (he said) "constituted an act of aggression as pernicious as if armed forces had been used".[32] M. Fuentes Ibañez of Bolivia complained that "Article 1 . . . did not mention intimidation or coercion, economic pressure or the blackmail exercised by powerful countries or countries possessing natural resources of primary necessity".[33] M. Ikouebe of Congo thought that the failure to protect third world countries against daily "sabotage, boycotts and other measures" was surprising in view of international declarations affirming the "sovereignty of States over their natural resources".[34] M. Jaipal of India insisted that in view of "modern techniques of coercion", the Definition should have included "economic pressures" and "interventionary and subversive operations".[35]

M. Bararwerekana of Ruanda (purporting to speak also for Zambia and other States) felt that the failure to include economic and ideological aggression exposed the Definition to being "overtaken by events", since these countries were already in "asphyxia" from the current economic crisis, referring, no doubt, to the oil boycott and soaring oil prices.[36] M. Bamba (Upper Volta) associated this complaint with the special vulnerability of landlocked States.[37] "What difference was there between the blockade of the ports or coasts of a State by the armed forces . . . and the economic blockade that a coastal State might impose on a neighbouring land-locked country?". There should (he insisted) be other guidelines covering non-armed aggression. Somewhat incongruously, M. Omar of Libya complained about the failure to cover economic aggression, and also military threat, and alien domination.[38] But M. Baroody of Saudi Arabia, as befitted the representative of the chief architect of the 1973 oil boycott, while agreeing that the Definition did not protect against economic aggression expressed, e.g., in boycotts and embargoes, applauded this fact rather than complained of it. Such acts, he said, "could not be regarded as aggression in the true sense, because they were really only a means of applying pressure, even though they might lead to aggression" (presumably the victim's reaction!).[39]

Such complaints about neglect of economic aggression could be taken to imply that the complainant States concerned interpreted the Consensus Definition as meaning that the acts in question were not "aggression", whether for the purpose of branding the State committing them as an aggressor, or for that of giving the victim legal grounds for self-defence, if necessary by arms.

This, however, is not *the only* way of understanding them. They could rather have meant that insofar as the Consensus Definition set out to clarify the meaning of "aggression", *it should have embraced all acts so characterisable,* and not merely those involving *armed* force. So understood, the view opposed to theirs would be that of States which, while recognising that aggression under the Charter was wider than use of armed force, nevertheless saw the focus on armed aggression as a *wisely limited first stage in the definitional enterprise.* Typical of the latter was the Soviet representative's already quoted view that though there were other forms of aggression, armed force alone had been taken up because it was the "most dangerous form of the illegal use of force".[40] And Special Committee Chairman Broms drew attention, when he opened the Sixth Committee debate, to Article 4 of the Consensus Definition which makes it clear that "the acts enumerated above are not exhaustive and the Security Council may determine that other acts constitute aggression under the provisions of the Charter." He stated further that this provision, seen in the light of Article 2, meant that the various practical alternative cases (presumably including economic duress) were covered.[41]

M. Broms also stressed that "other relevant circumstances" would under Article 2 base refusal of the Security Council to determine that a "first use of armed force in contravention of the Charter" was aggression, presumably because in the relevant circumstances it was found to be a response to unlawful force as an exercise of residual self-defence under Article 2(4) of the Charter.[42] Yet M. Broms did also use some language which could if carelessly read imply that only the question of armed aggression arose within the frame of the Charter. "Nearly all members", he said, felt that the Definition should be "drafted in the light . . . of the Charter and should concentrate on armed aggression". To draw the above implication would impute to him a simple *non sequitur,* or the assumption (which is gravely debatable) that the Charter term "force" in Article 2(4), as well as "threat to peace" in Article 39, embrace only coercion by force of arms. A more natural and legally sounder meaning would be to take the word "and" in the above sentence as a mere conjunctive with no consequential import. In other words, members wished the definition to be within the Charter frame *and also* that (*within that frame*) it should "concentrate" on armed aggression.

Similar ambiguities or even contradictions affected the positions of other delegations. M. Rydbeck of Sweden[43] flatly asserted, on the one hand, that economic aggression was "illegal" and "highly reprehensible", implying that the victim had liberty of proportionate response, presumably (in appropriate circumstances) by armed force. Yet M. Rydbeck was also, on the other hand, emphatic to deny any such inference. Insofar as "economic" aggression was not aggression within the Consensus Definition, he thought it did *not* give ground for "self-defence". "Economic" aggression was omitted so as to avoid diluting the notion of aggression, or provoking any such extension of the right of self-defence. But he was not willing to rest even on that level of apparent self-contradiction. For, in his very next breath, he seemed to admit that the Security Council's discretion in Article 2 to refrain from finding aggression in view of "other relevant circumstances" includes the consideration that the alleged aggressor was responding to economic "aggression". Yet, how can a flat assertion that "economic aggression", even though unlawful, cannot ground lawful exercise of armed self-defence since it is not "aggression" within the Consensus Definition, stand with a flat assertion that a first use of armed force *can* be exculpated on the ground that it was provoked by acts (such as "economic" aggression) which are not "aggression" within the Consensus Definition? Obviously, it cannot.

VII

Most delegations, certainly, took the positions that while the Consensus Definition extended only to armed aggression, this did *not mean* that acts-other-than-armed aggression could not legally constitute aggression. It meant only that "definition of economic and other forms of aggression would be tackled as soon as possible by the United Nations".[44] As M. Tabio of Cuba put it, economic aggression should not be lost sight of even if armed aggression were defined first.[45] Van Brusselen of Belgium said explicitly that economic aggression, though reprehensible and violative of international law, was "rightly excluded" from consideration because armed force was the most obvious matter.[46] So also, M. Ustor of Hungary declared that while his delegation condemned the use of "force" other than armed force, he was glad that the definition of armed force had been taken first, as the graver danger.[47]

M. Wehry of the Netherlands added to these simpler statements an argument based on the truncated enigma of Article 5(2) that "*a war of aggression*" is "a crime against international peace", while "*aggression*" gives rise to international responsibility".[48] The mere fact (he said) that in Article 5(2) "a war of aggression" is said to be "a crime against international peace", while mere "aggression" is there said only to "give rise to international responsibility", did not mean (M. Wehry thought) that "a war of aggression" could *not* give rise to such "responsibility".

He did not clearly explain why the converse should not also be true, so that "aggression" (as distinct from "war of aggression") should be a crime against international peace. And since aggression in this distinct sense had long been seen by many States to include non-armed aggression and, in particular, economic and indirect aggression, it is puzzling why he also said that Article 5(2) did not mean that *because non-armed force was not aggression*, therefore it was not unlawful, and did not create State responsibility. His assertion that the Consensus Definition had to be limited to armed force because Article 51 of the Charter referred only to self-defence against armed attack, certainly does not explain the puzzle; strictly Article 51 makes no reference to "aggression".[49]

Perhaps the nearest to a coherent view, in the Special Committee, of the Consensus Definition as it applies to economic aggression, was that presented by M. Rakotoson of Madagascar. While regretting the lack of express reference to economic aggression, he insisted that Article 2 was sufficiently flexible to extend to forms of aggression other than by armed force. For the Security Council was free to interpret the "relevant circumstances" which might indicate that even a first use of armed force should not be determined to be aggression, as including any provocative act of sufficient gravity. He thought such provocative acts might include, for example, certain acts of an economic nature, such as a maritime blockade, or of a psychological nature such as "racist propaganda".[50] The examples he offered are weaker than his analysis. Naval blockade is, in any case, stigmatised as aggression in Article 3(c) of the Consensus Definition itself; and *mere* racist *propaganda* is unlikely to threaten State survival. But the "strangulation" by oil boycott featured in President Ford's and Secretary of State Kissinger's 1975 warning that armed response could not be ruled out, would be an example *par excellence*. I assume in this example that the economic coercion involved is such that the victim's failure to respond by the means impugned as aggression, would spell the effective doom (in the words of Article 1 of the 1974 Definition) of the victim's "sovereignty, territorial integrity or political independence". No doubt, there may always be arguments as to whether this degree of severity of the coercion exists, but this does not dispose of the problem, any more than such arguments dispose of the problem of anticipatory self-defence.

The cogent conclusion of this account is, not that economic aggression is *"armed* aggression" within the Consensus Definition, but that self-defence against it might be licit even, in appropriate cases, to the point of use of *armed* force. Such an account can be soundly based under the Charter, insofar as the "force" forbidden by Article 2(4) (and perhaps also "threat to the peace" under Article 39) can reasonably be read as not limited to armed force, but as embracing extreme coercion (for instance, economic), or imminence of threat of the degree under discussion. "Economic aggression" on this basis could have these legal consequences under the Charter even though it is not expressly referred to in the Definition.[51] As already observed, the range of lawful force under the Charter is carefully preserved by the Consensual Definition itself. M. Tabio of Cuba[52] reminded his colleagues that the Charter prohibits threat or use of *force in any form and not merely armed force.*

By contrast with this clarity, the Swedish delegate's position above analysed[53] illustrates well the superficial—almost formalistic—view of the task of definition of aggression, recurrent throughout a half-century of debate. It ignores the truth that to deny to a victim State liberty of proportionate response to admittedly illegal acts of extreme gravity by a predatory State, is to sanction a *de facto* and possibly illegal and morally unjustifiable redistribution of global resources. For, to the extent that the resources of the victim can in fact be appropriated by acts which, despite their illegality and gravity, lie outside the definition, legal immunity against the victim's effective response is conferred on the illegal appropriator. Insofar as a definition operates thus to bar the only effective remedies available to victims of wrongs, its contents operate *de facto* to redistribute world resources. Blindness to this truth was more understandable before the oil boycott drama of 1973, than it can now be. Significantly, the only unequivocal suggestion that "economic" aggression was *not even unlawful* came from M. Baroody of Saudi Arabia. Certainly, the extreme coercive power through control of most of the world's fuel is much increased, if the victim of such an oil boycott imposed to force a change in the victim's foreign or domestic policies is legally stripped of any effective right of response. Correspondingly, this extreme coercion is reduced if a right of appropriate response is admitted expressly or implicitly by the terms of the Definition. The main point is that insofar as the terms of a definition of aggression which could be effective presuppose a redistribution of world resources among the States, it is absurd to think that such a redistribution could come about as a mere by-product of such a definition.

VIII

It is pertinent to note at this stage that it was mostly the Western States which, after it was clear that the text would omit any express reference to economic duress, defended this omission.[54] They used various rationales, many of them echoing rather mechanically their attitudes in the aggression debates of the 'fifties in a United Nations and a world very different from that of 1974.[55]

In the perspective of Section VII, an observer of the Fourth Special Committee does not need to be paranoid to stand in awe of the strategic blunders of the Western States. Granted that they finally agreed, with intense reluctance, to join in consummating the Consensus Definition, it is astonishing that in 1974, close after the oil boycott of 1973, they did not insist that economic duress, not even of the severity of the oil boycott, be expressly stigmatised as aggression. To leave so critical a matter in the purgatory of debate about interpretation was to treat the task of definition as a mere (or a bored indulgence of a) game of definition, at a time when the oil-duress spectre was actually stalking the world. A Western observer who *is* paranoid might even think that the fact that Libya and Saudi Arabia seemed to take mutually opposed views on this matter, and that most complaints against the neglect of economic aggression came from other Third World States, set a kind of trap into which Western States walked as in Rip Van Winkle sleep.

The main explanation appears to be that attitudes ingrained in Western diplomats over decades of argument about the definition of aggression blinded them to the new significance *for them* of the debate after 1973. It was a case of "Wolf!" being cried once too often. As late as 1971, it has been suggested, Washington's participation in sponsoring the Six Power draft was by way merely of showing some activity in an enterprise it regarded as quite useless.[56] Yet it might rather have been expected that the actuality of oil duress would suggest, after October 1973, that Western countries now had the strongest reasons to join in the long-standing concern of many Third World States, that extreme economic coercion should be sufficiently stigmatised with illegality to facilitate appropriate response. Western failure after 1973 to support the express stigmatisation of economic aggression, must be attributed to the above errors of approaching definition as a mere verbal exercise, or as a boring game that others wished to play, and (in either case), as Mr. Ferencz well suggests, as a vacuous enterprise. It certainly overlooked its importance in political warfare, and in the economic struggle for redistribution of world power and resources to be discussed in Chapter 7. A definition reached by consensus at that stage which excluded any specific reference to economic aggression, reflects strangely on the perspicacity, statesmanship, and even the enlightened self-concern, of the Western Powers.

The position of An Chih-yuan, of the People's Republic of China, seems at first sight no less politically naive. It had the flavour essentially of a public relations exercise in competing with the Soviet Union and the United States for leadership of the Third World. He attacked the failure of the Consensus Definition to include economic aggression, but was then at some pains to limit the meaning of "economic aggression", so as to point it at alleged United States and Soviet "plundering" of "the resources" of Third World countries. If the definition did not cover this, he claimed, it would do nothing "to serve the interests of the numerous small and medium-sized countries".[57] Even this preoccupation should not have blinded the Chinese delegate, any more than Western delegates should have been blinded, to the anti-Western import of the omission of express reference to economic duress, in a text formulated so soon after the oil boycott of 1973. Nor, even more significantly, did M. An Chih-yuan seem aware that, at this new post-oil-boycott stage of history, the express inclusion of economic aggression within the Definition would have benefited the United States and other western countries, as well as the Third World for which he was so anxious to speak.

IX

These conclusions can be given a certain degree of support by dint of the addition, late in the drafting process,[58] of the word "sovereignty" in the opening phrase of Article 1 of the Consensus Definition itself— "Aggression is the use of armed force by a State against *the sovereignty, territorial integrity or political independence* of another State . . . ". M. Jazic (Yugoslavia) urged its inclusion on the basis that "sovereignty" is "an essential element of the concept of the State . . ." which small countries in particular wanted included "in a general definition."[59] Indonesia's M. Joewono took the even vaguer ground that the "notion was a vital element in international relations".[60] Such grounds (unless they be mere rhetoric) imply that the "sovereignty" notion contains elements specially important for smaller States not covered by "territorial integrity" or "political independence", *simpliciter*. This could also be inferred from Article 2(1) of the United Nations Charter, affirming that the United Nations is based on the principle of the sovereign equality of all its Members, be they great or small. On the other hand, the main resistance to inclusion came from the Soviet Union, again on a rather vague ground—that "sovereignty" was superfluous alongside "territorial integrity" and "political independence".[61]

One might try to support the Yugoslav claim by arguing that while "territorial integrity" and "political independence" refer only to specific attributes like physical control of territory, and an existent independent government, "sovereignty" refers to some residue of attributes of Statehood beyond these. So that the inclusion of "sovereignty" might afford additional protection of these attributes, for instance, of freely making particular foreign or domestic policy decisions. A similar protection may, as already seen, be drawn from the provision of Article 2(4) of the Charter, obliging Members to refrain from "the threat or use of force against the territorial integrity or political independence of any States etc. . . .", if the word "force" is taken to include all kinds of extreme force, and not limited to physical violence. Article 2(4) would then forbid also "indirect" or "economic" aggression.

If, now, we try to reach this last result without Article 2(4), merely by reference to the inclusion of the "sovereignty" as well as "territorial integrity" and "political independence" in Article 1 of the 1974 Definition, the argument becomes self-defeating. For Article 1 by its terms stigmatises only aggression *by armed force*, and it is difficult to see how extended impact on the protected interests of the victim by the inclusion of "sovereignty" in the Article, if the aggression were (as there required) by armed force, would not in any case be "aggression" under Article 1, even had that Article referred only to "territorial integrity" or "political independence". In that sense the Soviet point that the reference to sovereignty was superfluous would be correct.

Any claim that addition of the "sovereignty" notion gives the victim an increased range of protection against coercion other than by armed force must rest, therefore, not on Article 1 itself, but on arguments by analogy about the range of other parts of the Definition. Thus an analogical argument from the additional protection due to sovereignty might affect the Security Council's consideration under Article 2 of "other . . . circumstances" in which an alleged aggression was but responding to an intrusion on its sovereignty. Or might, under Article 4, take such an intrusion into account in determining that though such an intrusion is not included in the acts enumerated in Articles 1-3, it may still consitute aggression.

For even if it were assumed that mere economic coercion could not impair "political independence" or "territorial integrity" as such so as to constitute aggression, the inclusion of the vaguely wider "sovereignty" notion, as also protected, may provide a sufficiently wider net to catch it. Such a wider net would obviously be advantageous for countries with little economic leverage for responding to industrial, financial and economic pressures.[62] Even without the reference to "sovereignty" in Article 1 of the Definition, this line of thought certainly underlay the Bolivian argument that a stigmatisation of *economic* aggression was to be inferred from the three Charter principles of "political independence", "non-interference" and "sovereign equality".[63]

Though pressure for stigmatising economic aggression came from the smaller powers, it is an error (as the 1973 oil boycott showed) to assume that major powers do not have a parallel interest in doing so. But Soviet resistance to inclusion of the sovereignty notion may be attributable to the feeling that such a reference might inhibit the spread of its economic and social system among small States, while its general alignment with the Third and Fourth Worlds and domestic supplies of essential commodities would sufficiently protect it from economic pressures. When M. Kolesnik finally explained the Soviet delegation's agreement "in a spirit of compromise to the inclusion of the word 'sovereignty' " in Article 1, he added that "violation of sovereignty in that context was to be interpreted as meaning *armed* encroachment on the territorial integrity or political independence of a State."[64] (Emphasis added.) In other words, "sovereignty" in Article 1 was to be read as a mere redundancy.

CHAPTER 8

Definition of Aggression and Redistribution of Power and Resources

I

The preceding Chapters have offered in the contexts of their specific subject-matters a variety of reasons for difficulties affecting the half-century-old enterprise of defining aggression, and even the value of the 1974 Definition. It is the cumulative effect of these reasons which guided me to the theme of the present Chapter on the relation of definition to the redistribution of global power and resources among the various States. In a real sense, therefore, the theme of this present Chapter is climactic on those that precede. I may therefore be permitted here to remarshal some of the reasoning which has gone before, by way of overture to this main theme.

The long effort to find a *legal* definition of aggression between States has certainly made clear that this is no mere lexicographic exercise, to describe the *usage of words*, nor mere taxonomic exercise, to classify the subject within the matrix of *knowledge*.[1] Its essential purpose is neither to describe the usage of the word "aggression" nor to classify the subject to which it refers, *but to prescribe rules of conduct for States.* Its aim is normative or prescriptive rather than descriptive. Moreover, and partly an independent point, the facts on which the rules to be prescribed are predicated are not simple external objects or acts—as, for instance, a territory, or a ship, or an armed attack or bombardment, but a relation between the conduct of States manifested through these and many other variable objects or acts.

To forget that a definition of aggression will thus prescribe rules to arise when there is a certain relation between the conduct of States is to conceal and confuse what is in any case an already hard prescriptive task of formulating norms and mutual restraint between sovereign power centres, which is at the heart of legal normative definition. The search is for a formula, to serve as a base of decision in crisis, which will produce the harmonious deployment of sufficient forces in the world of sovereign States to constrain other forces (which may be termed "aggressive") from operating in a manner unacceptable to those agreeing on the formula. This may seem an unduly complex way of referring to the deployment of military force, which is too often thought of as the central if not only factor in aggression situations. But this objection, by its very wrongness, affords clues to other truths.

First, it presupposes some absolute distinction between physical (military) force, assumed to be relevant to aggression, and other force, which is not. As repeatedly seen in this work, as well under the Consensual Definition as generally, other kinds of force bear at numerous points on the question whether State conduct is "aggressive". The difference between military force and economic or political force lies mainly in equipment and logistics: in terms of extremity of coercion the military may often be the milder.

Second, if the force that is relevant is not—as the very notion of power politics implies that it is *not*—merely military, we have to abandon any naive assumption that by prescribing against aggression we can produce a society from which "force" is *absent*. Any force is an organisation of demands, and there never has been any society or group of societies free of such force. The endless problem of civilisation is to control the forces operating in it, meaning by this not their abolition but that the equilibration into which they are brought is justifiable in terms of intelligible and accepted social objectives. If a legal definition of aggression is to serve this function in the international arena, it must take account not only of varied and changing fact ingredients of each situation, but also of the flexibility of techniques of equilibration, and the ethos of all the forces operating.

Third, this task is afflicted, as are so many socio-political problems, by tension between the need to abstract from the concrete reality in order to understand or handle it and the danger of abstractions becoming vacuities. For legal prescription, in particular, abstraction from the facts is a necessary preliminary to making rules, while abstraction which goes beyond a certain point ceases to be helpful for handling particular cases. If for "aggression-situations", the "facts" as abstracted down (i.e. the facts predicated by the rule) include only a geographical milieu, two or more States, and the movement of physical force, aggression virtually defines itself, in terms of these two or three external fact-elements, as some military movement across frontiers or against another State's ships or aircraft on or over the high seas. At this level of abstraction, "aggression" comes to refer to the external acts of one State, the putative aggressor. And this is at odds with the truism already mentioned, that whatever else may have to be said about aggression between States, it must *at least* refer to the relations between the conduct of both States involved.

II

The prescriptive (legal normative) rather than merely descriptive function of defining aggression, and the implications from this, are the theme of the present Chapter. Such a definition has to prescribe standards to which accepting States will commit themselves irrevocably in advance, regardless of future contexts and circumstances. By that commitment, States are to undertake: (1) to observe the standards themselves, whatever justifications they may in future feel for not doing so; (2) to accept grave penalties by way of sanction for violation; (3)

to join in coercive measures against States violating the standards, whatever justifications those other States might in future seem to have, and (4) to favour any State victim of such violation, however unworthy in the future circumstances they may deem that State to be. These are heavy undertakings. And even if a definitional text does not particularise these as *legal* obligations, they operate on the moral and political level.

In a general sense, this prescriptive nature of the task of definition may be thought not surprising, much less intimidating. It is in the nature of legal rules generally that they prescribe consequences for facts predicated in them, to be applied regardless of unique aspects of litigants or circumstances which may make the rule inapt or unjust for the particular case. What is intimidating in relation to aggression is still two-fold. First, is that in an international legal order the rest of which is in most other respects so sparse, uneven and ineffectual in the regulation of conduct, aggression would prescribe consequences which have such overriding importance for States. Second, is that the elements on which the prescription of such momentous consequences is predicated are so complex, including difficult value elements as well as external facts, and of so wide a range in space and time, and thus so difficult to abstract from and formulate in advance.

These intimidating aspects can, perhaps, best be seen by comparing this proposed prescription between States with typical municipal law prescriptions. Municipal systems of any maturity have a fairly adequate range of detailed rules for solving disputes of all kinds, in which the community's prevailing value-judgments about most aspects of men's lives have already been concretised. They have reliable collective processes for enforcing general observance of their rules, and for legislative adjustment of the social, legal and political arrangements to the minimal demands of justice and stability in the changing matrix of social life. The *effective* prescriptions of such a system are thus great in number and ambit. They do not stand or fall on any single overriding prescription anchored to a single indeterminate notion of illicit extreme coercion, such as is the aggression notion.

The drama of the aggression debate is that the society of States is not endowed like such a municipal order, and that therefore the prescription against aggression is really being offered as a virtual substitute for such an endowment. To fill such an ambitious role, the content of the definition would have somehow to make available detailed rules adequately covering the *meum* and *tuum* between States, reflecting the prevailing value-judgments. It would also have to make these rules tolerably effective by enforcement; and also assure in the face of change that the distribution of global power and resources is kept tolerably just by legislative change. And here precisely is the rub. For insofar as it is sought, in the *international* context, to prescribe abstract criteria for aggression which will at all approach these momentous tasks, they obviously cannot be of a simple nature, like the order in time of some concrete act like bombardment, or crossing of frontiers. In relation to the problems of a tolerably just and effective distribution of the world's resources, prescriptions based on such simple criteria are likely to turn out, especially for the yet unforeseen circumstances, to be technical, trivial and even fortuitous.

It is to be remembered also that it is for dealing with *future* crises that a definition of aggression is demanded. And this makes it even more fanciful to think that States will submit their major concerns (sometimes even their survival) *in advance, to such simple criteria.* If they are pressed to accept "aggression" as the cardinal object of prescription of the international legal order, together with some set definition of it, they are more likely to insist that it be such as to leave them free, in each application of it, to take their stand on what they see as the merits of each side, including the proportionality of reaction to wrong, in the full context of the relations of the States concerned leading to the alleged aggression.

III

This last point draws attention to the very nature of a legal "standard" as opposed to a "rule", as seen in municipal law requirements of "reasonableness", "fairness", "good faith" and "due process". Such prescriptions are predicated not on the mere finding of certain facts (as are simple rules like those as to parking, or shooting of protected game, or burglary), but also on the making of certain value-judgments on those facts as so found.[2] For this reason, I have elsewhere described such a standard as a "fact-value complex". The notion of aggression in international law is preeminently such a "fact-value" complex. This inbuilt reference to both facts and values is one of the deep reasons for the correctness of Charles de Visscher's much quoted comment on the aggression notion (when we recognise that for "subjective weighing of motives", he could equally have said "moral judgments"):

> Aggression, in the present state of international relations, is not a concept that can be enclosed in any definition whatsoever: the finding that it has occurred in any concrete case involves political and military judgments and a subjective weighing of motives that make this in each instance a strictly individual matter.[3]

Clearly the ambit of the "fact-value complex" involved in the judgment of international aggression will usually embrace vastly wider vistas of elements for deliberation, than even such standards as "fairness", "reasonableness" or "due process" found in particular precepts of municipal law. It will often involve not only the complex conditions of life of a whole people and a whole State, but those of two or more, impacting on hundreds of millions of human lives. The facts may, indeed, have an unlimited geographical or demographical range; and the resources whose distribution is at stake, and the standards of minimum life affected may range to the present limits and future expansion of man's global habitation and beyond, in outer space, and beneath the deep oceans.

With "aggression", as with "reasonableness" in a contract action, the exact ambit of relevant facts and values will vary with the circumstances of each case and nothing can dispense judgment from examining the full context. Yet, with the aggression standard the variables are far more numerous, complex, wide-ranging and unpredictable, and the decision to be made is an effort at instant legislation, by a single blow as it were, for a just and effective world order. A functional use of the notion of aggression would, in this light, demand that this vast ambit, with its innumerable future configurations, and without any adequate basis for apportioning rights among States by an effective international legislature, shall be taken into account by the applying organ in each aggression situation. The lack of a matrix of detailed rules, and of general effectiveness of such rules as exist, and of a legislature to adjust these rules to ongoing change, means that these functions would somehow have to be built into the scope and application of this single notion.

In short, the harshest difficulty is not that the enterprise of definition is thus legally prescriptive in effect. It is not merely that what is predicated in the definition is a fact-value complex. It is rather that the wide ambit of facts and values involved in this complex means that what is at stake is, finally, how the resources of the planet (meaning all the goods desired by States and their peoples) are to be apportioned among them.

The intuition of this point, quoted above from the late Charles de Visscher, is shared, though more vaguely, by others. Rapporteur Spiropoulos explained to the International Law Commission that aggression is a "natural notion", a "concept *per se* inherent in any human mind", a "primary notion".[4] It is vital to press, as is here attempted, beyond such a mere mystical *non possumus*.[5] The Rapporteur did reach this half-way point of observing that a determination of aggression "can only be given in each concrete case in conjunction with all constitutive elements of the concept of the definition." What needs also to be kept explicit is that this is precisely because the "aggression" notion is a fact-value complex of such vast range. The point, then, is not just that all the elements of the definition should be attended to. It is that these include *value elements* decisive for judgment, and that these, as well as the relevant fact elements, can be so wide-ranging as to affect the whole distribution of planetary resources among the States and peoples of the world.

IV

Proponents of particular contents of a definition may, of course, be quite inadvertent to their potential effect in the above respect, or for that matter, on their own State's interests. We saw in Chapter 7 the inadvertence of Western States to the bearing of proposals about economic aggression on their own post-oil boycott situation. But they are only rarely so naive or self-effacing, and even if they were always so, it would not change the bearing of the proposals on the distribution of world resources. Against the bench-mark of existing international law, particular offered definitions may tend to preserve the *status quo* of distribution. Or they may drive drastically to change or revolutionise this distribution. From the standpoint of proponents of a particular content, it is likely to favour the *status quo* as to those resources in which the proponent is affluent; and to support change or revolution as to those of which it regards itself as deprived. What an offered definition *with any substantive content* can rarely be, is merely neutral about the disposal of world resources.

In Europe between the two wars, for instance, the objective political reality behind demands for criteria centred on territorial frontiers lay in the fears of France and the other successor States about the stability of the Versailles territorial settlement, and the reluctance of other States to stand militarily behind their demands for assurance.[6] In this setting, even as Article 10 of the Covenant (the only one expressly referring to "aggression") faded into the background, efforts grew to define "aggression".[7] In the 'thirties, the continuing Soviet fear of interventionism was surely part of the reason for her similar concern with collective guarantees and the definition of aggression.[8] And it is useful to examine, in the same light, the Soviet proposed definition of aggression (presented to the Special Committee on October 23, 1956,[9] but first introduced in this precise form in 1953), presenting a Soviet view of the world at that time, when its control of the buffer zone of satellites had still not been threatened by the Hungarian and Czech affairs.

The first paragraph of the Soviet proposal covered the general areas of so-called "direct" or "armed aggression", which it defined in terms of the first commission of any of a series of acts, including declaration of war, invasion by armed forces or bombardment of the territory of another State, or attack on its ships or aircraft, or the landing or leading of land, sea or air forces inside its boundaries. Clearly, of all the Powers, the Soviet Union registered the greatest World War II territorial gains. The objective political meaning of a definition centred on armed invasion of territory and similar simple external acts would have been to give an extra stamp of legitimacy and collective guarantee to these gains (including the guarantee of those States at whose expense she expanded). Such guarantees may, as Soviet delegates urged, be implied in co-existence; the effect of the definition would still be to consolidate a co-existence highly favourable to the Soviet Union.[10]

The clause of the Soviet definition covering the landing or leading of forces inside the boundaries of another State without the permission of the Government of that State, or in violation of the conditions of their admission as regards length of stay or area of deployment, is also thought-provoking. As regards NATO forces in NATO countries, and Warsaw Pact forces in those countries, this clause seems fair and sensible on its face. The West may have felt that the consent of NATO Members to such movements between their countries is genuine in a sense in which that of satellite countries, is not. But even with more wide-eyed faith, the point remains. The buffer-zone of satellites by which the Soviet Union insulated the Russian heartland from the West, is a projection of her influence and power deep into the heart of Europe. As long as she can maintain it she attains three objectives: First, she reduces age-old fears of invading land armies from the great European plain. Second, however, by deploying her forces at will and manipulating satellite forces within that zone, she presents a sturdy *offensive* front towards West Germany, Austria, Yugoslavia and West Europe generally. Third, of course, this satellite zone, with its sturdy offensive posture towards Europe, is a mighty shield behind which the Soviet Union has continued to advance its objectives in Asia, and later, in the Middle East.

Despite, therefore, the appearance of Olympian impartiality of stigmatising as aggression the landing or leading of troops into a country affected without its consent, part at least of the political reality is quite otherwise. It is precisely in the satellites, so important for Soviet defensive and offensive power, where struggles are most likely to arise between two governments, one puppet, one not. As things seemed when she proposed this definition, Soviet troops would usually be present with the permission of the Government concerned, that Government being acceptable to, if not dominated by, the Soviet Union. By swallowing this part of the Soviet definition, therefore, the Powers would not only give their blessing to Soviet military domination of these countries. They would also brand in advance as the crime of aggression, the only recourse that might some day be open to themselves for assisting peoples held down by Soviet forces, after the clear overthrow by such peoples of the Soviet-supported regime. We do not here speak of Western military initiatives for European "liberation". But why should Western countries, even in the spirit of Helsinki 1975, *condemn themselves in advance as aggressors* if they should sometime feel compelled to come to the aid of people who have clearly rejected a Government, which then maintains them in subjection by the naked power of Soviet arms? Nor is the self-interested political import removed by the mere fact that in Hungary in 1956, and in Czechoslovakia in 1968,[11] the Soviet Union committed some grave miscalculations which would have led to her being hoist by her own petard, had she not been relatively immune as a nuclear Great Power with a veto from the penal code by which she wished to bind other States.

V

In the above ways the Soviet-offered definitions of the 'thirties and 'fifties marched with particular strategic demands of that State, and were centred on the condemnation of use of military force or the stationing of forces or the sending of armed bands across the frontiers. Other parts of the same definition bore a similar relation to Soviet economic demands. She proposed that such hostile military acts could never be justified by any "considerations of a political, strategic or economic nature", or of "capital invested", or any other particular interests; and, with even more studied particularity, that they could never be justified by the fact that the "victim" of any such acts has violated treaties, concessions or other trade rights of the reacting State or its citizens, ruptured diplomatic or economic relations, instituted economic boycotts, repudiated debts or the like.[12]

In a period when the Soviet Government's repudiation of Czarist Russian debts and other treaty obligations was a main source of Soviet-Western tensions, these studied denials of justification reflected Soviet economic demands just as directly as the acts it sought to stigmatise as aggression reflected its politico-military demands. On the latter front its proposals sought to sanctify territorial domains with which it was content; on the former (economic) front it sought a charter for subverting an economic order with which it was not content. Correspondingly, as to territory, the drive was to support existing international law; while as to economic interests the list of "no justifications" was custom-made for the carefree violation of the legal rights and legitimate economic interests of the Western States throughout the Middle East, Asia and Central and South America. For, in the absence of any collective means of righting such wrongs,[13] the definition would guarantee in advance to each wrongdoer virtual immunity from any effective measures of redress at all, and strip each wronged State of such effective redress for grave invasions of its rights and interests as had hitherto existed, by branding it as "aggression". Insofar, furthermore, as the Soviet Union adamantly maintained the exclusiveness of the Security Council's competence in the peace enforcement area, it was reserving, through its veto, its own liberty of interpretation as against minor States, and even (to the extent that they would feel more inhibited by the accepted understanding of an accepted definition) as against the other Permanent Members. (It should also perhaps be recalled, in this context, that to assess the objective reality of the intense Soviet-led campaign for outlawing nuclear weapons, we have to observe that it passed its zenith when the Soviet Union's stockpiling approached a level capable of basing substantial retaliation.)

This relation of proposed definitions to the proposing State's demands and ambitions, here illustrated through the Soviet's prominent role in the history of attempts to define aggression, continues into the contemporary debates. There has been detailed, for example, in the course of preceding Chapters, the persistent, sometimes controlling, and usually distorting, impact of Arab political strategies for the Middle East conflict on the work from which the present Consensus Definition emerged.[14]

By the same token, just as States which have shown disinterest and even distaste for the definitional exercise may not lack love of peace and security, so also the zealous promotion of definitions may not mean any special love of these ideals.[15] Demands for definition, and for particular definitions must, in prudence, always be checked for *their* objective political meaning. Very earthy objectives of some States may be spectacularly advanced by even the most general and high-sounding principles, endorsed in the utmost good faith by others.[16] Proposed definitions need to be examined, amid all else, also in terms, *cui bono?* and *cui malo?*[17] Which States' interests would benefit or be sacrificed by the proposed definition, over and above any common benefit or sacrifice to mankind?[18] To ask and answer that question may sometimes be the only way to understand how States may change their view even as to the possibility or desirability of seeking a definition.[19]

VI

Manoeuvring for a definitional text which will advance the proponent State's self-interests, and strike at its adversary's, is thus a central socio-political reality, side by side with noble aspiration for a text which will move States towards a more peaceful world in which there is a juster distribution among States and peoples. And perhaps the aggravation of the world's miseries by the socio-political reality of political warfare is an outcome that is to be expected—a turning sour—of the intellectual and technical hopelessness of realising the noble aspiration.

It is part of the present purpose to understand these interrelations. And we may here pause, before looking at the degree of awareness in the Fourth Special Committee of the bearing of its work on redistribution of world resources, to review the ground leading to the present point.

The campaign for advance definition seeks to prescribe precise limits for all future situations at which each State's liberty of self-assertion and defence of its legal rights and interests should end, and its duty begin to submit to invasion of these rights and interests by others. In its aspirational aspect (whether particular participants are conscious of this or not) the campaign thus covers a demand for a global redistribution of the powers and resources now respectively enjoyed by States in the legal and economic *status quo*. Moreover, the aspiration is to set new patterns of distribution by the prescriptions and proscriptions of the definition itself.

Yet it becomes ever clearer, even (or perhaps especially) after the Consensus Definition of 1974, why such a design has proved so intractable and hopeless. At the outset, the idea that a single definitional text, especially one which it is hoped can ground a quick decision in a crisis, could at one stroke (as it were) activate this redistribution, must be questioned. For not only is it to be expected that States, whose present rights and interests seem likely to be eroded by a particular text proposed, would resist the redistribution. It is also clear that other States, when they speculate about the unforeseeable circumstances of future crises, will be uncertain as to the fate of their *then* rights and interests, should the particular proposal now be adopted. This is the deeper meaning of the United States delegate's observation at one point in this endless debate[20] that the very acts which the Soviet Union offered (when "first" committed by any State) as the criteria of "aggression" might often, in the full context of future crises, constitute rather acts of "self-defence".

When what is at stake in the plausibly simple call for definition of aggression thus turns out to be a kind of planet-wide legislative redistribution of resources and prerogatives among the 145 States of the world, we should not expect any early success. And no success at all may be expected unless we become aware that such an enterprise, far from being achievable by finding a definition of aggression, will call for a preliminary *review of all the major legal precepts and institutions of international society*, as well as for a degree of consensus about the *norms of minimal justice* which are to control reform of the existing law in various situations. Such a comprehensive global reform cannot possibly be a kind of by-product of even the wisest and most cunning definition of aggression. We could not bring the socio-economic and legal orders in American or Soviet or any other municipal society into conformity with justice merely by a new prescriptive definition of the notion of unlawful "assault" or "unlawful trespass" to property, or a (for them) new notion of "aggression" carefully *defined*, even though these societies already also have comprehensive bodies of detailed rules, effectively enforced, and standing legislatures for continually reviewing them. How much more desperate, then, is the hope to bring such a transformation in the international legal order, with the inadequate coverage of its detailed rules, and their only sporadic observance and enforcement, as a mere by-product of a definition of aggression!

How far was this momentous import of the contents of a definition of aggression as setting, by the rules of State conduct it prescribes, directives for redistribution of global power and resources, present to the minds of those who worked on the 1974 Consensus Definition?

At first view there is a strange silence concerning it in the proceedings of the Fourth Special Committee. There are but one or two partial and muted hints. M. Verosta, for example, observed that the Committee was engaged in finding a definition which "not only stated what a word legally meant but was a part of the rule of law".[21] This correctly pointed out that the exercise was one of prescribing rules for States, rather than describing the usage of words. But it is not advertent to the basic value references involved in the notion—to the fact that the "aggression" notion, on which such prescriptions are predicated, is a fact-value complex, application of which will usually require reference to all the circumstances of action in a vast global and temporal context. Nor does it make explicit the resulting import for the distribution of world power and resources. Mr. Yasseen's observation that the work of the Special Committee showed that disputes about the meaning of "aggression" were not technical, but of a quite different nature, is open to similar comment.[22]

The dearth of such theoretical statements is not, however, so strange on further thought. It was to be expected, after all, that awareness of the import of the terms of definition on resource redistribution would manifest itself primarily in attitudes of States towards the effect of proposals *on their own particular interests*. These manifestations would take the form of striving to protect interests vested in themselves under the existing order, or of seeking to expose the interests of other States which they see as hostile to penetration or subversion by themselves or others. The present and preceding Chapters are replete with such manifestations.

They dealt at length, for example, with Soviet and Arab State strategies in advancing their policies through proposals for definition. Chapter 6, on armed bands and self-determination, is focussed on the essential confrontation in which third world States have demanded what is in effect a licence to use force to dismantle any existing State in the course of a struggle to "liberate" any people living under its sovereignty. Such a dismantling of selected target States is a method *par excellence* of global resource redistribution. In practice, this demand was targeted quite explicitly on Western or Western-aligned States, by the incorporation in the drafts of slogan-symbols such as "colonialism" or "racism". These specifications presumably reassured the Soviet Union that the demand would not be turned against its own hegemonial expansions, and suppressions, whether in the Baltic, the Ukraine, Hungary or Czechoslovakia. With some hedging, she was then able to support proposals designed to expose the Western or Western-supported interests.

In the controversies concerning economic and indirect aggression, discussed in Chapter 7, the crucial relation of the definitional limits to the maintenance or transformation of the economic *status quo* is also very readily apparent. It was seen how the simple assumption of the pre-1973 debates that the stigmatising of economic aggression would transfer power and resources from Western developed nations to developing nations, becomes more confused after the oil boycott of 1973 and the attendant price escalations. There are now two "Third Worlds", of which the more populous will be increasingly seen as the economic victims of Opec States, especially their dominant yet sparsely populated Arab members.

From the standpoint of the People's Republic of China, the economic villains of the economic scene were different again from those set up by the Soviet Union. When Chinese representative An Chih-yuan supported demands that the Consensus Definition expressly stigmatise economic aggression, he made quite clear that what must be caught is essentially "imperialistic". And by this he meant something different from what Moscow called "colonialist", since he focussed especially on United

States *and Soviet* "plundering" of the resources of Third World countries. If the definition did not cover this it was doubtful whether it "would do anything to serve the interests of numerous small and medium-sized countries."[23]

In these circumstances it is not surprising that the Consensus Definition did not clarify the problematic standing of "economic aggression". On this side, at least, the drive for redistribution has moved to more appropriate quasi-legislative *fora* of conferences of OPEC States and industrialised States (separately and together), the General Assembly with its Charter of Economic Rights and Duties of States, the Law of the Sea Conference and the governing organs of the World Bank and International Monetary Funds, the United Nations Conference on Trade and Development, "the Group of 77", and the like. I shall refer further to these in Section VIII below.

VII

When we thus bring the import of the terms of definition for redistribution of global resources from the level of the observer's theorising to the level of State postures—of claims, or resistance thereto, as regards particular resources—dramatic illustrations of it do reveal themselves. There was, for example, the virtual insurrection, as the adoption of the Consensus Definition approached, of a number of developing States, who complained that the draft definition threatened to deprive them of what they regarded as basic legal entitlements already vested in them.

The simplest paradigm of what worried them was the problem raised by a conflict between two States concerning the boundary lines between them. As to this, New Zealand's M. Baxter argued that the Consensus Definition was simply inapplicable to it since "the boundaries had not been agreed",[24] and (he thought) because Explanatory Note (a) to Article 1 of the Definition provided that the word "State" was used in the Definition "without prejudice to questions of recognition". It would result even without that Note, however, from the fact that where a State uses armed force across a disputed line which from its point of view is *not* the boundary, it is *from its own standpoint still using that force on its own territory*, and not against that of the other State. And M. Godoy[25] reached the same conclusion by an argument that the exculpation of a *prima facie* act of aggression, by reference to "other relevant circumstances" under Article 2 of the Definition, must include "action taken by a State to defend territory it considered to be its own". The difficulty of providing for this case of disputed land boundaries in a definition of aggression had long been recognised.[26] What emerged in the recent discussions was the potential extension by analogy of this stalemate wherever distribution of new resources or redistribution of old ones was subject to major conflicting claims of States.

This simplest case leads naturally to the protests of certain States, led by Kenya, that the stigmatising as aggression in Article 3(d) of attacks on the marine fleets of other States, would deprive the protesting States of their rights over waters within their maritime limits. The significance of this matter arises from the fact that a central controversy of the current series of much-tried and much trying Law of the Sea Conferences, concerns the claim of some States, and readiness of many others, to extend their national maritime limits to a width of up to 200 miles. Unless, therefore, the Consensus Definition expressly reserved the maritime rights of such claimant States from the prohibition of Article 3(d), its effect could be to deprive them of this part of their claimed maritime domains. On the other hand, of course, for the Definition to have licensed the littoral State to exercise force against foreign maritime fleets within a 200 mile range, would have deprived of their freedom of access to and use of the high seas, States which recognised only a lesser range of national waters. One way or another, then, *the definitional terms, ostensibly merely clarifying the limits of use of force, would have the effect of preserving or changing an existing distribution of maritime entitlements.*

It was in this context that the Paraguayan representative[27] invoked the reference to "other relevant circumstances" to be taken into account by the Security Council under Article 2 as protecting the use of force by such a claimant-littoral State "to defend territory it considered to be its own." But the States concerned pressed, though finally in vain, for an explicit dispensation.[28] M. De Soto of Peru introduced a draft statement,[29] the effect of which would have been to add an article to protect the coastal State's right to use force in waters such as contiguous zones and economic and archipelagic areas which it claimed to be its own national waters.[30]

In view of its confrontation with Iceland concerning the width of fishing zones and the fact that Iceland was a co-sponsor of the Peruvian draft statement, the United Kingdom position is of special interest. Mr. Steel argued that it would be far-fetched to treat Article 3(d) as impugning a coastal State's enforcement of its authority in accordance with international law, and therefore that an explicit dispensation was unnecessary *and even dangerous,* since it would imply that the trespassing craft "might be subjected to any degree of force ..." .[31] The British stipulation that the coastal State's measures should accord with international law, no less than the United States point that they should not be in contravention of the Charter,[32] would have begged the question.

The point here is merely to illustrate the momentous bearing of the contents of a definition of aggression on the distribution of the world's resources, here its maritime resources. Insofar as the Definition is regarded as operative against use of force by coastal States within their claimed waters, it necessarily places limits on their patrimonial rights. Insofar as on one or another of the above-mentioned grounds the Definition is regarded as inoperative in such disputed domains, it leaves the conflict *legally* open to settlement by negotiation or even by force.

This is virtually the effect of the inclusion, as a concession to the protesting States, of paragraph 10 in the Report of the Sixth Committee, providing that nothing in the Definition, and in particular Article 3(d), "shall be construed as . . . prejudicing the authority of a State to exercise its rights within its national jurisdiction, provided such exercise is not inconsistent with the Charter of the United Nations."[33]

Like a number of other delegates, M. Rosales[34] protested even then that his country "could not accept any limitation" (that is, under Article 3(d)) "of the right of coastal States to protect the marine resources within their jurisdiction." In apparent resentment of the failure of the Peru-led *démarche*, M. Balde (Guinea) added that there was "nothing more blind than international law when it was to be applied for the benefit of the third world countries."[35] But perhaps the final Peruvian comment on Article 3(d) is nearer the last word. "The intention", said M. Perez de Cuellar,[36] "seemed to be to make the actions of the coastal State conform to international law, but considering that the law of the sea was currently in the process of revision, it was difficult to know what international law meant." M. Kumi of Ghana[37] rounded off the outcome with the sensible and realistic aphorism that "the definition should not in any event be construed as prejudging any of the issues before the Conference on the Law of the Sea."

Though also illustrating the impact of a definitional text on the distribution of power and resources, the no less vexing problem of landlocked States had a different source and outcome. Article 3(c) stigmatised as aggression "the blockade of the ports or coasts of a State by the armed forces of another State." A number of States, including Afghanistan,[38] protested that the limitation of this clause to blockade of ports or coast by armed force might be interpreted to mean that blockade of landlocked States by transit States would not constitute an act of aggression—*expressio unius exclusio alterius*.

"Such a blockade," declared the representative of Bolivia, M. Ibañez, "might not fall within the conventional concept of armed aggression, but its economic and other effects would be such that it must be regarded as an act of aggression" against the land-locked countries.[39] An Afghanistan "Working Paper" proposed the addition at the end of Article 3(c) of the words: "as well as the blockade of the routes of free access to and from the sea of land-locked countries."[40] Such States were not content to leave the matter to bilateral or multilateral agreements.[41] Nor were they content to rely on the discretions of the Security Council to inculpate the land-blockading State under Article 4, or to exculpate their own response to a landblockade under Article 2.

At a late stage in the Sixth Committee, a compromise was reached under which a paragraph was inserted in the Sixth Committee Report stating that it was agreed that nothing in the Definition "and in particular Article 3(c) shall be construed as a justification for a State to block, contrary to international law, the routes of free access of a land-locked country to or from the sea."[42] Whether this Note adds any new guidance as to the meaning of blockade of ports or coast by armed forces, stigmatised by Article 3(c), is rendered problematic by the inclusion of the words "contrary to international law". For these refer us back to the very point at issue, namely, whether international law, in the absence of treaty, does forbid such blocking.[42a]

VIII

One dimension, therefore, of the enterprise of defining aggression, no less momentous than that of controlling violence between States is that of redistribution of the world's resources. The stormy and confused debates surrounding it merge with those surrounding demands for what has come to be termed a new international economic world order. The present book can only indicate something of the range of problems on which such debates are focused and the current literature which struggles to solve, or at least clarify, them.[43] This is an area for which the growth in numbers of new Members of the General Assembly, and Communist bloc support, reinforced now by the power of Arab oil-producing States, and the resulting "automatic majorities", have already been significant. Among other results of efforts in the General Assembly,[44] there may be mentioned Resolution 1803(XVII) of December 14, 1962, concerning each State's sovereignty over its natural resources, the adoption by the Sixth Special Committee in 1974 of a Declaration on the Establishment of a New International Economic World Order,[45] followed by a Programme of Action on the Establishment of a New Economic Order,[46] and the adoption on December 12, 1974 of a Charter of Economic Rights and Duties of States.[47]

The overall aim of these efforts has been well stated as that of increasing the developing countries' capacities to pursue their own development.[48] The *status quo* economic order, based on free trade ideas, is seen as favouring the strong against the weak "by distorting the terms of trade in favor of the former and by blocking the possibility of technological development by the latter,"[49] thus checking diversification of the economies of developing countries, and also as "incompatible with agricultural realities."[50] Within the above overall aim, a recurring theme of high priority is the need to improve the terms of international trade in favour of developing countries. A variety of ways of doing this are canvassed, including (1) some kind of indexation linking prices of their primary products and raw materials to that of manufactured products which they import;[51] (2) the setting-up of buffer-stocks of their products, to be released only when prices are at a stipulated level (supported, of course, by international funding);[52] and (3) the provision of new capital for developing countries by grants of additional blocs of Special Drawing Rights, once these become the special reserve asset of the International Monetary Fund;[53] and (4) of course, a constant pressure for removal of tariff barriers in favour of the exports of developing countries.[54] These, of course, are in addition to demands for increasing the more familiar modes of financial, technological and economic aid to these countries, and for more effective methods to mitigate the crushing debt burdens of many of them.[55] They are no longer made, as formerly, merely in terms of international benevolence, or even a duty of aid to poorer nations, or of narrowing the gap between rich and poor. They are now made rather in terms of the interdependence of all national economies, and of equitable and fair international adjustment benefiting both developing and developed countries.[56]

This context of struggle about a new economic world order bears upon the concern of many Third World Nations, discussed in Chapter 7, Sections VI and IX, concerning the absence of explicit reference in the 1974 Definition to economic aggression and the hopes that the reference to "sovereignty" in Article 1 might have some implicit bearing on it. If that reference to "sovereignty" is read in the light of the assertion in General Assembly Resolution 1803(XVII) of 1962 of the permanent sovereignty of a State over its natural resources,[57] interesting possibilities do indeed arise. As directed against the feared resumption of colonial economic exploitation, this earlier assertion of sovereignty meshes well with the later gropings for a new economic order. It might also form some ground for suggesting that such alien exploitation might even constitute aggression.

The more difficult and interesting questions lie beyond this. One of these, vividly symbolised in the 1973 oil boycott, is whether a State's "sovereignty" over its natural resources is so absolute that it can be used to withhold those resources as a means of extreme coercion to control the foreign or domestic policies of other States. Insofar as the word "sovereignty" in Article 1 has some implied reference to freedom of the State with natural resources from alien economic exploitation, would it not also imply a reference to the other State's freedom from alien coercion by the calculated withholding of such resources?[58] Second is the question whether, if the sovereignty over natural resources asserted in 1962 is to be regarded as absolute, this can be reconciled with the principle of "interdependence" of nations which the same nations have later claimed to be a cornerstone of the new economic order. In a world so interdependent, a State's disposal of its resources (which might seem a veritable paradigm of *the absence* of economic aggression against that State) could, if pressed to the bitter end, actually itself be used as a weapon of economic aggression against States which it deliberately deprives of these resources. If the principle of a State's sovereignty over its natural resources is to be seen as a cornerstone of the new economic world order, it cannot be in the sense in which that sovereignty is thus absolute.

It might have been thought that the cruel impact on developing countries of the Arab oil embargo and price rise would have brought this paradox home to developing countries, and that indeed it might have produced in them a deep hostility against these events. A subsidiary paradox thus arises that many developing countries much concerned about the failure of the 1974 Definition to deal with economic aggression, and hardest hit by the oil embargo and price rise, are still staunch apologists for the OPEC-cartel. Is this to be attributed to the developing countries' *fear* of OPEC retaliation, or to *hope* of substantial OPEC aid to ease their burdens,[59] or to a mere emotive exultation at the discomfiture of some of the richest Western nations, or perhaps all of these?[60]

Whatever the answer, it is clear that cartel operations of the 1973 OPEC type are at odds with proclaimed principles of the "New International Economic World Order".[61] Even if the OPEC *coup de monde* be seen as a mere necessary readjustment of global power, preliminary to the bid for such a new order, the harsh reality remains. The insistence of developing countries that their sovereignty over their natural resources must be absolute in order to protect them from economic mayhem by developed countries, at the same time as they excuse or even applaud that *coup*, is finally comprehensible only in one way. This is if they see the events of 1973 as a model for themselves of how to acquire sufficient bargaining power to wrest benefits such as increased export earnings from developed countries.[62] Yet, while their reaction could then be seen as comprehensible, and even rational, it would in no way warrant that their reaction, or consequent strategies, conformed to the principles of the "New International Economic World Order". Moreover, insofar as the 1962 Resolution on each State's sovereignty over its own natural resources may be invoked as a basis for legitimating such strategies of the developing world within a new world economic order, the economically advanced States would also be entitled to invoke it, in resisting the demands that they transfer still larger segments of their own resources and technologies for the benefit of developing countries.[62a] To say this is not to commend or condemn either position, but only to observe that the terms of world economic cooperation have to be prudently negotiated and cannot be laid down from on high by the General Assembly.

Present scepticism as to the decisiveness of the 1974 Definition and of current General Assembly resolutions concerning world economic ordering, for the actual economic relations of countries of the developing and developed States, should not be concealed. Nor should it be seen as belittling the wide-ranging and intense pressures on States to approach intractable world economic problems by arrangements, multilateral as well as bilateral, restricting the harsher demands and aspirations of economic sovereignty, and related imperialisms and autarchies. This, however, is but to state the problem, not to provide even a sketchy blue-print for its solution. So are principles about "equitable" redistribution of world resources, unless indeed "equitable" is understood in a stricter sense, as "equal". Certainly, "equality" is a most appealing and compelling symbol of our time.[63] But even an "equality" criterion carries with it momentous ambiguities, especially as to whether all *States* are to be equalised, *or all the men and women of the planet*.[64] And even if such criteria were universally accepted, and after these obstacles of thought about them have been overcome, demands for an "equal" redistribution would pre-require most radical social, political and economic changes in the developed countries. Among such changes the erosion of the responsibility of rulers critical for the democratic form of government is only the most startling.[65]

CHAPTER 9

Hopes and Loopholes in the Definition of Aggression

I

Central to claims made for the long "Consensus Definition" now embodied in Assembly Resolution 3314, is that it has "accomplished its main purpose of depriving a potential aggressor of the possibility of using juridical loopholes and pretexts to unleash aggression".[1] The Senegal representative added to this Soviet theme the prophecy that "there would no longer be any loopholes in international law of which an aggressor could take advantage".[2]

So far is this from the realities disclosed by the preceding Chapters that the Definition rather appears to have codified into itself (and in some respects extended) all the main "juridical loopholes and pretexts to unleash aggression" available under pre-existing international law, as modified by the Charter. Ambitions of delegations to narrow some major loopholes were usually balanced by the inclusion of provisions demanded by other States which efficiently neutralised the clarification proposed, and often produced new obscurations to boot. This is true even for the more concrete problems surrounding "armed aggression" and the legal liberty of self-defence against it. It is even truer as to the less concrete problems of "indirect" and "economic" aggression which, though not expressly mentioned in the Definition, may often be affected (and further complicated) by implications from its text and from its very silences. The status of extreme economic coercion, for example of the 1973 oil boycott and of legitimate responses to it under Article 2 (4) of the Charter, remains as legally problematic as ever.

Some of the "loopholes" for legal use of force by States arise, of course, as legal licences deliberately tolerated by the Charter itself. Situations in which Security Council action is blocked by the lawful use of the Great Power veto in face of an exercise of the right of individual and collective self-defence under Article 51, are only the best known and least disputed examples. No less important, though more chronically debated, are liberties of response by the victim State to "force" or "threat of force" used against it in violation of Article 2(4), *when such responses are not otherwise prohibited by the Charter*.

This is even apart from the plain legal impotence of any General Assembly resolution, including Resolution 3314, to impose legal obligations on Members over and beyond those already imposed by Charter or other treaty. This impotence has two sources, each in itself totally disabling. First, the Consensus Definition itself explicitly preserves, by several provisions, considered at length in Chapter 3, and rehearsed in Sections X-XI below, whatever may be the legal position under the Charter. Both the clear and the controversial loopholes under international law and the Charter are thus emphatically kept open rather than closed by the terms of the Consensual Definition. Second, even without these provisions, it would have been clear that the supremacy of the Charter text, and (with exceptions not here relevant) the incapacity of the General Assembly to impose new legal obligations on Members would produce much the same effect.

As to some of the "loopholes" and "pretexts", indeed, we have already seen that even apart from saving clauses, and the question of constitutional power, the very text of the Consensus Definition embodied in Resolution 3314 remains besieged by many mutually conflicting interpretations among the States concerned, at least as grave as those which it was the ostensible object of the definitional exercise to remove. So that we face the paradox that the closing off of "loopholes" and "pretexts" hailed by the Soviet Union as the great achievement is precisely what the Definition did *not* achieve.

This, moreover, is no mere *ex post facto* perception. On the contrary, as preceding chapters have also shown, States which joined in the Consensus showed ample awareness of persisting conflicts. They often made explicit, as part of the very ritual of "consensus", that they insisted on interpretations of the text which supported their earlier positions, when others among them persisted in interpretations supporting *their* earlier positions, regardless of the head-on conflicts between them as to "correct" interpretations.

It is indeed dramatic to the point of high tragedy—or is it low comedy?—that so many of the issues on which the Consensus Definition of 1974 is silent, or merely incorporates unresolved into itself the head-on conflicts between States, are rather central and critical for contemporary international crises and tensions. One main object of the preceding Chapters has been to examine the interpretations placed on the Definition by States who joined in the Consensus adopting it. I have done this by reference to a number of key issues central to the struggle for peaceful adjustment, this, after all, rather than draft refinements, being the context in which the Consensus Definition is to be judged. On most points, a comparison of *the conflicting interpretations after adoption* thus exposed with the conflicting State positions *which had previously blocked consensus,* will indicate the respects and extent to which the Consensus Definition merely built the conflicts into itself rather than resolved them. This will show (which is perhaps only the other side of the same coin) how far the "consensus" is, on critical points, a useful means towards peaceful adjustment, rather than a means of freezing these conflicts, or even reinforcing them towards an even more severe level of confrontation.

For the purpose of these comparisons, it is fair to choose, for exposing the pre-existing conflicts of position, the latest point in time before the "consensus" emerged, at which the prospect of reaching an agreed definition still seemed slight. I have chosen for this purpose the point in the Fourth Special Committee's work when the Soviet, Thirteen Power and Six Power drafts had already been well canvassed, and when the "Consolidated Text" and its notes of persisting conflicts of State positions, based on careful Reports of the Working Group and its Contact Groups, had just been presented. This, as seen in Chapter 2, Section II above, was in April-May 1973. At this point of time—to which I shall here refer as the pre-consensual stage—delegates were still questioning whether it was worthwhile continuing the effort.[3] At the other side, this point of time was also within a year or so of the Fourth Special Committee's adoption by consensus of the present text on 12th April, 1974.[4]

I shall, for the purpose of the above comparison, take a number of *foci* of matters unresolved by the Definition in an order moving from the simpler to the more complex. This will not follow the order of the provisions of the Definition, or the order of preceding Chapters. Care will be taken, however, to make the necessary cross-references, especially to the more detailed preceding discussions of each particular matter. I have chosen for this summation a dozen *foci* of conflicting State positions including, in items 7-12, some matters where the impotence of the Definition is conceded even apart from conflicts between State positions.

1. *Acquisition and Occupation of Territory as Aggression.*
2. *Relevance of Purpose and Intention to the Question Whether Acts of Armed Force Constitute Aggression.*
3. *Extreme Economic Duress and Aggression.*
4. *Non-State Entities (Peoples) as Aggressors or Victims of Aggression.*
5. *Self-Determination, "Wars of Liberation" and Aggression.*
6. *Aggression and Attack by Armed Bands and Volunteers.*
7. *Aggression In Relation to Disputed Territorial and Maritime and Other Domains.*
8. *Limits and Uncertainties Persisting from Supremacy of the Charter.*
9. *Aggression and Nuclear First Strike.*
10. *Effect of Security Council Refrainer from Determining Aggression.*
11. *Aggression Determination and the Veto.*
12. *Impact of the Charter on the Definitional Provisions.*

II

There was sharp division among States concerning proposals that acquisition or occupation of territory by armed force should, regardless of the lawfulness of use of such force, be unlawful and barred from recognition by States.

This division was already sharply outlined at the pre-consensus stage.

Article 6(2) of the Consolidated Text proposed that "no territorial acquisition or special advantage resulting from aggression is lawful nor shall it be recognised as such". Sharp dissent was registered by Egypt and other States, demanding that the words "resulting from aggression" be replaced by the words "resulting from the threat or use of force",[5] thus giving territory absolute protection against use of armed force regardless of the legality of such use. Similarly, it was proposed that the reaffirmation in Paragraph 7 of the Preamble that the territory of a State shall not be subjected to military occupation or other measures of force by another State "in contravention of the Charter", should be amended by the omission of those quoted words.[6] The gist of both proposals was clearly that even if the use of armed force were lawful, for example when used in self-defence under Article 51, the territorial State should be guaranteed the immunity of its territory. This is the more striking since literally its protection would enure even to a territorial State which had itself resorted to the unlawful armed attack, that is, to the armed aggression which made self-defensive action necessary.

Other States (including, but not limited to, Western States) found the proposed Article 6(2) entirely acceptable as expressing the existing legal principle *ex iniuria non oritur ius,* and resisted any emasculation of that principle. They pointed out, further, that this kind of provision was, in any case, concerned with the legal consequences of aggression once this is determined to have occurred, and not really with the definition of aggression. And even if legal consequences were to be regarded as relevant to definition, they did not see (turning a blind eye to Egypt's obvious collateral designs for her dispute with Israel) why territorial acquisition or military occupation alone should be singled out from many other such consequences.

All States, Oliver Wendell Holmes Jr. once observed, are built on the blood of men. In view of the role of armed force in the origins and territorial delimitation of almost all States, and even of its sadly continuing role in the escalation of armaments even in the Third World, the issue raised by Egypt was obviously of epochal importance. It is thus not surprising (as has been more fully described in Chapter 5) that the bid for so radical a legal change failed. The issue is perhaps the only important one on which the Consensus Definition did unequivocally choose between serious pre-consensual conflicts in State attitudes. This failure of Egypt and her supporting States to effectuate their demand that all acquisition of territory by force, even by lawful force exercised in self-defence, be forbidden, represents one of the few clear legal outcomes of the 1974 Definition on a disputed matter. The solution adopted favoured (as already seen) the principle *ex iniuria non oritur ius.* That principle was clear, however, quite apart from the work of the Fourth Special Committee on Defining Aggression; so that though unusual in the above respect, it did not represent a substantive achievement of the Consensus Definition.

This clear legal outcome as to acquisition or occupation of territory is, of course, reinforced by other provisions of the Definition. One of these, for example, prevents anything in the Definition from affecting the scope of the Security Council's powers in determining what is aggression and what measures shall be taken to deal with it (Consolidated Text, Preamble, paragraphs 2 and 4, and similarly in the final text). Another prevented it from enlarging or diminishing the scope of the Charter as to the cases in which the use of force is lawful (Consolidated Text, Article 7, and final text, Article 6).[7] It nevertheless still requires listing here as an example of failure of the Definition to quiet conflicts which had at an early stage blocked progress towards definition. For despite the clear confirmation by the Consensus of the existing legal principle, Egypt and other States continued to advocate their position as the correct one into their interpretations of the Definition after consensus. This phenomenon has been more fully described in Chapter 5, where it was seen that although clearly the Definition did not impugn the legal basis of occupations, such as that by Israel after 1967, this legal clarity could not conceal the political value to the Arab States of a number of collateral ambiguities in the language of this and other parts of the Definition. This political value was oriented, of course, to later exploitation of such ambiguities, in the marshalling by Arab States wielding oil and money power of "automatic" majorities in the expanded General Assembly. It is not likely to help towards a just and peaceful settlement of the Middle East conflict.

III

From earliest United Nations discussions (and indeed long before, under the League of Nations),[8] the question of the relevance of intention and purpose to commission of aggression was a main obstacle to agreed definition.[9] The Consolidated Text proposed in Article 2 that the first use of armed force in contravention of the Charter was prima facie evidence of an act of aggression, but that the Security Council might conclude that a finding to that effect was not justified "in the light of other relevant circumstances *including, as evidence, the purposes of the States involved*" (italics supplied). The italicized words adopted the gist of the long Paragraph IV of the (Western) Six Power Draft which set out at length the kind of purposes by way of impairment of the victim State which alone would render the various uses of armed force (there also listed) aggressive. It was thus explicit that, according as the Security Council may find, the priority principle (who used armed force first?) would operate only subject to a finding as to the respective purposes and intentions of the States in conflict. And other States also supported this relevance of State purposes.[10] At this pre-consensual stage the inclusion of any reference to purposes was so sharply contested that the Drafting and Contact Groups reported that "notwithstanding intensive negotiations it was not possible to find . . . a formula which would have been accepted by consensus."

The opposed position thus barring consensus at that stage was pressed by a number of States, demanding a more absolute operation of the principle of priority, by omitting, for example, the words "in contravention of the Charter" as well as the words "including, as evidence, the purposes of the States involved".[11] Egypt would also have deleted any reference to "other relevant considerations" of any kind.[12] This kind of position marched, of course, with the view of Arab States with an eye on the politics of the Arab-Israel dispute, seeking a similar absolute rule against territorial acquisition or military occupation regardless of illegalities of State conduct.

Between this flat disagreement at the pre-consensual stage and the final consensus, the Security Council's liberty to depart from the priority principle "in the light of other relevant circumstances" was maintained, but the particular express reference there to "the purposes of the States concerned" was omitted. Does this necessarily imply that the purposes of the States concerned should not be taken into account in determining whether acts constitute aggression? It has been seen in Chapter 4 that it is difficult to establish such an implication, involving as it would that the purposes of action cannot be "relevant" to such a determination.

As observed at length in Chapter 4, Sections III-VIII, both sides maintained that their respective and diametrically opposed positions represented the correct (and the only correct) meaning of the slightly amended Article 2 of the Consensus Definition.[13] So that on this point the Definition remains subject, after the consensus, to the same conflicting State positions which had been officially reported shortly before as barring consensus; namely, as to whether the *prima facie* stigmatised external acts would cease to be so because of the non-aggressive intention or purpose with which they were committed. Conflicting positions blocking consensus survived still after consensus, but now transmuted into conflicting interpretations of the Consensus Definition.

All this is, of course, an aggravation of other conflicts of position concealed within the apparent adoption by Article 2 of the test of priority, by which that State which first commits a *prima facie* stigmatised external act is the aggressor. This text, as also noted in Chapter 4, often faces intractable problems of fixing the moment in history from which priority is to be reckoned. Such problems, along with that of relevance of purposes or intentions, are only slightly covered from view by the provision in the same Article that the Security Council may hold, in the light of "other relevant circumstances", that it would not be justified in finding a *prima facie* stigmatised act to be aggression. And this same clause covers also the matter next to be considered, namely the conflict as to whether a *prima facie* stigmatised use of armed force may be exculpated as a lawful response to "indirect" and especially economic aggression. (See Chapter 4, Section IX, and Chapter 7.)

IV

Whether "aggression" embraced only armed aggression as distinct from other forms of extreme coercion, for instance economic coercion, had been disputed at least since 1953. (This earlier history is discussed generally in Chapter 1 and in Chapter 7.) The issue was to move to the centre of the international stage with the oil boycott imposed by OPEC Arab States as a part of the Egyptian-Syrian surprise offensive against Israel in October 1973. A substantial body of States continued to press in the Fourth Special Committee for inclusion of economic aggression. It was pointed out that the fact that even if the definition was only to deal with armed aggression that did not mean that economic coercion did not exist or could be ignored. In particular, the fact that an alleged aggressor's use of armed force had been in response to extreme economic coercion might be held by the Security Council to be among the "other relevant circumstances" which, under Article 2 of the Consolidated Text, might lead to the conclusion that a finding of aggression was not justified.

Opposed views at that pre-consensus stage, however, claimed that only armed aggression was the concern of the Security Council, that the resort to armed force was to be aggression not merely *prima facie,* but *per se.* An additional clause was indeed proposed which declared that "No consideration of whatever nature, whether political, economic, military or otherwise, may serve as a justification for aggression" (that is, for aggression within proposed Articles 1-3, all of which refer to armed aggression).[14] Taken literally, such a provision might be read to exclude response to extreme economic duress as a circumstance relevant to exculpation under Article 2. But such a literal reading would also negative a plea of self-defence against armed attack (supremely a "military" consideration), thus casting doubt on the literal interpretation. At the preconsensus stage of the Consolidated Text, however, there had been no decision as to the placement of such a clause.[15]

In the Consensus Definition no express reference was made to economic aggression, and the above clause negativing certain justifications was included as Paragraph 1 of the rather miscellaneous Article 5. The legal outcome, involving also the point that the "threat or use of force" forbidden by Article 2(4) of the Charter is not limited to *armed force*, has been examined in Chapter 1. What is very clear is that the above sharp conflicts of position at the preconsensual stage, persist after Consensus. In particular, it remains debated whether, if it was "economic aggression" which provoked the first use of armed force by its victim, this circumstance would be available as a "relevant circumstance" which, under Article 2 of the text, should lead the Security Council to conclude that "a finding of aggression would not be justified". The centrality of economic factors in the prospects for increased international tension or *détente,* especially after the 1973 oil boycott, gives major importance to the question whether international law sets any limits to the exercise of extreme economic duress. The Consensus Definition affords not even the beginnings of a clear answer.

V

Historically, as Chapter 7 has shown, the term "indirect" as applied to "aggression", despite the confused usage in the history, seems referable to either or both of two assumptions. One is that international aggression is a relation of State to State; a second is that armed hostilities have been used by one State against the other.[16] Article 1 of the Consolidated Text at the pre-consensual stage adopted both these assumptions, providing that "aggression is the use of armed force *by a State* against the sovereignty, territorial integrity or political independence of *another State . . .*".

The legal consequences of these assumptions touched some of the most sensitive nerves of Western and Third World States. So far as the *perpetrator* of aggression was concerned, Third World States, championing the right of peoples to struggle *by armed force* for self-determination were, of course, determined that *their* use of armed force should not stigmatise *them* as aggressors—that is, that "a State" should not (for this purpose) be interpreted to include such "a people". So far as the *victim* of aggression was concerned, the same advocates were no less obviously resolved that "State" should be read to include "a people" so struggling. Western States were opposed to this latter dispensation for non-State entities to use armed force, especially since it was proposed to extend it to any third States who chose to assist them in such armed struggles. The Soviet Union and the Soviet bloc States wished both to insist on the State-to-State requirement, and to support the use of armed force in "wars of liberation".

Already at this pre-consensual stage there had been attached to Article 1 an "Explanatory Note (a) (to remain unchanged from the Consolidated Text into the final text), which stipulated that the term "State" was used in the Definition "without prejudice to questions of recognition". As was shown in Chapter 7, however, this addition still left the main issue in conflict unresolved. For the phrase "questions of recognition" might refer merely to the question whether (the general conditions of statehood already being present) it made any difference whether, as between the alleged aggressor and victim States, the one had recognised the other.[17]

After consensus had been achieved, this question, whether "peoples" (as distinct from States) had some exceptional dispensation to use armed force, remained a bitter focus of conflicting interpretations of the Consensual Definition as between the main blocs of States. The Articles in relation to which these conflicting interpretations became manifest, were mainly Article 7, referring to struggles for self-determination (dealt with in the immediately succeeding Section VI), and Article 3(g), concerning aggression by sending armed bands (to be dealt with in Section VII).

As to the assumption that aggression involved State-to-State *armed hostilities*, the persistence of pre-consensual conflicts into conflicting interpretations of the adopted text, was manifest mainly on the issue of "economic aggression" discussed in the immediately preceding Section IV, and on the issue of vicarious aggression through the sending of armed bands (to be dealt with in Section VII).

It is eloquent of these persisting conflicts by way of interpretation that the Greek and Turkish Governments each felt immediately able to invoke draft provisions of the Consensus Definition to charge the other with aggression arising from the Cyprus Affair of 1973-74. So with the Soviet-Cuban and South African participants in the struggle to establish a Government for Angola in 1975-76. The equal division on the Angola issue among the States of the Organisation of African Unity, immediately before the success of the Cuban intervention, displays dramatically the helplessness of the Consensus Definition.

As already noticed, the oracular caveat in Explanatory Note (a) to Article 1 of the Consensus Definition that its use of the term "State" is "without prejudice to questions of recognition" or of Membership of the United Nations, brought little light to such matters. The Indonesian military activity in East Timor early in 1976, which culminated in its virtual annexation, was not in *direct* conflict with any other pre-existing State. It is difficult to see how Explanatory Note(a) helps *the application of this Definition* as between Indonesia and the Fretilin forces struggling for independence. This is because it remains most obscure and debatable, even with Explanatory Note (a), whether and in what sense that Definition is limited to State-to-State aggression. And, of course, it was arguable that (as with Angola) East Timor still lacked at the time of the military intervention concerned the stable government necessary for statehood.

VI

Paragraph 6 of the Preamble of the Consolidated Text referred to "the duty of States not to use armed force to deprive people of their right to self-determination, freedom and independence". Article 5 of the same Text proposed to save the right of self-determination of peoples in terms going in three respects beyond what was later to be included in Article 7 of the Consensus Definition. First, the draft Article 5 explicitly reserved a people's right to use force in such struggles. Second, it implied that they had a right to receive assistance of third States in this use of force. Third, this right to use force was to extend also to "peoples under military occupation". The licence of "peoples" *to use force* against

States under whose sovereignty they lived, and of third States to support them in this, was strongly denied by many States, especially Western States. On all these heads, especially the first two, these proposals were adamantly resisted, especially (but not only) by Western States. The Soviet Union and other Soviet *bloc* States were, for example, zealous, even while predictably supporting self-determination claims, to deny that anything in the Definition could affect a State's right to take "police action" against dissident movements. At this pre-consensual stage the Drafting Committee reported that "there was no general agreement as to the text to be adopted".[18]

In the text which emerged on this matter in Article 7 of the Consensus Definition, all express reference to use of force by peoples under military occupation was excised, and a vague reference to their "right . . . to struggle . . ." was substituted. Paragraph 6 of the Preamble had also had added to it, at the end, the words "and territorial integrity". I have, in Chapter 6, examined in detail these and other changes, and the conflicting interpretations still offered of them which here concern us. The final result was to preserve the above preconsensual conflicts into the question of interpretation whether the right of peoples to "struggle", includes the right to use armed force against the parent State, and the corresponding question as to the right of third States to support such struggles by force. The additional phrase about "territorial integrity" to Paragraph 6 of the Preamble increased this indecisiveness since this is an attribute of sovereign States rather than peoples "struggling" for self-determination which may, indeed, often have no defined territorial base. The new reference to territorial integrity might thus be interpreted as forbidding, rather than licensing, the use of force by third States in support of a "struggle" for self-determination against the target State. It marches with this view that the Working Group refused to attribute "sovereignty and territorial integrity" as rights *of peoples* parallel to their right of self-determination, saved by the future Article 5.[19]

If we anticipated that the final Article 7 would leave the conflicting positions much as they were at the preconsensual stage, we would thus be profoundly correct. Nowhere are the equivocations and silences of the Definition better designed to preserve, in the form of conflicting interpretations of the text, the conflicts which seemed at the preconsensual stage to block progress towards consensus. And, as seen in Chapter 6, on no matter are the post-consensus assertions of contradictory interpretations more numerous and vociferous. The preconsensual confrontation of those who made and those who resisted demands that insurgent peoples and supporting third States be licensed to use force, was metamorphosed into a gross conflict of interpretation between States which insist that the "struggle" reserved as lawful by Article 7 of the Definition includes armed struggle, and others which deny this. The mere fact that words in the preliminary Consolidated Text expressly licensing force were deliberately omitted from the Consensus Definition, in no way inhibited States favouring the licence to use force from arguing that on a fair interpretation it was licensed by the Definition. All this appears very clearly from the rehearsal in Chapter 6, Section V.

Claims were flatly asserted, by way of interpretation, that use of force by non-State entities (and any States supporting them) against established States is always lawful in furtherance of the "inalienable right of self-determination", which some even placed on the same overriding level as the "self-defence against armed attack" under Article 51 of the Charter. This was asserted to follow from declarations of the General Assembly, as well as from the oracular Explanatory Note(a) to Article 1 of the Consensus Definition itself, that the term "State" is there used "without prejudice to questions of recognition or to whether a State is a member of the United Nations." (See Chapter 6, Section II.)

On the other hand, many States, including Western States, insisted that by its terms the Definition dealt only with State-to-State aggression. Some States, as already noted, continued to insist that the Definition in no way inhibits "police action" by an established State within its own sovereign domains. (See Chapter 6, Sections VI-VIII.) These Communist-bloc States, of course, also gave strong support to the above claims that force may be used in the struggle for self-determination. They tried to secure the best of both worlds, by stressing that only struggles against "*colonial*" or "*racist*" oppressors were saved by Article 7. The Chinese Representative reduced this Soviet tactic to some degree of absurdity by designating as the relevant struggles those against "imperialist" oppression, with which he expressly associated the Soviet Union as well as the United States.

The stalemates and cross-purposes thus surrounding the permitted limits of "struggles" for self-determination under the Definition are compounded by a whole series of further unresolved problems, on some of which judgment in a particular case is likely to depend.

First, the question *which peoples* are the beneficiaries of the saving clause in Article 7 is even more dubious than even the vagueness of such terms as "colonialist", "racist" or "imperialist" suggests. If, indeed, the references to "self-determination" in the Charter and in General Assembly declarations have established some legal (as distinct from political) principle, the legal marks for identifying a "people" having this entitlement—the "self" entitled to "determine" itself—remain at best speculative. Those who do not recognise this as a problem will do well to recall the continuing stream of violence arising from it, of which the affairs concerning Katanga, Biafra, Cyprus and Angola, Lebanon, Bougainville and now Zaire, are contemporary warnings.

This, moreover, is a burning issue, not only for the birth and early years of new States. It may be a critical one for some of the oldest and most powerful States. Thus, in the form proposed in the Consolidated Text, Preamble, Paragraph 6 and Article 5, the Definition might have invited scrutiny of questions concerning the legal rights of the Baltic peoples overrun by the Soviet Union at the opening of World War II, not to speak of her armed actions against the Hungarian and Czecho-slovak peoples in 1956 and 1968. And such rights might even at some time be invoked by the Welsh and Scots in the United Kingdom, not to speak of the Indians and Blacks of the United States, the Aborigines of Australia, and the Chinese of Malaysia. Though the revision of Article 5 in what became the final Article 7 inserted the qualifying phrase "peoples under colonial and racist regimes or other forms of alien domination", these terms are vague enough to leave such claims open in the future.

The specification "colonial and racist" will no doubt protect such Soviet adventures as long as Third World majorities in the United Nations maintain their present orientations. But persistent Chinese charges of Soviet "imperialism", as well as Soviet and satellite insistence that the Consensus Definition does not bar "police" action by a State within its own territory, indicate that the issues involved are not finally closed. They have certainly not been resolved by the equivocations of the Helsinki Declaration of 1975, despite the surrounding rhetoric.

It is, of course, a hard truth for this problem, as well as that of competing claims to self-determination which follows, that it is often the direct armed action of third States which conditions (if not actually creates) the "self" which demands "self-determination", not to speak of the "self" which succeeds. On such issues the Consensus Definition speaks with no discernible voice at all.

Second, Article 7 is directed solely to peoples oppressed by States and gives no guidance for cases (increasingly important today) of competing claims of two or more peoples for self-determination with regard to the same territory. The rights of the Katangan and Biafran and South Vietnamese peoples are mostly water under the international bridge, whatever the merits of those outcomes. But the bloody struggle in Lebanon in 1975-76 involving local insurgency by Lebanese Leftist forces allied with Palestine Liberation forces localised in Lebanon, opposed by the Christian Rightists and also by other Palestinian forces trained in and despatched from Syria, then by regular Syrian forces, later renamed Arab "peacekeeping forces", signal again the increasing intimacy between civil strife, wars of liberation or self-determination and international aggression. So does the claim of the Palestine Liberation Organisation to dismantle and replace the State of Israel. Here again, the Consensus Definition says little that is pertinent and plain. The controverted doctrine of the legitimacy of "wars of liberation" only adds to the confusion where, as in Lebanon, the "inalienable right of self-determination" can be equally invoked by both peoples engaged in a "struggle" to vindicate it.

The France-Comoros affair of 1976 neatly illustrates the present point.[19a] The fact that the island of Mayotte alone did not join in the overwhelming vote of the people of the Comoros four-island Archipelago of December 12, 1974, in favour of independence, led France to hold a special referendum on Mayotte on February 8, 1976. No less than

99.4% of the Mayotte people were then to vote to remain an integral part of France. On February 6, 1976, Comoros, which had meanwhile been admitted to the United Nations, and other States sought in the Security Council to have this French action declared an interference in Comoros' internal affairs, from which France must desist. Comoros even declared that it was a "flagrant aggression". The draft resolution to the above effect, sponsored by Benin, Guyana, Libya, Panama and Tanzania, received 11 votes, with Italy, the U.K. and U.S. abstaining, but was defeated, naturally, by a French veto.

No one seriously challenged the reality that while "the people" of the other three islands overwhelmingly wanted independence, the people of Mayotte overwhelmingly wanted to remain integral with France. "Self"-determination, therefore, pointed both ways, according to which "self" was regarded as entitled to this right. What was the bearing on this question of the facts that (1) all four islands were, under a French law of 1912, a single administrative unit, or (2) that after the vote of December 12, 1974, the Comoros unilaterally proclaimed its independence on July 5, 1975, and (3) that thereafter, on December 31, 1975, the French Parliament (under its exclusive constitutional power to that end) recognised the independence of the three islands, but provided for a referendum on *its* future to be held in Mayotte on February 8, 1976, or (4) that the General Assembly, by Resolution 3385 (XXX) of 1975, admitted Comoros (embracing *all four* islands) to U.N. Membership, or (5) that France by abstaining rather than vetoing allowed the corresponding Resolution concerning Comoros' admission in the Security Council to pass?

The central issue is, of course, whether the "self" entitled to self-determination of peoples consists only of the four islands together, either because they were while under French rule a single administrative unit, or because the General Assembly had admitted them *qua* single entity to Membership. Or whether the people of Mayotte were entitled also to this right. Neither the Charter references nor the plethora of Assembly declarations and recitals of the self-determination principle offer any solution to such a problem. Indeed, paragraph 4 of the principle as stated in the 1970 Declaration of Principles ... Concerning Friendly Relations of States (Res. 2625 (XXV) seems to support the French argument rather than that of Comoros. It provides:

The establishment of a sovereign and independent State, *the free association or integration with an independent State* or the emergence into any other political status freely determined by a people constitute modes of implementing the right to self-determination by that people.

Yet, of course, precisely the contrary view can be inferred from the wide affirmation of the 1960 Declaration on the Granting of Independence to Colonial Countries and Peoples (Res. 1514 (XV)) of the principle of *territorial integrity* of Territories destined for independence. (Emphases added.)

The impasse here involved for the imputation of aggression to the parent State for alleged encroachment on the inchoate political independence of peoples claiming self-determination, when the "self" which is entitled to self-determination is itself in dispute between the peoples concerned, has a wider theoretical interest. It is somewhat analogous to the impasse which we have already seen to face the notion of aggression when the aggression charged is across disputed boundaries into territory of which the invader claims that it is sovereign. If the latter be regarded as a legal impasse caused by legally undetermined entitlements *in the dimension of space,* the former might be regarded as an impasse created by legally undetermined entitlements *in the dimension of time.* The answer depended on whether France's prior (and still unrenounced) claim of sovereignty could support the Mayotte claim to self-determination, or whether Comoros' later assumption of independence for all four islands precluded the Mayotte claim.

Third, the problem of competing self-determinations becomes even more intractable to handling by the Definition, where the competing claims and accompanying military activities, punctuated by actual wars, armistices and cease-fire agreements, *have been made over long historical periods.* We have seen that the test of priority of resort to armed force in Article 2 presupposes a fixed point in time from which priority is to be calculated. (See Chapter 1, Section VI, Chapter 4, Section IV.) Does one fix the aggression in the Cyprus Crisis of 1974 from the action of the Greek officers who led the *coup d'état,* or the Turkish response by invasion, even assuming that the 1974 crisis can be severed from the earlier struggles? Is the critical date of the Middle East Crisis 1973 or 1967, or the first Arab States' attack on Israel in 1948, or is it at the Balfour Declaration in 1917, or at the Arab invasions and conquest of the 7th century, or even perhaps at the initial Israelite conquest of the thirteenth century B.C.? The priority question, as well as the self-determination question, become even more baffling when, in the course of such a long time-span, a later developing nationalism arises, like the Palestinian, which claims to override retrospectively the sovereign Statehood already attained by the competing people. (See Chapter 5 above.)

A fourth aggravating problem should perhaps here be added, concerning the phrase "forcibly deprived" of "the right of self-determination", which in Article 7 now delimits the range of peoples entitled to "struggle" for self-determination under that Article. It corresponds to the recital in Paragraph 6 of the Preamble of "the duty of States not to use armed force to deprive peoples of their self-determination". Does "forcible deprivation" refer only to future or at least contemporary acts? Or does it embrace all such deprivations which have occured, at however remote a time, in the establishment of a State now existing? Considering that most, if not all, well-established States have been founded by armed force, if not by conquest, commonsense would indicate the need for some statute of limitations. But, of course, one of the most current assumptions among Third World States is that a State exercising sovereignty over a people seeking self-determination within its territory, even if it has done so for centuries, must be deemed to be in a continuous state of armed attack against that people forcibly depriving it of its self-determination. The theorem proposes that such a State be deemed in law to be in a standing condition of armed aggression, thus giving the people concerned and supporting third States the licence (or "privilege" or "liberty") to use armed force in individual collective self-defence. It presents one basis for the interpretation of "struggle" in Article 7, to include the use of armed force. As has been seen in Chapter 6, the theorem does not go without criticism even by protagonists of "wars of liberation", and alternative theorems were there also discussed.

VII

The story of efforts to outlaw "war" has, ever since the League of Nations, been harassed by various devices of States for evading the legal precepts. Not least among these has been the concealment of a State's resort to use of armed force, by making this resort vicarious, or claiming that the persons acting are only "volunteers" and not part of its armed forces. The modern history of such resorts include post-World War I counter-revolutionary moves against the Soviet Government; the "volunteers" on both sides in the Spanish Civil War; and the intervention of Chinese "volunteers" in the Korean War; the hosting and equipment by Arab States of terrorist bands later featured as a miscellany of "military arms" of "the Palestine Liberation Organisation"; the sending of Soviet "civilians" to support the armed forces of one or other of the Arab States from 1967 to the present time; and Cuban and Soviet support for the leftist contenders for control of Angola in 1976.

Certainly, all engaged in the enterprise of definition were sharply aware of the need to clarify at what point responsibility for armed aggression would attach to a State thus acting vicariously, cutting through fictions and evasions. Prior to and apart from the Consensus Definition, international law attributed deliquency to a State which in its territory knowingly hosted or sent armed bands to operate against a neighbouring State. It gave to the victim State rights of self-help, extending to entry onto the culprit's territory (at least in hot pursuit) to abate the depredations, if that State was not willing or able to do so.

The provision in Article 3(g) of the Consolidated Text, listing the sending of armed bands against another State as an act of aggression was somewhat more permissive towards alleged aggressors than these rules of traditional international law, and than many past proposals on the matter, for instance, by the Soviet Union. It apparently reduced the guilty activities from organising, encouraging, assisting or sending armed bands, to merely that of "sending". Even then it qualified the range of guilt by requiring that the resulting acts of armed force against the target State must be "of such gravity as to amount to the other acts of aggression listed above in the definition." (Which had a rather circular ring to it.) The final words of Article 3(g) "or its open and active participation therein" created further doubts as to whether, indeed, other activities than "sending" might be caught in certain circumstances.

At this pre-consensual stage, State positions were in head-on conflict. Some pressed to expand the range of guilty activities. Indonesia wanted to include "support" as well as "open and active participation".[20] The United States wished to stigmatise not only sending but organising, encouraging the organisation, assisting and knowingly acquiescing as well as sending, and not only "armed bands, groups, irregulars or mercenaries", but also "volunteers".[21] Guyana would have included "organizing and supporting" as well as "sending", and so would Uruguay.[22] And there were other objections that Article 3(g) was too narrow and omitted acts which should be covered.[23] Other States, on the contrary, wanted further to emasculate even Article 3(g). There were objections even to the stigmatisation of "open and active participation therein" at the end. Syria, Iraq and Egypt, like the "non-aligned" Thirteen Power Draft, Article 7, urged that this activity should be removed from the list of acts of aggression and declared neutrally to be a mere "breach of the peace". Algeria approached the same object more obliquely by asking that Article 3(g) be expressly derogated from by the opening words of Article 5 (later to become Article 7 of the Consensual Definition) in favour of peoples struggling for determination.

At the pre-consensual stage, therefore, the Drafting and Contact Committees understandably observed that there was no general agreement on the text they offered.[24] In the text which achieved Consensus, the confrontation concerning armed bands was preserved in a concealed form. On the one hand, Article 7 did contain a clause that Article 3 (*not merely Article 3(g)*) should not derogate from the right to struggle for self-determination in Article 7. On the other hand, however, any explicit licence for use of force in self-determination struggles was deleted. So that the Algerian non-derogation proposal was adopted in form but rejected in substance, and the issue was turned into conflicting interpretations of the word "struggle" in Article 7, already summarised in Sub-Section 6 above.

In sum, therefore, what the 1974 Definition contributed on aggression by sending "armed bands" was a somewhat emasculated restatement of the rule of international law, beclouded, however, by the tendentious and disputed proviso in Article 7 concerning the right of "a people" to "struggle" for self-determination, and of third States to give it support. On no issue of interpretation, as observed above, were the States joining in the consensus so starkly at odds, as on whether the word "struggle" includes the use of armed bands contrary to Article 3(g).

The effect of so reading it would be to neutralise, for most practical purposes, the express stigmatisation as aggression of such use of armed bands in Article 3(g). We have given reasons (Chapter 6, especially Sections V-VI) for thinking this self-frustrating and rather untenable. But the fact that the Consensual Definition makes the point seem even arguable gives for the future a certain spurious *political* legitimacy to devices of indirect armed aggression, which the preexisting rule of international law condemned as unlawful. Here, as elsewhere, loopholes and pretexts were extended rather than closed off. While objections to the *limited* references to indirect aggression were dominant in the pre-consensual change discussions in this area, a theme which dominated the post-consensus statements was the inadequacy of express provisions concerning it.

VIII

The limitations of the aggression notion in relation to disputed boundaries have long been recognised, for the earliest notions of aggression were centred on the armed crossing of frontiers. The limitations arise from the fact that where frontiers are disputed, both sides can claim to be acting within their own domains. There is here the initial paradox that while the most simple and intuitively felt notion of aggression is armed trespass across a frontier, it has also long been agreed that this notion is not helpful when the frontier line is in debate. While it is thus recognised that the test of armed crossing of frontiers is inadequate, this should not blind us to the fact that resort to armed force over disputed frontiers remains a cardinal class of contemporary warlike conflicts.

Contemporary trends, indeed, may tend to increase rather than decrease the spread and gravity of conflicts as to both territorial and marine entitlements of States. Thus, the States of Black Africa, now that the first stage of liberating nationalisms and decolonisation is almost over, are likely to become increasingly restless within the pencil and ruler boundaries so debonairly drawn by the Congress of Berlin in 1878. Lines which thus often ignore tribal, geographical, strategic, and economic function are likely to come into controversy as the united front against Western colonialism yields to concern with questions internal to the Black African region. Even the existence of an original treaty basis for the frontiers later accepted by newly established Black African States, gives no assurance against future disputes. The treaty basis of Sino-Indian frontiers, which had proved stable for a half-century, did not prevent the People's Republic of China, on the basis of nascent doctrines about unequal treaties and treaties made under duress, from bringing those frontiers to unpleasant life in the 'sixties. Tribal divisions, restlessness and irredentism may yet make the doctrines of "unequal treaties" and "wars of liberation" as powerful in political warfare among Black African States *inter se,* as it has proved against Western States. (See Chapter 1, Sections III and IV.) President Amin of Uganda, on February 16, 1976, as this chapter was being written, played the overture to this phase, even as the problems of Southern

Africa were still unsolved. He made major territorial claims against both Kenya and the Sudan, to further which he added that Uganda had at present no intention to make war on those neighbours, but merely to point to the mistakes of the former British ruler in fixing the Kenya-Uganda frontiers.

The Consensus Definition, it was agreed on all hands, reduces not at all the intractability of land boundary disputes for definitions of aggression, and there was no serious division of opinion about it, either before or after Consensus was achieved. What is clear by silence, and by inferences drawn by some from Explanatory Note(a) to Article 1, explaining that the word "State" is used "without prejudice to questions of recognition", as to land frontiers, was also made clear as to maritime entitlements by express caveat to the Definition. (On Explanatory Note (a), see Chapter 6, Section III.) This declared its provisions to be without prejudice to the rights of littoral States to act in waters within their national jurisdiction, conformably to the United Nations Charter.[25] The effect is, of course, that armed action such as that of Iceland in vindication of her disputed claims of national jurisdiction in a widened exclusive fishing zone (as well as reasonable responses thereto by other States such as the United Kingdom) are not affected one way or the other by the contents of the Definition. Apart, therefore, from any restraints or controls arising from the Charter or other treaties binding the parties, armed action arising from this conflict as to maritime frontiers is left to customary arbitraments of negotiated agreement or force. As seen in Chapter 8, a whole range of conflicts, solutions to which still escape the third (1976) Conference on the Law of the Sea at New York, is similarly out of reach of the Consensus Definition.

This close bearing of a definition of aggression on the momentous issues of planetary distribution of the various regions and uses of the oceans and the resources they contain (not to speak of the uses and resources of continental shelves and the ocean bed) points to a deeper meaning of the task and its difficulty. In both its aspiration and political warfare aspects, the undertaking is a demand for global redistribution of powers and resources now enjoyed by the respective States in the legal and economic *status quo*. A definition which forbids the use of kinds of coercion by which alone particular States or groups of States can assure the security of their rights and legitimate interests under the existing order, exposes those rights and interests to appropriation by others. Manoeuvring for a definitional text which will advance the proponent State's self-interests, and strike at its adversary's, is thus a central socio-political reality, side by side with noble aspirations for a more peaceful world in which there is a juster distribution among States and peoples. It was to be expected that States whose rights and interests seem thus exposed by a particular text, will resist that text and the redistribution which it threatens. No less clearly other States, to whom such rights and interests are exposed by the definition, may support and press them. Still other States will be uncertain about the effect of a text on *their* rights and interests, and will prefer a text which by silence or ambiguity leaves them escape hatches in the future, but now unforseeable, circumstances.

When what is at stake in the plausibly simple call for definition that now turns out to be a kind of planet-wide legislative redistribution of powers and resources among the 145 States of the world, we should not expect any easy success from the Fourth Special Committee. Such a success, far from being achievable by "finding" a definition of aggression calls rather, first of all, for a review of all the major existing legal precepts and institutions of international society—in short of the existing legally supported politico-economic order. What this requires is a consensus not so much about phrases in a definition, as about the norms of minimal justice among mankind which would control and guide this reform of the existing law in various situations. I have examined at length the available approaches to these norms of justice, and the special difficulties of approaching them in international rather than municipal contexts.[26] Certainly such a comprehensive global reform cannot be approached as a mere by-product of an exercise in definition of aggression, however skilful, cunning and wise the draftsmen and diplomats whose labours produced it.

IX

This stocktaking of vital matters unresolved by the 1974 Definition is, I hope, a sufficient comment on the diplomatic claims quoted at the start of Section I, that the "loopholes in international law" for aggressors have been closed. Claims of this nature, concealing the power-political realities behind the language of peace-directed idealism, when they proceed from representatives of States, may be but tactful expressions, filling oratorical time without impairing or committing State interests. They may also be an oblique salute to the expected value to States concerned of built-in ambiguities as future political weapons. It is far less easy to understand such concealments in serious scholarly analysis.

Among the most diligent running commentaries on the work of the Fourth Special Committee have been those of Benjamin B. Ferencz. They have been notable for their important insights, as well as for an optimism often verging on wishfulness.[27] His account after the achievement of the Consensus Definition, in a volume collecting 539 pages of United Nations documents, with a 59-page analysis of the text, brings both these qualities to a striking level.[28]

Hope, of course, springs eternal, especially when it is for the long-dreamed-of peace and harmony of mankind. Mr. Ferencz closed his earlier study of what he called "the last mile" of the race for definition —immediately before the "fragile consensus"—with a confident plea. It was that since only a "few points" of non-agreement existed, the Fourth Committee should by compromises now obey the renewed instruction by the General Assembly to define aggression as soon as possible, even with imperfections. "The most important thing about defining aggression is to define it."[29] He was prepared, as it were, to put aside the major interests, sometimes involving the very survival of States, which depend on those few points of conflict. For this purpose, he seemed disposed to encourage what he criticised in the final outcome, namely, consensus "regarding the phrases in the text", but not regarding their "meaning"— thus reducing the negotiations to a matter of verbal exercise, and drafting skills, and to a count of clauses still to be settled by these. After all, he finally pleaded, defining aggression is only the beginning.

Yet his own detailed critique[30] could not conceal that a definition so full of gaps and equivocations, papering over the severest current conflicts, either by omission or by building them unresolved into the text, is not even a beginning. Even if triumphant as a verbal exercise, it may still (as I have just shown) be a vacuity in relation to the control of war. My own more detailed analysis is even more severe. And I shall also shortly show that the Consensus Definition, by its very gaps and equivocations, has produced a new armoury of weapons of political warfare, which may well herald a new level of confrontation and tension, quite negative in its bearing on the cause of peace. For some States which are particular targets of manipulated majorities in the General Assembly, the gaps and equivocations of the Consensus Definition may be "the beginning" only of grave political and military wrongs to which they are unlikely to submit.

The present work, and especially Chapters 4 to 8, shows that on crucial points the hailed Consensus Definition was only as to phrases, not as to meaning. This was a mere shell of definition, wrapped in a mere shell of "consensus". So wide open does its meaning remain to opposed interpretations on critical issues, that it cannot seriously be thought to guide States and United Nations organs as to their duties for the avoidance and control of war. Its final reality, I have shown in this and the preceding Chapter, is likely to lie in the verbal weapons of political warfare which it provides for use in contexts extraneous to that authentic objective. Mr. Ferencz climaxed his own chronicling of the negotiations with an overall analysis, Article by Article, of the final Consensus text which finally emerged, which I have already examined at length elsewhere.[30a] He there acknowledged that others may criticise the Definition on the following grounds: (1) "Consensus" had too often not signified "agreement", but merely that "States refrained from voicing their doubts and objections". (2) The ambiguities, omissions, and internal inconsistencies of the Definition make it subject to conflicting interpretations on very critical matters. (3) Any guidance which it might provide has, in any case, no binding effect on the Security Council (or, as one might add, on anyone else).[31]

The learned author is nevertheless concerned, in the end, to defend the Consensus Definition. The main gist of his defence is that the Definition cannot be disregarded, that its norms will tend to become binding norms, that they will deter national leaders from breach of them, and will enable "the public" better to understand the actions of States in relation to peace. All this is almost in the same breath as he had just chastened the silences, ambiguities, internal inconsistencies, and built-in conflicts of interpretations on decisively critical matters. Such being the text, the praise can at best amount to little; and if we envisage that these shortcomings may sharpen the weapons of future political warfare, praise might turn into warnings about new temptations for potential aggressors. Indeed, the Author himself almost steps back to make this self-correction (but scarcely sufficiently so). The definition, he says, reflects both the adhesion of old nations to traditional values, and defence of their positions, and the brandishing of fledgling sovereignty by new nations demanding equality and justice. It reflects the fears and doubts of an unevenly developed community of nations, with short-term gain often preferred to long-term survival. "Terrorism, the killing of diplomats and use of armed force . . . are in some parts of the world defended as legitimate means for attaining legitimate ends while elsewhere they are condemned as the most atrocious of crimes". And on his own account, the States adopting these violently contradictory positions on such matters can still invoke the Consensus Definition to support them.[32]

Mr. Ferencz is really unable to show that any features of the Consensus Definition have relieved the world to any degree of this and other aspects of harsh reality. His reflections lead him back to the generality that "definition, codification, adjudication and enforcement are all essential steps towards a rule of law", that all of these depend on common acceptance by States, and that fear of failure is no excuse for inaction.[33] But even if we were to agree that "definition" *in general* is a first step to "the rule of law", that still does not cancel the fact that the central provisions of *this* so-called "Consensus Definition" are, even by his own criteria, but *an agreement on phrases with no agreement as to their meaning.*

We can perhaps acquiesce in Mr. Ferencz's final thought that "the consensus definition, despite all its imperfections, is . . . a visible re-affirmation of the indomitable hope that there must be legal limits to the use of armed force." But this is only because, like most of mankind, we would still applaud this indomitable hope, even though the Consensus Definition had done nothing to advance it. For the fact remains that, even after making full allowance for diplomatic understatement or hyperbole, the discrepancies between the achievements claimed for the Consensus Definition, and the gross functional inadequacies revealed by objective examination of it, are extraordinary.

X

We have been comparing the conflicting attitudes of States concerning what conduct should be stigmatised as aggression which at first blocked achievement of the Consensus Definition, with the position as to these same matters after its achievement. There is also involved, in evaluating the claims made for the Consensus Definition, consideration of doubts and uncertainties as well as conflicts. To have substance, the claims made for the Consensus Definition (for instance, as to deterring aggressors, enlightening States or guiding United Nations organs) would require the elimination, or at least substantial reduction, of the many chronic doubts and uncertainties concerning the Charter provisions as to the limits of lawful use of force, and the powers of United Nations organs in relation thereto.

Without seeking to exhaust the list,[34] some of these may here be brought to mind.

(a) Article 2(4), forbidding certain kinds (what kinds?) of "threat or use of force";

(b) Articles 10-12, giving the General Assembly certain powers (what powers?) to discuss and recommend on questions relating to maintenance of international peace and security, subject to certain limitations (what limitations?) as compared with the legally superior Security Council competence and action mentioned in the next three subparagraphs;

(c) Article 24, giving the Security Council "primary responsibility" (what other body (if any) has secondary (or other) responsibility?) for the maintenance of international peace and security;

(d) Article 25, by which Members agree to accept and carry out the decisions of the Security Council in accordance with the present Charter. (Does this refer only to decisions under the Chapters VI, VII, VIII, and XII referred to in Article 24, or as the International Court of Justice advised in the *Namibia Case*,[35] to any resolutions which the Security Council is competent to adopt?);

(e) Article 39, empowering the Security Council to determine "the existence of a threat to the peace, breach of the peace, or act of aggression". (What is the relation of each of these terms to "threat or use of force" prohibited in Article 2(4) above?)

(f) Chronic doubts also surround Article 51 which, at the end of the Chapter on peace enforcement, makes an overriding reservation to States of "the inherent right of individual and collective self-defence". (What is the relation of the terms "threat or use of force" in Article 2(4) and "threat to the peace, breach of the peace or act of aggression" in Article 39 to the "armed attack on a Member of the United Nations" in Article 51?)

(g) In this same Article 51, do the words "if an armed attack occurs" mean "after an armed attack occurs" so that target States must wait and receive the first blow, however dire (as in nuclear warfare) the consequences, before they can lawfully act in self-defence—the problem of "the sitting duck"? Or do those words *merely describe the kind of peril* against which they are entitled, even in advance of its appearance, to take self-defensive action—the converse problems of anticipatory self-defence?

Impatience or unease of States in face of such doubts as to the meaning of the Charter on fundamental matters must have contributed to the drive for an "authoritative" definition of aggression. It might, therefore, have been expected that these matters would have become the subject of keen controversy and debate at the pre-consensual stage. Among the 35 Members of the Fourth Special Committee, whose attitudes and interests conflicted so sharply on the critical issues listed in the preceding sections, were there corresponding conflicts as to the removal of these doubts concerning the limits of lawful resort to force under the Charter?

It is extraordinary that among States so *parti pris* and articulate on other critical matters, little or no interest was shown at the Committee session which produced the Consolidated Text in this vast jungle of legal uncertainties surrounding the basic Charter provisions. Article 7 of the Consolidated Text (which was left untouched in Article 6 of the Consensus Definition) provided that "nothing in this Definition shall be construed as in any way enlarging or diminishing the scope of the Charter, including its provisions concerning cases in which the use of force is lawful". Only one single State proposal relevant to it was recorded by the Working Group,[36] that of Uruguay. This proposed the adoption of what I have called the "idealist-restrictive" interpretation of the Charter, namely, that the only lawful uses were (1) by the Security Council or agencies authorised by it for maintaining or restoring international peace; and (2) in exercise of Article 51 self-defence. I have elsewhere discussed and criticised this and competing views.[37] But the outcome of the fourth Contact Group's discussions on this matter was only to observe that the Sponsors of the Thirteen-Power Draft "had not taken a final decision on the question of the legal uses of force".[38] That Draft in Paragraph 3 had reformulated the Article 51 self-defence provisions in a manner suggesting two changes: first, that only armed attack "by another State" (therefore, presumably, not "indirect aggression") could activate self-defence; second, more ambiguously, the substitution of the words "in the case of the occurrence" for the words "if an armed attack occurs" in Article 51 of the Charter, in an order which *might* exclude anticipatory defence.

This comparative disinterest in the removal of the plague of legal uncertainties surrounding the Charter provisions is indeed strange *if we assume that the participants even at this pre-consensual stage were mainly driven forward by the aim of providing States and United Nations organs with guidance of precision and clarity as to the limits of lawful use of force.* And this for two reasons. First, because the effect of Article 7 of the Consolidated Text (final Article 6), as well as other provisions of it to be mentioned shortly, is to preserve every doubt and uncertainty concerning force and the Charter, including those enumerated above, thus flying in face of the main objective. Second, because acquiescence in this legal *status quo* "solution" contrasts with the sharp contentiousness at that stage on so many other issues.

This strangeness, however, is tied to the assumption that the major drive of the enterprise, at this stage, was towards precision and clarity of the law. To escape from it we have to test this assumption and, perhaps, seek other hypotheses as to what the drive was. Two possibilities present themselves. One is that participant States were at this stage primarily concerned not with any beneficial effect of greater precision and clarity in controlling force between States, or guiding United Nations organs, but rather to maximise the value of the definition to themselves as an instrument to be invoked in support of their own political objectives, or to minimise its value as an instrument invoked by others against themselves. On this alternative hypothesis the definition is envisaged, above all, as an instrument of political warfare. Insofar as a State could not secure acceptance of the definitional terms which thus optimise its own political interests, the Political Warfare Drive was at any rate to neutralise any prejudicial effect of the terms on its interests. *For this latter purpose* precision, clarity and the closing of loopholes, far from being necessary, were on the whole undesirable, at any rate if any substantial price had to be paid for it. What was rather sought was the continued availability of loopholes or pretexts upon which States could fasten to support their own national policies, or attack those of their adversaries, in suitable forums. And, of course, for Third World and communist States (and in particular for the dominating Arab bloc), the forum most in view was the General Assembly with its so-called "automatic majorities" on a wide range of global questions.

The other possible drive, extraneous to that of peace-seeking, may be called that of United Nations Verbal Celebration or Face-Saving. It has to be seen against the background of repeated failures in the preceding quarter-century of United Nations efforts to define aggression, efforts which, with those of the earlier League era, have been surveyed in this and several earlier Chapters. By 1972, failure also threatened the Fourth Special Committee. The need to produce some kind of formula or other that could be said to be "accepted", and thus save the face of the General Assembly and its Committees, does indeed seem to have loomed ever larger in the final operations of the Working Group, the Contact Groups, and the Committee itself. A United Nations success this time would not only save face but be all the more impressive in view of so many earlier failures.

For this purpose, any formula which could plausibly be said to be accepted would suffice, regardless of its functional aptness to the peace-serving tasks. We shall highlight, especially in the concluding Chapter, the numerous words and incidents which evidence the prominence of this United Nations Face-Saving Drive. It will suffice, for the present point, to note that the tendency of this drive was to find forms of words which were ambiguous so far as they referred to the most serious conflicts in State attitudes, or to avoid referring to such conflicts altogether. Clarity and precision were therefore qualities rather to be avoided than sought: for to seek them would have destroyed even the superficial verbal level of consensus. This, perhaps, is the true "fragility" which the architects of the "consensus" were so desperate to protect.

XI

In the light of the preceding Section, the placidly conservative attitudes of the participants to the jungle of legal problems affecting the Charter provisions as to the use of force, loses much of its strangeness. Far from seeking to resolve the notorious doubts and uncertainties concerning the meaning of the Charter as to the limits of lawful use of force, the Consolidated Text was meticulously emphatic in negating any intention or effect of the Text by way of modifying in any way the Charter provisions.

Paragraph 2 of the Preamble recalls in the identical language of Article 39 the Security Council's responsibility to determine any threat to the peace, breach of the peace or act of aggression. In case anyone might see any difference, Paragraph 4 of the Preamble recites that "nothing in this definition shall be interpreted as in any way extending or diminishing the provisions of the . . . Charter with respect to rights and duties of the organs of the United Nations." (These paragraphs still remain in the Consensual Definition with no serious change, though the words "affecting the scope of" were substituted for "extending or diminishing", and the words "functions and powers" for "rights and duties" of United Nations organs.)

Article 1 of the Consolidated Text reproduced the substance of Article 2(4) of the Charter with no clarification of the critical word "against", but with four changes increasing the problems of interpretation of Article 2(4). It substituted "armed force" for "threat or use of force", leaving in the air the question what are the permissible responses to the "threat or use of force" prohibited by Article 2(4) which is *not* armed force. As seen in Chapter 7, Section IX, it added "sovereignty" to "the territorial integrity and political independence of any State" protected by the prohibition in Article 2(4), opening the way for new questions whether a people "struggling" for self-determination can be said to have sovereignty, even if it has no territorial base or political independence. Third, it substituted inconsistency with "the Charter" for the inconsistency with "the Purposes of the United Nations" in Article 2(4). The latter phrase refers clearly enough to Article 1 of the Charter, which alone raises ample problems. The new reference to "the Charter" at large must compound these problems. So, fourth, does the concluding phrase in the Consolidated Text, apparently qualifying the whole Article: "as set out in this definition". There was, perhaps, one point on which the Consolidated Text *might* have clarified the Charter. The words "however exerted", tentatively added after "armed force" in Article 1 of the Consolidated Text, might have gone some way to solve a pre-existing problem as to whether Article 2(4) prohibited "indirect" as well as "direct" threat or use of force. But, as we shall later see, this exception proves the rule, *for these words were finally excluded from the corresponding article of the Consensus Definition.*

Article 2 of the Consolidated Text setting out the test of "the first use of armed force" (priority) and the Security Council's discretion "in conformity with the Charter" in applying it, would raise difficulties enough, even without the qualification placed on the priority test in it by the words, "in contravention of the Charter". This qualification was retained in it against all arguments that it was redundant. The effect of its retention is to make doubly (if not triply sure) that all room to manoeuvre formerly available due to disputed interpretations of the limits of lawful force under the Charter continues to be available. (Article 2 of the Consensus Definition still retains the same qualification.)

In Article 5 of the Consolidated Text, the right to use force and seek and receive support "in order to exercise their inherent right of self-determination" is qualified in some way difficult to determine by the words "in accordance with the principles of the Charter". The matter is not made easier by the absence *in the Charter* of any reference to "the inherent right of self-determination", though (as seen in Chapter 6) some less solemn (and less binding) international instruments later came to use the phrase.

Among the most difficult Charter problems requiring review, moreover, was the relation of the overriding liberty of self-defence against armed attack in Article 51 to Article 2(4) prohibiting certain threats or uses of force, and to Article 39 on determination of aggression. No less were the problems within Article 51 of anticipatory self-defence and preparations for self-defence, on which in some aspects the legality of the Nato and Warsaw security pacts depends. Neither the Consolidated Text nor the Consensus Definition mention self-defence, much less preparations therefor, or anticipatory self-defence. Yet, clearly, the participants were conscious of the need for greater clarity. For instance, the Thirteen Power Draft proposed (presumably in clarification of Article 51 of the Charter) that self-defence could only lawfully be used "in case of the occurrence of" an armed attack (as distinct from "if an armed attack occurs") *by another State*. One effect of this would have been that indirect attack, e.g. by sending "armed bands", would not activate the victim's right of self-defence. The six Powers (Australia, Canada, Italy, Japan, U.K. and U.S.), however, wanted a wider formula, leaving it open that self-defence might be available even against such less direct forms of "aggression", and that anticipatory defence might be lawful.[39] The final omission of both proposals is the more significant in view of the fact that, because of Soviet opposition, no requirement appeared in either text setting any limit of proportionality to self-defensive response. The Charter position, with all its problems, was thus scrupulously preserved, not only (as already seen) by explicit saving clauses, but also by simple silences.

In case the above saving clauses and omissions did not sufficiently preserve and incorporate the problematics of Charter interpretation into the Definition of Aggression, Article 7 of the Consolidated Text (with which Article 6 of the final Consensus Text is identical) provides a comprehensive saving clause for them all. It provided: "Nothing in this Definition shall be construed as in any way enlarging or diminishing the scope of the Charter, including its provisions concerning cases in which the use of force is lawful."

Among the main results of this overall control by the Charter, even after the 1974 Definition, are the continuing uncertainties concerning (1) aggression and anticipatory self-defence; (2) the related problem of nuclear first strike and preemption; (3) the effect of Security Council *non*-determination that an aggression has occurred; and (4) the related hard fact of the Great Power veto.

The standing of the claim to invoke anticipatory self-defence to the charge of aggression, is among the most controverted of legal issues under the Charter. As with economic aggression, this matter is not expressly mentioned in the Consensus Definition. Can anything be implied? At first blush, the priority principle in Article 2 might seem to bar anticipatory self-defence. At no point in the drafting, however, was there any serious chance of this principle being left unqualified. It is qualified in two main ways (even apart from the use of a Great Power veto).

First, to be caught by Article 2, the acts concerned must not only have been committed first; they must also have been committed "in contravention of the Charter". Insofar as the admissibility of anticipatory self-defence is disputed under the Charter, including Article 51, it must also remain disputed under Article 2, a point re-emphasised by the scrupulous barring by Article 6 of any "enlargement" or "diminution" of the scope of lawful use of force under the Charter. Second (as also seen in Chapter 3, Sections V and VI, and Chapter 4), Article 2 expressly goes on to declare as to any act which is *prima facie* aggression under it, that the Security Council may, in the light of "the relevant circumstances conclude that a determination that an act of aggression has been committed would not be justified . . .". Whatever one may think of the parties' merits in any particular case, it is clear that it may be a "relevant circumstance" that the accused State acted in response to a threat from the other State, which left it no other alternative save to submit to its own destruction.[40]

The problem of preemption in nuclear warfare is a particularly difficult case of anticipatory self-defence. The United Nations Charter itself received its main structure before nuclear weapons came into full view. The major nuclear Powers, to this day, regard the problems raised as beyond clear control by the Charter.

Suppose Soviet military intelligence (or *mutatis mutandis* that of the of the United States) received what was regarded as indisputable evidence that a hostile State was poised to launch a nuclear attack by MIRVs against its strategic and population centres at a zero hour 12 hours ahead. Would it be "an aggressor" if it did not wait until after the attack before it made appropriate response, if possible by non-violent dissuasion or deterrence, but at a pinch, if need be, by armed force. We would be naïve to think that the target would regard itself as barred from armed response, and obliged to await its own destruction, hoping only that its second strike capacity, whether in hardened silos or on and under the oceans, would remain available for retaliatory measures. It would be naïve even if (as is not the case) the Charter and the Definition clearly excluded anticipatory self-defence. While the Consensus Definition 1974 was (unlike the Charter) worked out in full awareness of the exigencies of nuclear warfare, it is (as seen in Chapter 4, Section V) no more illuminating than the Charter concerning this aspect of it.

The Security Council has exclusive power under Article 39 of the Charter to determine aggression, which includes its discretion to refrain from determining it. And this is still so under Article 2 of the 1974 Definition itself, when it finds that "other relevant circumstances" do not justify a finding of aggression. State interpretations still divided, after the Consensus Definition, as to whether a *"prima facie"* aggression was an aggression even if the Security Council refrained altogether from a determination. Since, in historical fact, the Security Council had never up to 1974 determined conduct to be aggression, this is a momentous question, now left still momentously open.

A particular consequence of the exclusive power of the Security Council is that the Definition cannot prevent any Permanent Member of the Council from vetoing a determination either that there has or has not been an aggression. On this ground alone, China's delegate observed that the pretensions that the Definition would deter aggressors were without foundation.[41] For it is also to be recalled that Permanent Members may use their vetoes to immunise, not only their own actions, but those of any other State they choose to protect.

By this provision, as well as by the paragraphs of the Preamble and of Articles 2 and 6 just referred to, and the saving in Article 4 of the power of the Security Council under the Charter to determine acts to be "aggression" under the Charter even if not caught by the Definition, it is clear that no legal liberty to resort to force which a Member enjoys under the Charter can be taken away *by the Consensus Definition*. The Definition thus submits itself to the Charter, just as the Charter imposes itself on the Assembly Resolution which contains the Definition:

and the great controversies which surround a number of the Charter licenses, also surround the definitional text.

XII

In proportion as pre-existing doubts and uncertainties as to the limits of lawful use of force under the Charter were thus mostly preserved or even compounded, Paragraph 8 of the Preamble of the Consolidated Text was stripped of all but wishfulness. That paragraph expressed the conviction that the Definition ought to "deter" potential aggressors, "simplify" determination of acts of aggression and action to suppress them, and "facilitate" protection and assistance to the victim. Paragraph 9 of the same Preamble itself (both paragraphs surviving into the final Consensus Draft) neutralised to a degree the wishfulness of Paragraph 8. It expressed the belief that though "the question whether an act of aggression had been committed must be considered in the light of all the circumstances in each particular case", it was still desirable to frame "basic principles" to guide such determinations. It is most unlikely that a judgment unique to "all the circumstances in each particular case" can be controlled by "basic principles" clear enough to deter potential aggressors acting in future, equally unique circumstances.

The way in which the Committee escaped, even at the pre-consensual stage, from the above contradiction between Preamble, Paragraphs 8 and 9 was to make clear in the body of the Definition that the criteria laid down *were not criteria in the sense that their application in a particular case was decisive.* They did so by three mechanisms, each sufficient in itself. First, they put beyond doubt that finally only the Security Council can determine whether an aggression has occurred. (Consolidated Text, Preamble, Paragraphs 2 and 4, and Article 7, surviving into the Consensual Definition, where Article 7 became Article 6.) In doing this everyone was fully aware that that body had not in more than 20 years ever determined an aggression to exist, and that every Permanent Member, in any case, had a veto. Second, they asserted in Article 2 (*which is similar in the final Consensus text*) the inconclusiveness of the criteria in the Definition, by reminding that body of its freedom to apply them (or rather *not* to apply them) "in the light of other relevant circumstances". Third, they provided in Article 4, as read with the above reference to "other relevant circumstances" in Article 2, that the definition was to be virtually open at both the exculpating and inculpating ends. So that even though the criteria might seem to be met, a finding of aggression need not follow (Article 2); and, also, "the Security Council may determine other acts as constituting aggression under the provisions of the Charter". (Article 4, also similar in the Consensus Definition.)

The effect of these escape mechanisms is to denude the criteria of any cogent *directive* effect, even if we do not worry about legally binding effect. So that the result appears to be not greatly different from what it would have been if the Special Committee had indeed drawn the correct inference from the uniqueness of each case by offering a *nunc dimittis* before the conclusion of its task.

The only objectives achieved are again seen to be those I have above designated as drives of Political Warfare, and of United Nations Verbal Celebration or Face-Saving. Criteria of aggression, open at both the inculpating and exculpating ends, and required to be applied *in the light of all the circumstances of each individual case,* by a body with exclusive discretion, of which each of the five Members has a veto, leave the field quite clear for determinations (or absence of them) according to the expediencies of the decision-maker, and for the play of naked power politics to fix what these expediencies are in each case.

Perhaps to guard against any last chance that some new clarity or certainty might still emerge for the limits of force lawful under the Charter, a number of delegations were later to secure the addition to the Consensus Definition of a new final Article 8. This provides that "in their interpretation and application the above provisions are inter-related and each provision should be construed in the context of the other provisions". Its effect is to require all dubieties, whether from the Charter or the text of the Consensus Definition, to be compounded together on any matter on which they may bear.[42]

The seal seems to be further set on this dispiriting story by the fact that the General Assembly in its Resolution 3314(XXIX) adopting the Definition by consensus, did not attempt to give any binding force to the Definition even as against individual Members. And as against the Security Council, it did not more than "recommend that it should, *as appropriate,* take account of that Definition as guidance in determining, *in accordance with the Charter,* the existence of an act of aggression."

CHAPTER 10

Consensus or Conflict?

I

When we look with hindsight at the Pyrrhic achievement of the 1974 Consensus Definition, we may well wonder how even the hope could have persisted that such obviously head-on conflicts of State interests could be resolved sufficiently to close all loopholes against aggressors, identify aggression, and foster the true spirit of *détente*. Yet even after failure in this had become writ large in the terms of the Consensus Definition itself, commentators are still found giving credence to such claims made, for example (as seen in opening the last Chapter), by the Soviet Union.

The reasons for failure, though conclusive, are not indeed simple to state. Some of them arise from the very complex and rather fundamental nature of the difficulties which would have to be overcome before such a hope could be realised. These difficulties are unhappily durable and remain as operative today as they were in frustrating the numerous meetings of the General Assembly's Fourth Special Committee prior to the emergence of the Consensus Definition, and as they were for four decades prior to that in hundreds of formidable debates of League of Nations and United Nations bodies. They have been canvassed in preceding Chapters, but they should perhaps be brought together in the present context. And in this context what demands explanation is not only the failure of a fifty-year search, in which so many intellectual and political talents have been engaged. For what the Consensus Definition has added to this failure, which also demands explanation, is the collusive celebration of this latest failure by hailing it as a success. A Consensus on verbal formulae which are simply equivocal, vacuous, or silent about the deepest conflicts of State interest which the enterprise had for fifty years struggled in vain to resolve, is now offered as its consummation.

A preliminary puzzle, examined in Chapter 1, is as to why the enterprise was thought necessary at all for peace enforcement in the legal context of the United Nations Charter. And this for three reasons. First, because the organ with exclusive competence, the Security Council, was vested with plenary powers of peace enforcement without the need for determining the existence of an aggression. For Chapter 7, Article 39, of the Charter makes no distinction of legal consequences between "threat to the peace", "breach of the peace" or "act of aggression". Moreover, second, as a practical matter, the Security Council had never found it necessary to make a determination of aggression.[1] And, finally, even the most precise definition, free of loopholes (if one could be found), could not control determinations by the Security Council, since each of the five Permanent Members is free to use its veto to bar a particular determination.

It was, significantly, not in the legal context of magisterial peace enforcement *by the Security Council* under Chapter 7, but rather of efforts to create peace-keeping machinery by voluntary cooperation of Members under the General Assembly Uniting for Peace Resolutions, that the United Nations quest for a definition of aggression began in earnest. For this purpose, of serving as a trigger in crisis, the aggression notion and its application had to be free of head-on conflicting views as to which State was at fault in the circumstances most likely to arise. Moreover, since by hypothesis the cooperation would be sought *in a crisis,* the triggering notion had to be capable of yielding judgment *quickly.*

In one respect, namely its emotive inspirational overtones, the aggression notion does seem apt for triggering voluntary cooperation among States. Provided it could be given a definition both comprehensive and precise enough, the aggression notion does seem to have sufficient affect for this purpose. The hard question is whether the above conditions for successful use of the aggression notion to trigger voluntary cooperation in a crisis could *also* be met.

First, it is probably fair to say that those who are sanguine about defining aggression tend to assume that conflicting State standpoints concerned *the discovery* of the meaning of *the word* "aggression", whereas the States engaged in negotiating for an authoritative definition assume that their task is *to give* to the word (*or prevent it being given*) particular meanings which will advance or hinder (as the case may be) the interests of the respective States. The reality, in other words, revealed by fifty years of argument, is that the conflicts blocking success were not about discovering the meaning of a word, but about which State interests a definition *should be made to favour or disfavour*—about which shall be furthered and which shall be cut back by the meaning *given* to the notion. In general, as might be expected, States favour meanings which protect their vested interests, as France and the U.S.S.R. favoured meaning focused on crossing of frontiers when they were concerned to consolidate territorial gains, or the Arab States now favour meanings which imply that Israel is legally bound to withdraw from all occupied territories. States oppose meanings, on the other hand, which prevent them from advancing their interests, as many "non-aligned" States in their strategy of securing redistribution of power and resources as against Western States seek to exclude "wars of liberation" from the ambit of "aggression".

Second, moreover, States can only foresee with precision the effects of a definition on their respective interests for a comparatively short term into the future. Of course, their solicitude also extends into the longer term, when the circumstances become rather unforeseeable, and therefore what their interests will be becomes uncertain. This combination of solicitude and uncertainty about the longer term future tends to lead States to want to include appropriate equivocations, and mutually neutralising contradictions or silences, into the definition, to serve as escape hatches for their interests as they may in the future see them.

Third, however, as soon as a definition includes such escape hatches, its application to the circumstances of a future crisis is likely to become all the more debatable and contentious, thus blocking quick cooperative action. Not only the States at variance, but also many third States whose voluntary cooperation is sought in handling the crisis, will tend to draw different meanings from the equivocations, contradictions, or silences, leading to conflicting conclusions as to which side is the aggressor. Other third States will have the sincerest doubts and hesitations about this, paralysing rather than inspiring the will to cooperate. Both of these effects undermine the inspirational value of the aggression notion as a trigger for decision and action, which *ex hypothesi* in a crisis must be quick. Third States forming opposed judgments as to which side is an aggressor, will obviously not cooperate together: States paralysed by doubts and hesitations will not act at all.

In sum, therefore, the Security Council does not legally need the aggression notion, or a precise and comprehensive definition of it, to exercise its magisterial powers of peace enforcement. For the General Assembly such a definition, if it could be agreed, would be psychologically useful for inspiring voluntary cooperation in crisis; but for the reasons just given such a definition is not politically and factually attainable.

II

I have presented the obstacles thus far as if they were mainly the outcome of self-regard by States, and of disregard by them for the great ideals of controlling resort to force by States. It is important now to observe that such attitudes of States are not necessarily cynical or irresponsible. Their attitudes reflect, even if crudely, an instinctive understanding of the functions which a precise and comprehensive legally binding definition of aggression (were it attainable) would fulfil in the world arena. First, those States with more capacity for a kind of action prohibited by the Definition, would thereby be legally deprived of that superior capacity and of the resources which could be protected or commanded by it. Second, States better endowed with non-prohibited capacities, for instance of expropriating foreign assets found within their sovereign domains, or extorting concessions by inflicting strangulation by oil boycotts, would (when we assume these not to be stigmatised) be confirmed in these capacities and in any resources they could extort from other States by their use. These effects would be intensified if use of the victim's capacities to respond were simultaneously stigmatised as aggression.

So that another reason why defining aggression is so difficult, is that efforts to define it immediately bring into issue most momentous political, strategic and economic conflicts between States. A demand for a particular content of definition is a demand for global redistribution of resources, corresponding to the lines drawn between prohibited and non-prohibited capacities of States. Once this is recognised, we should expect confrontations between States in debates on the definition of aggression, closely similar to those found in conflicts about world resources still under explicit negotiation for distribution. A topical instance is the current series of Conferences on the Law of the Sea as to the distribution of resources of waters bordering and beyond the continental shelf, and in and under the deep oceans. Chapter 8 considered some of the direct impacts of conflicts about this distribution in the final debates on the Consensus Definition. Certain coastal States condemned one clause as in effect depriving them of the jurisdiction they claimed over adjacent oceans up to the 200 miles limit. It would, they said, stigmatise as aggression their use of force there against foreign ships—a use of force which in their view was a lawful exercise of jurisdiction. Landlocked States also complained that their rights of passage to the ocean and to non-adjacent States were being destroyed by the failure of the Definition to stigmatise blocking of land access.

This direct relation of the contents of definition to planet-wide legislative redistribution of world power and resources thus became patent in particular fields, even to States less endowed with power and diplomatic experience. But, of course, in a rapidly changing world, particular States may occasionally be inadvertent to such implications, or prevented by given situations from acting on their advertence. As seen in Chapter 7, some powerful, wealthy and diplomatically well experienced States were apparently inadvertent in these recent debates to the possible side-effects of not including provisions concerning extreme economic duress (e.g. the oil boycott), and of the role to be left by default to the General Assembly.

The vital legislative nature of such an enterprise of redistribution explains, of course, why definitional debates so often conceal the ploys and stratagems of political warfare. More importantly, for our purpose, it is perhaps the deepest reason why a definition which is both generally acceptable and functionally effective seems beyond our reach. A planet-wide redistribution of resources among the 140-odd States of the world really presupposes an overhaul of all the foundations and the precepts of international law, based on common acceptance by all of norms of minimal justice applicable to all men and women of the world. *We should never have expected to be able to make such a redistribution as a mere by-product of a legal inquiry about the meaning of aggression.*

III

Even when we recognise the momentous *legislative* implications of the drive for definition of aggression, false analogies between the municipal and international spheres still tempt us to underrate the problem. If the primacy of the public peace—the exclusion of private violence—was attained in municipal societies as a phase of establishing municipal legal orders, why may international society today not be at precisely that phase? And is not attainment of a satisfactory definition of aggression essential for this phase?

We are now, of course, in an unstable age in which exclusion of private violence can no longer be taken for granted in many municipal societies. Even, however, if they were all stable, there are powerful reasons why the municipal analogy does not really support the hope that we can find a satisfactory definition of aggression as a first step to the elimination of violence between States.

The public monopoly of force in municipal societies presupposes that there is already a legal order distributing the goods of life in a way generally acceptable, at least to those members of the community strong enough to challenge the legal order by use of private force. Such distribution is always, of course, imperfect, and even if it were perfect at a particular time, changes in social and economic life constantly create imperfections. So that, second, the stable public monopoly of force in municipal societies also presupposes the routine operation of legislative institutions to bring the legal distribution into conformity with emerging conditions, values, and centres of power. And in societies with responsible government, the adequacy of this redistribution is periodically tested by general elections. Moreover, third, the municipal legislative distribution is regularly enforced by the executive, if necessary by public force.

Would private force remain out of the picture in a municipal society which awoke one morning to find that there was no longer any parliament to make and change laws, as well as no executive power capable of enforcing the laws as they exist, and no courts with jurisdiction to hear complaints? In such a society legal rights could be adjusted either by direct agreement between all members of society or by naked force. How far could we expect agreement always to be reached, and naked force always to be excluded? Yet, of course, this is, in substance, the normal condition of the so-called society of States. No legislature capable of redistributing world resources is even in sight; nor is there effective adjudication and enforcement of the present legal distribution. The law concerning some resources—for instance of the oceans and ocean beds—is still inchoate. There is no effective collective redress for even the gravest wrongs, much less for progressive collective adjustment of law to minimum standards of justice.

It is in such a society that this single notion of "aggression" is being asked to perform, for the States of the whole planet, most of the major tasks which in municipal society are performed by criminal, constitutional and administrative law, not to speak of the law of property, civil wrongs and procedure.[2] It is being asked to do this, moreover, while still respecting those minimum standards of respect for law and justice between States which lack, as just observed, any present assurance other than the aggrieved Party's own self-assertion of its rights and interests. All this, we believe, is part of the deepest ground for the tragic paradox that the very factors which spur efforts to define aggression also doom it to failure. And it is a new level of this paradox that, even after the achievement of the Consensus Definition has been celebrated, it is doomed to remain fundamentally barren for the purposes for which definition is needed.

If we now return to the false analogy of municipal systems, it is worth observing that they do not use notions like aggression, whether defined or not, as the major means of distributing resources and enforcing the distribution when made. The main structures of municipal law rest on an elaborate multitude of prescribed and enforced rules about land and other patrimonial rights, rights of personality, trespass, arson, defamation, assault, larceny, rape, and the like, in which the community has already crystallised and embodied its current standards and values in specific detailed rules. In international law, such specific rules are still largely unformed, and often (as now, with many aspects of the law of the sea and the seabed) the subject of harsh contention. It is attractive to think that this and the other deficiencies above mentioned can be made good at one stroke by defining aggression: but it is a vain hope.

We have observed on the failure of various shortcuts, for instance, of the priority in time of some defined act, such as the first declaration of war, bombardment, or crossing of the frontier.[3] They failed even before the appearance of nuclear weapons. In the present nuclear age when a State's very survival may depend on accurate anticipation of the enemy's attack, so that each side may sincerely feel that only by preemption can it hope to survive an impending enemy assault, the prospects for such precise shortcuts must fade even more. The 1974 Consensus Definition left this question (like so many others) intact by building contradictory positions into its terms, expressly saving in Article 2 the Security Council's power to exculpate in the light of "relevant circumstances". This compromise admits the truth that if we are to use the notion of aggression for crisis-handling, each application of it still prerequires an assessment of the merits of both sides in the conflict, in the light of the whole course of their relations, including the proportionality of reaction to wrong.[4] Except in such rare cases as the Nazi invasions of Czechslovakia and Poland, the agonising and time-consuming problems of the "just" and "unjust" causes of war[5] still interpose themselves despite two generations of effort to substitute more "sensible", "objective", "externally verifiable" and instant tests, such as use of armed force across a frontier.[6] In historical fact, as was to be expected, the "short-cut" tests have never approached acceptance, unless qualified by references such as those touching "legitimate defence", "self-defence" or "provocation", or now, in the 1974 Consensus Definition, "other relevant circumstances". As soon as we qualify them thus, we admit by the back door the very questions of justice vainly ejected by the front door.

All this reinforces the suspicion already raised elsewhere, that to make peace enforcement dependent on acceptance of an objective, instantly applicable definition of aggression, is to put the cart before the horse. This single notion, much less such a definition of it, cannot suffice as a substitute for the vast bodies of law, and the complex and sensitive institutions, still required to delimit effectively the tolerable *meum* and *tuum* of international life.[7] If, pending such happy development, we are to use the aggression notion at all, progress depends on the establishment (necessarily gradual) of appropriate trusted organs to apply it as best they can.[8] And we seem still so far from the emergence of such trusted organs that the prudent course is rather to discontinue the effort to base collective peace enforcement action primarily on the notion of "aggression".[9]

IV

The most plausible ground offered for attaching importance to the Consensus Definition is that in 1954 "the United Nations put aside its work on a Draft Code of Offences Against the Peace and Security of Mankind and an International Criminal Court, until the question of defining aggression could be resolved. *After much effort that missing piece has now been produced.*" (Italics supplied.)[10] It is certainly clear that we cannot ignore the question whether, however negative the value of the Definition for peacekeeping and peace enforcement between States, it may nevertheless be of positive importance in relation to the establishment of an International Criminal Court to try individuals for the crimes *inter alia* of aggressive warmaking.

We referred in discussing the relevance of intention as an element of aggression, to certain differences between, on the one hand, the peacekeeping and peace enforcement function, and, on the other, the international criminal law enforcement function. Historically, in the launching of the United Nations definitional enterprise, the two functions stimulated and reinforced each other. The criminal law aspect emerged from the London Charter, under which the major war crimes of World War II were tried by the International Military Tribunal at Nuremberg. This in turn inspired the work of the International Law Commission on the Draft Code of Offences against the Peace and Security of Mankind, and the Draft Statute of an International Criminal Court. The peacekeeping and peace enforcement aspects emerged sharply after the entry of the General Assembly into that area under the Uniting for Peace Resolutions of 1950. While the general orientation of the 1974 Definition is towards peacekeeping and peace enforcement, Article 5, paragraph 2, providing that a "war of aggression is a crime against international peace", seems oriented towards the punishment of individuals.

I have suggested above[11] that one of the major obstacles which blocked progress towards an International Criminal Court was that it was so heavily centred on punishment of the crime of aggressive war-making—"the planning, preparation, initiation or waging of a war of aggression"—included in the indictments before the Nuremberg Tribunal. It is certainly clear that in 1954 the General Assembly suspended work for the creation of an International Criminal Court until the problem of defining aggression, for which it had meanwhile begun to establish its series of Special Committees, had been solved.[12] The postponement was intended ostensibly to give States time to examine the bearing of the definition adopted on the possible creation of such a tribunal. And, of course, insofar as it was taken for granted that the tribunal would have jurisdiction over this offence, this time would afford the States opportunity to consider whether they were prepared to accept jurisdiction over themselves in relation to it—whether as automatic jurisdiction over this offence, or as one of a list of offences in respect of which States might accept the optional jurisdiction of the tribunal.

The fact that the work for an International Criminal Court had thus been postponed till after aggression had been defined, made it plausible in 1974, after the Consensus Definition was adopted, to think that the work for such a Court could now proceed, for instance, by the International Law Commission revising its earlier Draft Statute, and in due course in the General Assembly. The matter, indeed, was presented in this way before the Fourth Special Committee by Legal Counsel of the United Nations, when he opened the Working Session from which the Consensus Definition emerged, on 11th March, 1974.[13] One could speculate, therefore, that the prospect of a resumption of work on the Statute of such a Court was a prod towards consensus on the definition of aggression. There is, however, little evidence of deep interest of any State in this aspect. Only M. Wehry of the Netherlands, of the many delegates present, touched upon it; and the sentence he devoted to it does not seem important in its context.[14] For the rest, the members, not only of the Special Committee, but of the Sixth Committee, showed virtually no interest in it.

Even if all States had felt prodded into consensus by the prospect of progress in establishing an International Criminal Court, this in itself would not necessarily mean that the attainment of the Consensus Definition now makes such progress much more likely. As to this latter, we have to distinguish the formal question whether work towards that Court could resume, from two other more important questions of substance. To the first, *the formal,* question, the answer is clearly yes. Insofar as the General Assembly in 1954 postponed work on the Court till the completion of work on the definition of aggression, the completion of the latter, however imperfect, equivocal or vacuous its text, fulfils the condition of deferment, and enables work on the Court to resume. This clear affirmation, however, is as trivial as it is positive so far as State action is concerned, though it has, of course, some importance for the duties of the United Nations Secretariat, and the expenditure of its funds.

The two *substantial* questions are a different matter. First, even if the 1954 deferment was until the completion of the work of definition, it would in no way follow that such completion would give any real promise that a plan for an International Criminal Court could be devised which the General Assembly would accept and on which States would agree to confer jurisdiction. This would be so even if the Definition reached were perfect by tests of clarity, comprehensiveness and orientation in good faith towards the tasks of peace-keeping and peace enforcement. *For the absence of a definition of aggression may have been only one obstacle, and but a minor one,* standing in the way of establishment of an International Criminal Court in 1954. The outcome might finally depend upon *the other* obstacles. My own analysis already cited shows that this precisely was the case.

Second, even if we assumed that the absence of a satisfactory definition of aggression was the only obstacle in 1954, the question would still remain whether the terms of the 1974 Consensus Definition are sufficiently satisfactory to remove *that* obstacle. To this I will now turn.

V

The present work has shown acute and far-reaching conflicts between particular States and between main blocs of States as to the limits of lawful use of force, and corresponding limits of aggression. It has also shown that these conflicts continue on after and despite the Consensus Definition. So that States continue to interpret that Definition in quite contrary senses for the situations most likely to cause contemporary crises. The Consensus Definition continues in this way to proclaim the truth that States will decline to submit to an *authoritative definition* of aggression unless, on the major points, they are free by dint of its ambiguities or silences to put their own meaning to it.

How does this bear on the prospects of acceptance by States of jurisdiction for a new Court over charges of aggression against their own leaders, or over charges which they make against leaders of other States?[15] One answer would be that the very confrontation of opposed interpretations makes such a jurisdiction both apt and necessary. But this proves, on examination, to be as fallacious as it is facile, since the competing conflicts of interpretation are, as it were, built into the Definition, or tolerated by its silences or other equivocations, and the Court could not *ex hypothesi* act in accordance with all of the conflicting views on the matter before it. To do so would reduce its activity to some kind of barren stalemate, and finally to rather grotesque farce. It would be barren because on the critical points, as we have seen, the competing interpretations are in head-on conflict. It would be grotesque since to give judgment for either side, without embracing either of the opposed interpretations, could only be, if at all, on the basis of artificial distinctions unrelated to the intentions and interpretations entertained by the parties.

It is, on the other hand, conceivable that the Court could, in the process of adjudicating, build up from the interpretations of one side or the other, or from its own original interpretation, a body of jurisprudence pertaining to aggression. Since, however, States would envisage this possibility in the course of determining whether to set up such a Court, it is a fair, if not inescapable, assumption that this would lead States to refuse to establish it or, at any rate, to refuse to accept any jurisdiction of it over aggressive war-making. Over nearly fifty years States have resisted advance commitment to an authoritative meaning of aggression, except one on which they were able to place unilaterally an interpretation tolerant of their own respective interests. It would be a miracle if, now, they were willing to present to a new body of independent judges the power to place an authoritative interpretation on a text so calculatingly open to opposed interpretations. The fact that national leaders might have to face such a Court on capital charges turning on such interpretations, is only a final mark of the miracle which would be required.

I do not believe there are any portents of such a miracle. And insofar as one cannot be expected, it must be stressed that the above *formal* sense in which the Consensus Definition may be said to have cleared the way for resumption of work on a Draft Statute of an International Criminal Court in no way advances the prospects of actually establishing a Court to which States will entrust the question whether their leaders or other officials, much less they themselves, have been guilty of the crime of aggressive-warmaking. The fact, indeed, that the 1974 Definition is susceptible on so many important matters to diametrically opposed interpretations, insofar as it would leave so much to the independent choice of the judges as to a particular crisis, produces a self-defeating paradox. Even anyone sanguine enough to have believed that the attainment of an agreed definition of aggression was a prerequisite for the establishment of an International Criminal Court having jurisdiction over aggression, would have to acknowledge that the nature and terms of the Consensus Definition of 1974 have made the creation of such a jurisdiction more improbable than ever. This may explain, at least in part, the singular lack of either attention or enthusiasm of States to this aspect of their work, in which Professor Suy of the Secretariat tried hard, as seen above, to interest them. The fact that many Third

World and Communist States are (as Sections IX-XI will show) antici-
pating with some satisfaction that the General Assembly may become
the body which *de facto* will "interpret" the Consensus Definition, is
not inconsistent with this analysis. The "automatic" majorities favouring
the interests of these States give them a confidence in outcomes from
the General Assembly which a body of independent judges can certainly
not inspire.

It is too sweeping to say with Robert-Louis Perret that the creation
of an International Criminal Court must fail because of "the fact that
the strong tyrannical tendencies still looming amongst the nations of the
world are a total negation of any idea of a duty owed by man toward
his neighbor."[16] It is only for a Court with jurisdiction over matters as
critical to State survival as determination of aggression, that pessimism
can be so absolute. I stated the reason for this pessimism as regards this
particular head of jurisdiction some years ago as follows:

> Submission to an international criminal court of a standing nature
> (and therefore free of the vice of unilateralism) to try crimes of
> aggressive war-making would limit this claim of States to freedom of
> action at precisely its most obdurate point. So that it is not really
> surprising that while the drive to establish a standing jurisdiction [for
> this crime] is both ethically and psychologically strong, it has also
> shown itself diplomatically and politically as rather impotent.[17]

We have already sufficiently explained the heavy stake of States
generally in what conduct is stigmatised as aggression and thus pro-
scribed. States which submitted themselves to binding determinations
by a Court on this matter would obviously be subject to disadvantageous
inhibitions as compared with States not so submitting. With the nuclear
Super Powers, there will be the additional inhibiting factor that such
submission would (legally at any rate) blunt their superior capability to
use armed force in defending their interests and value-commitments, as
well as the converse of this, namely, their ability to impose their interests
and value-commitments on others. It only reinforces this point to say
that binding legal obligations would not deter a Super Power which saw
the chance of imposing its world hegemony. So that even if (what
cannot be expected) both sides submitted questions of determination of
aggression to the jurisdiction of a Court, the all-fateful advantage would
rest with the lawless and the faithless side.

It is often said that in the present world no Super Power will seek
world hegemony, knowing as it must that a major nuclear war would
entail its own as well as its enemy's destruction. But this, too, is not free
of some wishfulness. From the standpoint of each centre of nuclear
armed power, its own destruction is a matter not of certainty but of a
certain degree of risk, which is a function in turn of its military and
technological preparedness, the intelligence resources and strategic and
planning skills and nerve power of its decision-makers, and many other
factors. When the stakes are so momentous in terms of both loss and

gain, only virtual certainties not mere risks of self-destruction can banish the search for security through hegemony, however senseless this may seem to onlookers who do not have to make the dire decisions involved. To imagine that both Super Powers would grant jurisdiction over issues of aggression to an independent International Criminal Court, would presuppose that somehow their traditional power-structures and related ideological commitments have already disappeared, and been replaced by some new planetary order. We have as yet, alas, no inkling as to how these two presuppositions can be made true, save that afforded by the intuitive wishfulness of our yearning for peace. In the kind of final resort represented by the Washington-Moscow nuclear confrontation, the contemporary search for peace—whether by the determination of aggression or by nuclear arms control and limitation or (for that matter) by *"détente"*—is not an unconditional commitment to international peace by the States concerned, but rather a sort of more cautious *modus vivendi* for the time being.

The above are some of the reasons that led this writer to the view, in his paper entitled "Range of Crimes for a Feasible International Jurisdiction",[18] that if an International Criminal Court is to come into being, it will have to be a tribunal whose jurisdiction *quoad materiam* is *not* centered on the crime of aggressive war-making. The converse of this, *pace* Professor Perret, is that such a Court with a more modestly delimited jurisdiction may well be within our reach. Insofar as the adoption of the Consensus Definition 1974 formally fulfils a condition set in 1954 for resuming work for the establishment of an International Criminal Court, it may thus permit progress towards such a Court—but (by a singular paradox) only towards a Court whose jurisdiction *does not cover the crime of international aggression*. And the truth—which also resolves the paradox—is not so much that attainment of a definition of aggression will help to establish the Court, but rather that this condition for further work to establish such a Court *should never have been set by the General Assembly*. For this preliminary condition did not then and does not now correspond to any practical relation between the two.

VI

This remarkable package of ambiguities, concealed conflicts, confusions and frustrations of definition was certainly given the label of *consensual* acceptance. The representatives responsible were not, of course, so naive as to be untroubled by the notion of a "Consensus" so potently riddled with basic conflicts. They were, indeed, very zealous and fertile in producing soothing formulae. M. Klafkowski of Poland, for example, comforted himself for the conflicts of interpretation with the thought that "any compromise . . . could be the subject of different interpretations", so that post-consensus conflicts of view were almost inevitable.[19] And, indeed, the commonest formula for covering the obvious incongruity of a Consensus Definition which was but a vehicle for relaying conflict, and whose outcome was thus negative, was to bedeck this outcome with spuriously positive compliments.

M. Bracklo of West Germany thought it "reconciled" different and "sometimes diametrically opposed views", but drew comfort from the fact that the Preamble, paragraph 4 and Articles 2 and 6, "left the powers of the Security Council unaffected".[20] But, of course, in terms of precise meaning necessary to close loopholes, the saving of the Security Council's powers (not to speak of the range of lawful force) was really (as indicated in preceding Chapters, especially Chapter 3, Sections III-VIII, and Chapter 9, Sections X-XII) a negative rather than a positive factor. It was to preserve and further extend rather than to close loopholes. M. Ustor of Hungary thought that incorporation of unresolved conflicts on crucial matters into a "Consensus" merely exemplified the juristic commonplace that "uncertainty could not be eliminated from law". This truth, he thought, was especially pertinent to the regulation of force and aggression, where "the possible conjunctions of fact remained indefinitely various".[21] Yet, of course, the "uncertainty" commonly associated with law is not usually *deliberately* created by incorporating the most crucial conflicts *unresolved* into a "Consensus" text. And it is even rarer for the architects of such confusing structures then to have the temerity solemnly to declare that they have thereby "closed" all "loopholes".

Some participants did, indeed, come near to calling a spade a spade. Canada referred to the limits of what could "in realism" be demanded of the definition. Of course, it reflected "compromise" on all sides, and "inevitably opened the door to differing interpretations".[22] It continued the fifty years' history of the enterprise, enshrining within its ambiguities the continuing efforts of States to impose definitions restricting the use of force by disfavoured States and permitting its use by favoured States. It is at this last point that the representative transcended mere apologetics and reached the harsh politico-legal realities. What had changed in the last fifty years (the Canadian delegate thought) was not the deep and chronic conflicts, but merely which States from time to time were favoured or disfavoured by which other States, in relation to them. And he capped the realism by noting that after Resolution 3314, as before it, the central legal and political fact was that discretion to determine aggression was vested in the Security Council *which had never yet exercised it.*

Consistently held, such an analysis could lead States to join in the Consensus Definition only with tongue held firmly in the cheek, or at least with deep scepticism as to its value. What had emerged, observed M. Rosenne of Israel, was a non-reasoned text, subject to "conflicting" and "irreconcilable interpretations".[23] M. Garcia Ortiz of Ecuador thought that the "consensus"[24] was certainly an "elegant" way of resolving difficulties, "but . . . the text : . . was not satisfactory . . . ." That was why his delegation would have abstained if the draft resolution had been put to the vote." Bolivia, through M. Fuentes Ibañes, joined Paraguay in "astonishment" at the Sixth Committee proceedings on the landlocked States proposal,[25] which had also been the occasion of Ecuador's immediately preceding comment. Bolivia, he said, would have abstained if a vote had been permitted, and he deplored the contempt shown by the Soviet Union for the delegations concerned.[26]

Perez de Cuellar[27] joined Canada's general point to his particular grievances. He observed plainly that a definition incorporating the conflicting positions within it left the matters in conflict undefined. While on matters of general interest his country was willing (he said) merely to qualify the consensus by oral reservation, "it could not pass over in silence a provision the adoption of which might endanger a national interest." He was referring to the possible implication from Article 3(d) that Peru's policing operations against foreign ships within the 200 miles limit which it claimed as national waters, might be stigmatised as aggression. He thought that even if "it had taken 50 years . . . to produce the draft definition . . . , it would be better to conclude that its work was not complete[28] than to impose an unsatisfactory definition on the international community". With related anxieties as to landlocked States, M. Ghaussy of Afghanistan[29] warned that the "consensus" was reached by "consultation" without any vote. It did not mean that the difficulties had been overcome or that reservations were not "in order".[30] India, indeed, as a transit State, complained that it had not even been "consulted" in the "consensus" on this matter.[31] M. Lekaukau (Botswana) declared that "as a sponsor of A/C 6/L 900 [on landlocked States] his delegation had had to agree to a compromise of Article 3(c) . . . although it had not been offered any convincing reasons for not including that text in the draft definition itself."[32] It had simply been threatened with having to bear responsibility for failure of the Definition if it did not acquiesce.

VII

It did not dispose of such complaints for the Soviet representative to explain that the text, "instrument of consensus that it was, . . . could not completely satisfy everyone", and that any attempt to change (the draft) would disrupt "the broad compromise" and threaten the "many years of work" since 1933.[33] If, indeed, as the present analysis establishes, the Consensus Definition merely incorporates unresolved the more crucial pre-existing conflicts of position, then it is worse than an understatement to admit that it did not "completely satisfy everyone". It is a very misleading caricature of the realities. By that light, the "many years of work" would still have amounted to very little for the advancement of peace. The resulting Consensus Definition could then be called an achievement only in the negative and rather circular sense, that if the fifty years of effort had not achieved even this, they would not have achieved even this.

Such deceptive euphemisms from many States bestrew the final apologetic path to "consensus". A bare sampling will suffice. For M. Van Brusselen the lack of precision was explained by the fact that "since the concept itself was not clear, it had not been possible to embody it in a subtle definition based on a set of objective criteria."[34] Special Committee Chairman Broms and others observed smugly upon the "careful balance" of the definition.[35] A chorus of others enjoined that the text should not be amended, "since its very vagueness or ambiguity might be the basis of its balance".[36]

VIII

The Fourth Special Committee's Rapporteur, M. Sanders of Guyana, declared in opening the Sixth Committee debate on October 8, 1974, that "the definition had been reached by consensus and was extremely fragile. Almost every word was of significance and the result of really tough negotiations".[37] "Consensus" resulting from "really tough negotiations" had indeed produced a frightening cluster of fragilities. First, a collusive ignoring of the critical conflicts now embodied within the Draft. Second, a sophistic celebration of the face-saving or contradictory verbal formulae used to conceal them. Third, an accompanying sigh of relief that after fifty years anything at all, however useless and in some respects dangerous, could be reported as in some sense "agreed".

Such an achievement might save somewhat the faces of the General Assembly and of its Fourth Special Committee on Defining Aggression. Its irrelevance to peace or even the reduction of tensions was sadly illustrated almost immediately. M. Boulbina of Algeria, after repeating ritually that the definition was open to differing interpretations, pointed out that the reaffirmation of these differing interpretations, after the consensus by "certain Powers, including Permanent Members of the Security Council, *could nullify all the efforts made to arrive at the delicate compromise.*" (Italics supplied.) He instanced the "reintroduction" of the intent element into Article 2 of the Consensus Definition by interpretative statements of a number of States. This, he said, was "tantamount to destroying the compromise", and led his delegation to wonder about the real scope of the text proposed by the Special Committee.[38] M. Petrella of Argentina climaxed his expression of faith in the future influence of the Consensus Definition by adding that it would be of little use without "good faith".[39] As the present study has shown, this particular conflict as to the intention element in aggression is but one of many on which critical State conflicts which had blocked agreement prior to the "consensus" of 1974 were calculatingly read back into the "consensus" by interpretation of the newly adopted text.

It adds but another wry footnote to both the meaning of "consensus" and the prospect of good faith in all this that the final meetings of the Sixth Committee on 26th November, 1974 were disturbed by an unseemly fracas as to whether some States Members of the Sixth Committee were to be blocked by a majority of States politically and ideologically opposed to them from being co-sponsors of the draft reso-lution which finally presented the Consensus Definition to the General Assembly.[40]

IX

In this account we have not yet sufficiently described an objective of the definitional enterprise which some States certainly entertained, and of which we see rather explicit evidence in post-Consensus inter-pretations of the Definition. This is the objective of extending the General Assembly's influence, as against that of the Security Council, in matters of maintaining and restoring and enforcing international peace and security. Under the Charter provisions, Articles 10-12, the General Assembly's powers extend only to maintenance of peace, and even within that area do not extend to give that body power to make decisions legally binding on Members. An uncertain degree of influence of that body over the whole area has, however, been asserted (though subject to continuing, but now decreasing, resistance from the Soviet Union and satellite States) under the Uniting for Peace Resolutions, as well as under cover of concern with self-determination of peoples. And the constant pressure of "the group of 77" (now counted at 110 at the 1976 Unctad Conference) for further expansion of independent General Assembly activity, and for pressure by it on the Security Council in particular matters, has become a contemporary commonplace.

The new definition of aggression (as here repeatedly seen) has surrounded the whole area of peace enforcement with an ever denser entanglement of doubts and ideologically and economically based con-flicts of interpretation about the limits of lawful use of force. Corres-pondingly, there is likely to be a continuing if not an increasing shortfall of Security Council performance in this area.[41] It was, of course, such shortfall which heralded the initial expansion of the General Assembly's activity under the Uniting for Peace Resolutions after 1950. There might well, then, be expectations among leaders of "the Group of 77" (and more) of further accretion of business and power to the General Assembly. A plausible basis for this accretion could be envisaged in the very terms of the old Uniting for Peace Resolutions. For, be it recalled, those Resolutions were conditioned on failure of the Security Council "to exercise its primary responsibility for the maintenance of inter-national peace and security in any case where there appears to be a threat to the peace, breach of the peace, or act of aggression."[42] The further fact that the General Assembly was now the formal source of the allegedly "authoritative" Consensus Definition of aggression would obviously add self-confidence if not "political clout" to Members seeking such an enhanced role for the General Assembly.

It is to be stressed that this objective marches well with the other two extraneous objectives of Political Warfare and United Nations Verbal Celebration or Face-Saving which I shall recall in the succeeding Section. For all of them it is immaterial whether the definition had the clarity and precision required for its success as a guide to States and United Nations organs determining cases of aggression. Indeed, for this objective, as for the general Political Warfare objective, lack of pre-cision and clarity may be an advantage rather than otherwise. What is necessary is merely that any ambiguities and confusions are tolerant of the proponents' own *parti pris*. Once that is achieved, States pressing for expansion of the General Assembly's powers could expect that the view-point which they favour would be supported by the "automatic majorities" on which they can now rely on many conflicts, especially with Western States. The rest could be left to the practical precept of United Nations law, that each major organ controls its own proceedings, even so far as concerns the operation of the Charter entailed in those proceedings.

In ultimate analysis, of course, this drive to enhance the role of the General Assembly because majorities in that body may be expected to cooperate readily in using United Nations pressures for the furtherance of certain national or bloc policies, is a wholesale version of "the Political Warfare Drive" of definition,[43] largely at odds with the original drive of definition for deterring aggressors and guiding United Nations organs responsible for maintaining and restoring peace. It is thus a very special form of this drive. It does not merely, like campaigns to legiti-mise the use of force in alleged "wars of liberation", or to stigmatise military occupation as aggression regardless of lawfulness of origin, seek to ensure outcomes of particular struggles which further the advocate State's or bloc's particular foreign policies. It is a drive to appropriate all effective decision-making in the whole area to the furtherance of the advocate States's particular foreign policies, by steady encroachment of the General Assembly into the sphere of the less manipulable Security Council. As such, it brings into question the whole future of the General Assembly, a matter to which I shall return in the concluding Section.

X

The theme of this concluding Chapter has naturally been the bearing of the General Assembly's achievement of the Consensus Definition on the strengthening of the prospects of peace between States. We do not need to pitch the claims for this achievement at the ambitious level set by Soviet eloquence of "depriving" potential aggressors of all legal loop-holes and pretexts through which they can unleash aggression. Even pitched at the modest level of relevance and bearing on the *mere* narrowing of such loopholes and pretexts, the claims have been shown to be a travesty of the truth.

As pointed out, however, in Chapter 9, Section X, and here further developed, it is an error to think of the Consensus Definition in terms solely or even mainly of the objective of strengthening prospects of peace between nations. Even if the Consensus Definition was not an achievement in those terms, we can still understand claims of achievement in terms of other—it is true rather extraneous—drives. One drive we there designated as the Political Warfare Drive, another as the United Nations Verbal Celebration or Face-Saving Drive.

The Political Warfare Drive has been exemplified at a hundred points in the preceding pages. All States are sensitive to the impact of the terms of definition on their own national policies and those of their adversaries, which is what political warfare is about. This is so even if not necessarily all—or even most—States feel the definitional operation as such to be an instrument of political warfare.

Two States for whom it has manifestly become such an instrument are Egypt and the Soviet Union. And this pair of examples is perhaps all the more fascinating because, in certain important areas, the Soviet drives frustrated the Egyptian. Egypt, as we have indicated at length in Chapter 5, exerted strenuous pressure to include in the definition some clause or phrase in relation to acquisition of territory, which would cast doubt on Israel's legal rights under international law, in territories occupied in the 1967 War. A no less major concern of Soviet national policies proved however to be a main reason for the Egyptian failure in this regard. For if mere "threat or use of force" *regardless of lawfulness* were to invalidate titles (as Egypt wished the Definition to assert), many past Soviet positions, for instance in the Baltic States and in relation to satellite powers, might come into question. Though past, these positions were still of contempory importance to her; and untold future positions might become exposed to political attack. The Soviet Union's stern insistence (with other States) on the final determinative authority of the Security Council (for instance, in the Preamble, Paragraph 2, and in Articles 4 and 6) was, of course, her main defence. But she could not overlook, despite present alignments in the General Assembly favourable to her, that a majority in that body might some time choose to use the Consensus Definition against her. So that she was no less stern in maintaining all the room to manoeuvre provided by the doubts and uncertainties as to the meaning of Charter provisions concerning the limits of lawful force under the Charter.

Accordingly, as previous Chapters showed at length, the Soviet Union insisted that any reference to invalidation of titles must be grounded not on a mere threat or use of force, but only on such use "in contravention of the Charter" (Preamble, Paragraph 7) or on "aggression" (Article 5(3)). Her insistence on these qualifications was as dogged as the efforts of Egypt and other Arab States to have them omitted or at least overlooked. In terms, moreover, of either the Egyptian or the Soviet political warfare objectives, whether offensive (as with Egypt) or defensive (as with the Soviet Union), what was important was not clarity and certainty to close loopholes against future aggressors, but only sufficient plausibility within the unclarity and uncertainty to serve their present *ad hoc* concerns.

The same is to be said as to the other objective which Chapter 9, Section X, showed to be in strong play, especially during the last-minute building of the so-called consensus. This was the desire to minimise the frustration and humiliation both of the United Nations as an organisation, and its Member States, resulting from more than 20 years of hitherto fruitless efforts to find an "authoritative definition" which would yield the dreamed-of guidance for United Nations and Member State action. It was there termed the "United Nations Verbal Celebration or Face-Saving Drive". If the conflicting attitudes of States which blocked full success could not be overcome, so as really to close the loopholes, then at least forms of words should be found which accommodated the conflicting attitudes sufficiently to secure adoption by "consensus". Such adoption would at least avoid the humiliation of again confessing failure. It could, indeed (as the opening Section of Chapter 8 showed that it was), be hailed as a United Nations triumph. For this objective, too, clarity and precision of indications sufficient to deter aggressors, etc., was not necessary—indeed, perhaps quite the contrary. Clarity and precision on the important matters chronically in conflict would prevent the only kind of accommodation—that on the mere verbal level—which might be within reach.

On the hypothesis here presented, that the decisive drives were those of Political Warfare and United Nations Verbal Celebration or Face-Saving, the fact that conflicts which seemed unbridgeable as late as 1972 were so quickly replaced by the "consensus" of 1974, ceases to be so startling. Insofar as participants were concerned with possible use of the definitional terms as weapons of political warfare, proposals and counter-proposals and confrontations were not in vain, even if the operative value of the resulting "compromise" terms of the Definition for advancing peace were nil. The conflicting positions had to be articulated in order to be accommodated by mutual negation. By the same token, insofar as the text was to accommodate them, it had to become rich in ambiguities and even self-contradictions, thus preserving the conflicting positions as conflicts of interpretation.

This hypothesis also explains the related paradox (adverted to in Chapter 3, Sections V-IX, and Chapter 9, Sections X-XII) that whereas conflicts were so many and so sharp on many great issues, there was no serious disagreement on the point that the Definition should meticulously preserve the exact provisions of the Charter, including the many well-known doubts and uncertainties already surrounding them. Insofar as the above extraneous drives require doubts and uncertainties as a medium of operation, no proposals, counter-proposals, or confrontations were *necessary* in order to build the doubts and uncertainties of Charter interpretation into the Definition. *All that was needed was to ensure that nothing in the Definition clarified those already notoriously present in the Charter.* That being done, States would be able to continue to use their own interpretations of the doubtful and uncertain provisions in their political warfare, just as they had done hitherto. Moreover, the reassertion of the sanctity and unchangeability of the Charter provisions would also give rhetorical support to the twin United Nations Verbal Celebration Drive. Yet, of course, in terms of the ostensible peace-seeking drive for authoritative definition, the clarification of the problems of the Charter provisions as to use of force *should* have been at the heart of the whole enterprise.

XI

Above all, however, it is the encroaching role of the General Assembly which is critical for understanding the dangers implicit in a Consensus Definition of aggression into which the gravest conflicts between States are covertly built, for later "application" by that body. For that encroachment threatens at a time when the overarching issues are of equitable distribution of world resources. We are in an epoch of discovery of new worlds, of the oceans, the ocean bed, of outer space, and of technological re-exploration of the old worlds, as surely as 16th and 17th century Europe opened up the Americas and the Indies.

This is not a time when any State, let alone the Western States, can afford to submit supinely to the edicts of hostile majorities, counted, vote for vote, without distinction down to the most mini-of mini-States, especially when those edicts lack moral or legal basis. What is in issue is no mere objection to particular resolutions, but the checking and arrest of the strategic design of certain States to use the General Assembly for imposing their arbitrary will on others. Such a use of the General Assembly violates both the words and the spirit of the Charter, which strictly withheld this kind of power from that body.

It is, of course, true that in the first decade of the United Nations, before the first "package deal" for extended membership and the flood of new Members arising from decolonisation, the Western Powers, and in particular the United States, were disposed to extend the functions of General Assembly majorities which they felt able to control. Western sponsorship of the Uniting for Peace Resolutions was a fruit of this period, although, as I have shown elsewhere, these Powers were careful, even then, not to attribute to the General Assembly powers to impose legally binding obligations on Members.

In the decade following the package deal on membership in the 'fifties, the General Assembly was able to promote the achievement of decolonisation of most dependent territories, by measures which were often sponsored by Soviet, Asian and African bloc Members, but also mostly cooperatively received by Western States. The flood of new Members following decolonisation more than doubled overall Membership of the Organisation and swung the voting in the General Assembly drastically against Western interests. Even then a certain restraint and law-abidingness of outcome was assured by the continued economic independence and relative power of the Western States. Early American leadership in assuring international economic aid for raising to tolerable levels the standard of life of the poorer nations, assured a degree of deliberation and give and take on both sides.

That fruitful balance was destroyed—quite apart from the sheer predominance in numbers of the Communist, Asian and African blocs—by the economic crises of the 'seventies affecting even the strongest Western Powers, aggravated by the drastic rise in energy costs, the shift of unprecedented financial power to a few sparsely populated OAPEC States, and the continuing threat of the extreme coercion of the oil boycott. The tables were in a sense turned, *both as to voting majorities and as to economic vulnerability*. Correspondingly, the restraint and give and take which kept the General Assembly's activities within reasonable and on the whole lawful bounds in the 'sixties, have given way. States struggling with long-term economic crises no longer receive the consideration formerly accorded to major contributors to aid funds for poorer States whose votes dominate the General Assembly.

It is tempting to become bemused with the ironies of the reversal of Western positions in the General Assembly, and to dismiss Western anxieties in terms of what is good for the goose being good for the gander. Such a response, however, conceals the very substantial differences between the position in the first decade of the United Nations, and that which now casts its shadow over the fourth decade. One is that the former Western-led majorities did not attempt to arrogate to the General Assembly overall powers of binding decision, including that of imposing legal obligations on Members. Second, even the recommendatory or hortatory power of the General Assembly was invoked for the most part with a certain restraint and attention to general principles *vis-à-vis* Communist bloc and Asian and (later) African bloc interests. Decolonisation under General Assembly auspices owes as much to American anti-colonialist ideals as to Soviet self-interested pressures and initiatives. Third, at no point did the United States or other Western countries use the kind of extreme coercive power for wholesale control of votes which is now manifest in the operations of OAPEC. Such a power was theoretically open to the United States, especially in the years preceding the Soviet nuclear breakthrough. Western interests never did, however, regularly assert the assured power of marshalling automatic majorities regardless of the merits, now asserted by OAPEC-Soviet operations with Third World votes.

Despite facile goose and gander and pot and kettle arguments, therefore, it is still necessary to call attention to the fact that the present phase of tyranny of "automatic" majorities in the General Assembly creates unprecedented dangers for some of its Members and for most of the principles of the United Nations, not to speak of international law. The stakes are momentous, not only in terms of the control by the Western Powers of their own destiny, but of the recovery of the West to a point again capable of contributing to the economic advancement of the developing nations. So that, however their interests may appear in the short run, the poorer States of the developing world have, on a slightly longer view, a heavy involvement in these same stakes.

The present writer observed, seventeen years ago, that the General Assembly's claim to represent "the conscience of mankind" could become "a protective shield for predatory and imperialist designs against Western States and an execution chamber for any State that tried to defend itself against these designs".[43] This would be inevitable, I then said, if "through a regular stacking of votes regardless of the merits, it committed a *détournement* of the moral authority of that body". These trends were apparent even before the gross *coup d'état* (or should we say *coup de monde*?)of the oil boycott in support of the aggressive surprise attacks of Egypt and Syria on Israel, of October 1973. The question thus raised in 1958 for the then long-run future has become now a most urgent and important question for the immediate future. The General Assembly is rapidly becoming a committee to execute the will of the Soviet and Arab oil-producing nations manipulating the numerically overwhelming votes of African and Asian States. As this pattern continues (and, most tragically, also imposes itself in the Specialised Agencies such as Unesco and the I.L.O.), the question will become increasingly urgent—How long will the target States permit themselves to continue to be led, one by one, issue by issue, step by step, like sheep to the slaughter?

No doubt, the submissiveness of Western States since 1973 has been mostly due to the brooding threat of renewal of the economic coercion of the oil boycott—a kind and degree of coercion which is certainly a candidate for the title of "economic aggression". In part, however, it was also due to the notion that even such extreme economic coercion is free of legal restraints applicable to strictly military coercion, and is somehow also immune from legitimate defensive action of the victims.[44] The dangers threatened by this chaotic state of affairs may now have arrived. Intransigent and irresponsible majorities in the General Assembly can now, by placing spurious self-serving interpretations on the ambiguities and silences of the Consensus Definition, use it as a political weapon against whichever are the target States for the time being. This would increase enormously "the clout" of that body's *de facto* usurpation of magisterial power. The dangers to the Organisation itself are almost as great as those to target States. The Great Power veto in the Security Council was based on recognition that the choice was not between an international security organisation with the veto and one without the veto, but between an international security organisation with a veto and no international security organisation at all. The general *lack* of authority of the General Assembly (with a few express exceptions of marginal importance to international security) to take decisions legally binding on members, *was a corollary of this same principle for a body where voting goes by simple majority or even two-thirds majority.*

Insofar as the General Assembly now seeks to arrogate such magisterial authority to itself, it imperils also its true moral and hortatory role in international security matters. As it becomes a mere weapon in one side's political armoury, the effect is to consolidate rather than resolve hostile alignments, to harden rather than temper negotiating positions, and deprive States subject to its pressures of any but military alternatives. Even in terms of the need to avoid military confrontations threatened States may conclude that until these patterns disperse, the only practical step may be a collective withdrawal, not only of budgetary contributions, but of their continued participation. They will certainly recognise, sooner rather than later, that their continued participation is an important source of the legitimacy sought by the manipulating blocs. Such a withdrawal, even if it did not cripple the Organisation by budgetary emasculation, would leave it as a rather empty shell—the fruits of a Pyrrhic victory in the hands of the Third World.[45]

Appendices

General Note: The main General Assembly documents relating to the defining of aggression are listed in Appendix 1. They include *inter alia* the Reports of the Sixth Committee and of the Fourth Special Committee, but repetitious minor items are not listed. Sixth Committee proceedings at the Twenty-Ninth Session are there also listed in detail. Appendix 2 reproduces the three main draft proposals considered by the Special Committee, followed in Appendix 3 by the Consolidated Text which was the basis of the Committee's final deliberations. Appendix 4 reprints the more relevant parts of the diffuse Declaration of Principles of International Law Concerning Friendly Relations and Co-operation Between States, 1970 (Resol. 2625 (XXV)), and Appendix 5 reprints Chapters I and VII of the United Nations Charter. The full text of the 1974 Definition and the covering General Assembly Resolution 3314 (XXIX) of December 14, 1974 are reproduced in Appendix 6.

. . . . .

APPENDIX 1
LIST OF PRINCIPAL U.N. DOCUMENTS RELEVANT
TO THE DEFINITION OF AGGRESSION

Note: The texts of these documents other than the SR series are reproduced in vol. 2 of B. B. Ferencz, *Defining Aggression . . .* (1975) *passim*. And see also Appendices 2-5.

GENERAL ASSEMBLY, OFFICIAL RECORDS

Fifth Session, Annexes, Agenda Item 72. Doc. A/C. 1/608 USSR Draft Definition of Aggression, 4 Nov., 1950, pp. 4-5.

Fifth Session, Resolution 378 (V). Duties of States in the event of the outbreak of hostilities, 17 Nov., 1950, pp. 12-13. Resolution 380 (V). Peace through Deeds, 17 Nov., 1950, pp. 13-14.

Sixth Session, Supp. No. 9 (A/1858)—*Report of the International Law Commission*, 16 May-27 July, 1951, pp. 8-14.

Sixth Session, Annexes, Agenda Item 49. *Report of the Sixth Committee* A/2087, 29 Jan., 1952, pp. 12-17.

Seventh Session, Annexes, Agenda Item 54. Report of the Sixth Committee, A/2322, 17 Dec., 1952, and Draft Resolutions, pp. 81-91.

Ninth Session, Supp. No. 11 (A/2638)—*Report of the Special Committee on the Question of Defining Aggression*, 24 Aug.-21 Sept., 1953, pp. 1-15.

Ninth Session, Annexes, Agenda Item 51. Report of Sixth Committee, A/2806, 2 Dec., 1954, pp. 9-12.

Twelfth Session, Supp. No. 16 (A/3574)—*Report of 1956 Special Committee on the Question of Defining Aggression*, 8 Oct.-9 Nov., 1956, pp. 1-33.

Twelfth Session, Annexes, Agenda Item 54, *Report of the Sixth Committee*, A/3756, 27 Nov., 1957, pp. 1-7.

Twenty-Second Session, Annexes, Agenda Item 95. Report of the Sixth Committee, A/6988, 15 Dec., 1967, pp. 4-8.

Twenty-Third Session, Agenda Item 86—*Report of Special Committee*, Question of Defining Aggression, A/7185/Rev. 1, 4 Jun.— 6 Jul., 1968, pp. 1-40.

Twenty-Third Session, Agenda Item 86, *Report of Sixth Committee*, A/7402, 13 Dec., 1968, pp. 3-8.

Twenty-Fourth Session, Supp. No. 20, A/7620, *Report of Special Committee*, 24 Feb.-3 Apr., 1969, pp. 1-39.

Twenty-Fourth Session, Agenda Item 88, *Report of Sixth Committee*, A/7853, 10 Dec., 1969, pp. 1-7.

Twenty-Fifth Session, Report of Special Committee, Supp. No. 19, A/8019, 13 Jul.-14 Aug., 1970, pp. 1-68.

Twenty-Fifth Session, Agenda Item 87, *Report of Sixth Committee*, A/8171, 19 Nov., 1970, pp. 1-7.

Twenty-Sixth Session, Supp. No. 19, A/8419, *Report of Special Committee*, 1 Feb.-5 Mar., 1971, pp. 1-46.

Twenty-Sixth Session, Agenda Item 89, *Report of Sixth Committee,* A/8525, 19 Nov., 1971, pp. 1-8.

Twenty-Seventh Session, Supp. No. 19, A/8719, *Report of Special Committee,* 31 Jan.-3 Mar., 1972, pp. 1-23.

Twenty-Seventh Session, Agenda Item 88, *Report of Sixth Committee,* A/8929, 7 Dec., 1972, pp. 1-9.

Twenty-Eighth Session, Supp. No. 19, A/9019. *Report of Special Committee,* 25 Apr.-30 May, 1973, pp. 1-28.

Twenty-Eighth Session, Agenda Item 95, *Report of Sixth Committee,* A/9411, 10 Dec., 1973, pp. 1-15.

Twenty-Ninth Session, Supp. No. 19, A/9619, *Report of Special Committee,* 11 Mar.-12 Apr., 1974, pp. 1-42.

Twenty-Ninth Session, Agenda Item 86, *Report of Sixth Committee,* A/9890, 6 Dec., 1974, pp. 1-3.

U.N. Secretariat, ST/LIB/32, 24 Oct., 1973, Definition of Aggression, A Select Bibliography, pp. 1-13.

.   .   .   .   .

SUMMARY RECORDS OF PROCEEDINGS OF THE SIXTH COMMITTEE ON THE
QUESTION OF DEFINING AGGRESSION—(DATE OF DISTRIBUTION IS IN
BRACKETS FOLLOWING DATE OF EACH MEETING.
ALL DATES ARE IN 1974.)

A/C.6/SR. 1471, 8 Oct. (10 Oct.); A/C.6/SR. 1472, 9 Oct. (11 Oct.); A/C.6/SR. 1473, 10 Oct. (15 Oct.); A/C.6/SR. 1474, 11 Oct. (15 Oct.); A/C.6/SR. 1475, 14 Oct. (16 Oct.); A/C.6/SR. 1476, 15 Oct. (18 Oct.); A/C.6/SR. 1477, 15 Oct. (17 Oct.); A/C.6/SR. 1478, 16 Oct. (21 Oct.); A/C.6/SR. 1479, 18 Oct. (23 Oct.); A/C.6/SR. 1480, 18 Oct. (22 Oct.); A/C.6/SR. 1481, 21 Oct. (24 Oct.); A/C.6/SR. 1482, 22 Oct. (25 Oct.); A/C.6/SR. 1483, 23 Oct. (25 Oct.); A/C.6/SR. 1484, 24 Oct. (28 Oct.); A/AC. 134/SR. 110-113, 11 Mar. to 12 Apr. (18 July).

APPENDIX 2

THREE MAIN PROPOSALS BEFORE THE SPECIAL COMMITTEE

(appearing as Annex 1 to the Special Committee's 1970 Report, G.A.O.R. (XXV), Supp. No. 19 (A/8019), pp. 55-60, and reprinted in G.A.O.R. (XXVIII), Supp. No. 19 (A/9019), pp. 7-12.

A.   *Draft proposal submitted by the Union of Soviet Socialist Republics (A/AC.134/L.12)*

The General Assembly,

Basing itself on the fact that one of the fundamental purposes of the United Nations is to maintain international peace and security and to take effective collective measures for the prevention and removal of threats to the peace, and for the suppression of acts of aggression or other breaches of the peace,

Noting that according to the principles of international law the planning, preparation, initiation or waging of an aggressive war is a most serious international crime,

Bearing in mind that the use of force to deprive dependent peoples of the exercise of their inherent right to self-determination in accordance with General Assembly resolution 1514 (XV) of 14 December 1960 is a denial of fundamental human rights, is contrary to the Charter of the United Nations and hinders the development of co-operation and the establishment of peace throughout the world,

Considering that the use of force by a State to encroach upon the social and political achievements of the peoples of other States is incompatible with the principle of the peaceful coexistence of States with different social systems,

Recalling also that Article 39 of the Charter states that the Security Council shall determine the existence of any threat to the peace, breach of the peace or act of aggression and shall decide what measures shall be taken in accordance with Articles 41 and 42 to maintain or restore international peace and security,

Believing that, although the question whether an act of aggression has been committed must be considered in the light of all the circumstances in each particular case, it is nevertheless appropriate to formulate basic principles as guidance for such determination,

Convinced that the adoption of a definition of aggression would have a restraining influence on a potential aggressor, would simplify the determination of acts of aggression and the implementation of measures to stop them and would also facilitate the rendering of assistance to the victim of aggression and the protection of his lawful rights and interests,

Considering also that armed aggression is the most serious and dangerous form of aggression, being fraught, in the conditions created by the existence of nuclear weapons, with the threat of a new world conflict with all its catastrophic consequences and that this form of aggression should be defined at the present stage,

Declares that:

1. Armed aggression (direct or indirect) is the use by a State, first, of armed force against another State contrary to the purposes, principles and provisions of the Charter of the United Nations.

2. In accordance with and without prejudice to the functions and powers of the Security Council:

A. Declaration of war by one State, first, against another State shall be considered an act of armed aggression;

B. Any of the following acts, if committed by a State first, even without a declaration of war, shall be considered an act of armed aggression:

(a) The use of nuclear, bacteriological or chemical weapons or any other weapons of mass destruction;

(b) Bombardment of or firing at the territory and population of another State or an attack on its land, sea or air forces;

(c) Invasion or attack by the armed forces of a State against the territory of another State, military occupation or annexation of the territory of another State or part thereof, or the blockade of coasts or ports.

C. The use by a State of armed force by sending armed bands, mercenaries, terrorists or saboteurs to the territory of another State and engagement in other forms of subversive activity involving the use of armed force with the aim of promoting an internal upheaval in another State or a reversal of policy in favour of the aggressor shall be considered an act of indirect aggression.

3. In addition to the acts listed above, other acts by States may be deemed to constitute an act of aggression if in each specific instance they are declared to be such by a decision of the Security Council.

4. No territorial gains or special advantages resulting from armed aggression shall be recognized.

5. Armed aggression shall be an international crime against peace entailing the political and material responsibility of States and the criminal responsibility of the persons guilty of this crime.

6. Nothing in the foregoing shall prevent the use of armed force in accordance with the Charter of the United Nations, including its use by dependent peoples in order to exercise their inherent right of self-determination in accordance with General Assembly resolution 1514 (XV).

B. *Draft proposal submitted by Colombia, Cyprus, Ecuador, Ghana, Guyana, Haiti, Iran, Madagascar, Mexico, Spain, Uganda, Uruguay and Yugoslavia (A/AC.134/L.16 and Add. 1 and 2)*

The General Assembly,

Basing itself on the fact that one of the fundamental purposes of the United Nations is to maintain international peace and security and to take effective collective measures for the prevention and removal of threats to the peace, and for the suppression of acts of aggression or other breaches of the peace,

Convinced that armed attack (armed aggression) is the most serious and dangerous form of aggression and that it is proper at this stage to proceed to a definition of this form of aggression,

Further convinced that the adoption of a definition of aggression would serve to discourage possible aggressors and would facilitate the determination of acts of aggression,

Bearing in mind also the powers and duties of the Security Council, embodied in Article 39 of the Charter of the United Nations, to determine the existence of any threat to the peace, breach of the peace, or act of aggression, and to decide the measures to be taken in accordance with Articles 41 and 42, to maintain or restore international peace and security,

Considering that, although the question whether aggression has occurred must be determined in the circumstances of each particular case, it is nevertheless appropriate to facilitate that task by formulating certain principles for such determination,

Reaffirming further the duty of States under the Charter of the United Nations to settle their international disputes by pacific methods in order not to endanger international peace, security and justice,

Convinced that no consideration of whatever nature, save as stipulated in operative paragraph 3 hereof, may provide an excuse for the use of force by one State against another State,

Declares that:

1. In the performance of its function to maintain international peace and security, the United Nations only has competence to use force in conformity with the Charter;

2. For the purpose of this definition, aggression is the use of armed force by a State against another State, including its territorial waters or air space, or in any way affecting the territorial integrity, sovereignty or political independence of such State, save under the provisions of paragraph 3 hereof or when undertaken by or under the authority of the Security Council;

3. The inherent right of individual or collective self-defence of a State can be exercised only in case of the occurrence of armed attack (armed aggression) by another State in accordance with Article 51 of the Charter;

4. Enforcement action or any use of armed force by regional arrangements or agencies may only be resorted to if there is decision to that effect by the Security Council acting under Article 53 of the Charter;

5. In accordance with the foregoing and without prejudice to the powers and duties of the Security Council, as provided in the Charter, any of the following acts when committed by a State first against another State in violation of the Charter shall constitute acts of aggression:

(a) Declaration of war by one State against another State;

(b) The invasion or attack by the armed forces of a State, against the territories of another State, or any military occupation, however temporary, or any forcible annexation of the territory of another State or part thereof;

(c) Bombardment by the armed forces of a State against the territory of another State, or the use of any weapons, particularly weapons of mass destruction, by a State against the territory of another State;

(d) The blockade of the coasts or ports of a State by the armed forces of another State;

6. Nothing in paragraph 3 above shall be construed as entitling the State exercising a right of individual or collective self-defence, in accordance with Article 51 of the Charter, to take any measures not reasonably proportionate to the armed attack against it;

7. When a State is a victim in its own territory of subversive and/or terrorist acts by irregular, volunteer or armed bands organized or supported by another State, it may take all reasonable and adequate steps to safeguard its existence and its institutions, without having recourse to the right of individual or collective self-defence against the other State under Article 51 of the Charter;

8. The territory of a State is inviolable and may not be the object, even temporarily, of military occupation or of other measures of force taken by another State on any grounds whatever, and that such territorial acquisitions obtained by force shall not be recognized;

9. Armed aggression, as defined herein, and the acts enumerated above, shall constitute crimes against international peace, giving rise to international responsibility;

10. None of the preceding paragraphs may be interpreted as limiting the scope of the Charter's provisions concerning the right of peoples to self-determination, sovereignty and territorial integrity.

C. *Draft proposal submitted by Australia, Canada, Italy, Japan, the United Kingdom of Great Britain and Northern Ireland and the United States of America (A/AC.134/L.17 and Add. 1 and 2)*

The General Assembly,

Conscious that a primary purpose of the United Nations is to maintain international peace and security, and, to that end, to take effective collective measures for the prevention and removal of threats to the peace, and for the suppression of acts of aggression or other breaches of the peace,

Recalling that Article 39 of the Charter of the United Nations provides that the Security Council shall determine the existence of any threat to the peace, breach of the peace, or act of aggression and shall make recommendations, or decide what measures shall be taken in accordance with Articles 41 and 42, to maintain or restore international peace and security,

Reaffirming that all States shall settle their international disputes by peaceful means in such a manner that international peace and security, and justice, are not endangered,

Believing that, although the question of whether an act of aggression has been committed must be considered in the light of all the circumstances of each particular case, a generally accepted definition of aggression may nevertheless provide guidance for such consideration,

Being of the view that such a definition of aggression may accordingly facilitate the processes of the United Nations and encourage States to fulfil in good faith their obligations under the Charter of the United Nations,

Adopts the following definition:

I. Under the Charter of the United Nations, "aggression" is a term to be applied by the Security Council when appropriate in the exercise of its primary responsibility for the maintenance of international peace and security under Article 24 and its functions under Article 39.

II. The term "aggression" is applicable, without prejudice to a finding of threat to the peace or breach of the peace, to the use of force in international relations, overt or covert, direct or indirect, by a State against the territorial integrity or political independence of any other State, or in any other manner inconsistent with the purposes of the United Nations. Any act which would constitute aggression by or against a State likewise constitutes aggression when committed by a State or other political entity delimited by international boundaries or internationally agreed lines of demarcation against any State or other political entity so delimited and not subject to its authority.

III. The use of force in the exercise of the inherent right of individual or collective self-defence, or pursuant to decisions of or authorization by competent United Nations organs or regional organizations consistent with the Charter of the United Nations, does not constitute aggression.

IV. The uses of force which may constitute aggression include, but are not necessarily limited to, a use of force by a State as described in paragraph II.

A. In order to:
(1) Diminish the territory or alter the boundaries of another State;
(2) Alter internationally agreed lines of demarcation;
(3) Disrupt or interfere with the conduct of the affairs of another State;
(4) Secure changes in the Government of another State; or
(5) Inflict harm or obtain concessions of any sort;

B. By such means as:
(1) Invasion by its armed forces of territory under the jurisdiction of another State;
(2) Use of its armed forces in another State in violation of the fundamental conditions of permission for their presence, or maintaining them there beyond the termination of permission;
(3) Bombardment by its armed forces of territory under the jurisdiction of another State;
(4) Inflicting physical destruction on another State through the use of other forms of armed force;

(5) Carrying out deliberate attacks on the armed forces, ships or aircraft of another State;

(6) Organizing, supporting or directing armed bands or irregular or volunteer forces that make incursions or infiltrate into another State;

(7) Organizing, supporting or directing violent civil strife or acts of terrorism in another State; or

(8) Organizing, supporting or directing subversive activities aimed at the violent overthrow of the Government of another State.

APPENDIX 3

CONSOLIDATED TEXT OF THE REPORTS OF THE CONTACT GROUPS AND OF THE DRAFTING GROUP

(being Appendix A to the Special Committee's 1973 Report, G.A.O.R. (XXVIII), Supp. No. 19 (A/9019), pp. 15-21)

Preambular paragraphs

Basing itself on the fact that one of the fundamental purposes of the United Nations is to maintain international peace and security and to take effective collective measures for the prevention and removal of threats to the peace, and for the suppression of acts of aggression or other breaches of the peace,

Recalling that Article 39 of the Charter states that the Security Council shall determine the existence of any threat to the peace, breach of the peace or act of aggression and shall make recommendations or decide what measures shall be taken in accordance with Articles 41 and 42 to maintain or restore international peace and security,

Recalling also the duty of States under the Charter of the United Nations to settle their international disputes by peaceful means in order not to endanger international peace, security and justice,

Bearing in mind that nothing in this definition shall be interpreted as in any way extending or diminishing the provisions of the United Nations Charter with respect to rights and duties of the organs of the United Nations,

Considering also that since aggression is the most serious and dangerous form of the illegal use of force, being fraught, in the conditions created by the existence of all types of weapons of mass destruction, with the possible threat of a world conflict with all its catastrophic consequences, aggression should be defined at the present stage,

Reaffirming the duty of States not to use armed force to deprive peoples of their right to self-determination, freedom and independence,

Reaffirming also that the territory of a State shall not be violated by being the object, even temporarily, of military occupation or of other measures of force taken by another State in contravention of the Charter,

Convinced that the adoption of a definition of aggression would have a restraining influence on a potential aggressor, would simplify the determination of acts of aggression and the implementation of measures to stop them and would also facilitate the protection of the lawful rights and interests of the victim and the rendering of assistance to the victim,

Believing that, although the question whether an act of aggression had been committed must be considered in the light of all the circumstances in each particular case, it is, nevertheless, appropriate to formulate basic principles as guidance for such determination,

General definition of aggression
Article 1

Aggression is the use of armed force [however exerted] by a State against the sovereignty, territorial integrity or political independence of another State, or in any other manner inconsistent with the Charter of the United Nations, as set out in this definition.

Explanatory note: In this definition the term "State"

   (a) is used without prejudice to questions of recognition or to whether a State is a Member of the United Nations, and

   (b) includes the concept of a "group of States".

Questions of priority and aggressive intent
Article 2

The first use of armed force in contravention of the Charter shall constitute *prima facie* evidence of an act of aggression provided, however, that the Security Council may in conformity with the Charter conclude that a determination to that effect would not be justified in the light of other relevant circumstances, including, as evidence, the purposes of the States involved.

Acts proposed for inclusion
Article 3

Any of the following acts, regardless of a declaration of war, shall constitute an act of aggression:

   (a) The invasion or attack by the armed forces of a State of the territory of another State, or any military occupation, however temporary, resulting from such invasion or attack, or any annexation by the use of force of the territory of another State or part thereof;

   (b) Bombardment by the armed forces of a State against the territory of another State or the use of any weapons by a State against the territory of another State;

   (c) The blockade of the ports or coasts of a State by the armed forces of another State;

   (d) An attack by the armed forces of a State on the land, sea or air forces, marine and air fleets of another State;

(e) The use of armed forces of one State which are within the territory of another State with the agreement of the receiving State, in contravention of the conditions provided for in the agreement or any extension of their presence in such territory beyond the termination of the agreement;

(f) The action of a State placing its territory at the disposal of another State when the latter uses this territory for perpetrating an act of aggression against a third State with the acquiescence and agreement of the former;

(g) The sending by or on behalf of a State of armed bands, groups, irregulars or mercenaries, which carry out invasion or attack involving acts of armed force against another State of such gravity as to amount to the acts listed above, or its open and active participation therein.

Provision on the non-exhaustive character of the list and the clause on minor incidents

Article 4

The acts enumerated above are neither exhaustive nor do they prevent the Security Council from refraining from the determination of an act of aggression if the act concerned is too minimal to justify such action.

Conversely, the Security Council may determine other acts as constituting aggression under the provisions of the Charter.

The right of peoples to self-determination

Article 5

None of the preceding paragraphs may be interpreted as limiting the scope of the Charter's provisions concerning the right of peoples to self-determination or as preventing peoples under military occupation or any form of foreign domination in their actions against and resistance to such alien domination from using force and seeking or receiving support and assistance in order to exercise their inherent right to self-determination in accordance with the principles of the Charter and in conformity with the Declaration on Principles of International Law concerning Friendly Relations and Co-operation among States in accordance with the Charter of the United Nations.

Legal consequences of aggression

Article 6

Aggression constitutes [   ] against international peace giving rise to responsibility under international law.

No territorial acquisition or special advantage resulting, from aggression is lawful nor shall it be recognized as such.

Legal uses of force, including the question of centralization

Article 7

Nothing in this definition shall be construed as in any way enlarging or diminishing the scope of the Charter including its provisions concerning cases in which the use of force is lawful.

*
* *

The following wording has been considered, but it has not been decided where it should be inserted:

"No consideration of whatever nature, whether political, economic, military or otherwise, may serve as a justification for aggression."

Comments contained in the reports of the contact groups and of the drafting group

Preambular paragraphs

With regard to the sixth paragraph, two members of the drafting group reserved their position until related provisions of the operative text have been agreed upon. One member reserved his position as to the substance of the paragraph, asking that a reference be made to the principle of territorial integrity.

With regard to the seventh paragraph, one member proposed that the word "armed" be inserted before the word "force". One member approved the addition of the word "armed". One member objected to the words "in contravention of the Charter" at the end of the sentence.

Article on "General definition of aggression"

One member of the relevant contact group proposed that the words "[however exerted]" be replaced by "in any form" and that the text read "inconsistent with the *principles and purposes* of the Charter". Another member proposed that the text should read "inconsistent with the *principles and provisions* of the Charter". One member proposed to delete the words between brackets in view of the inclusion, in the list of acts of aggression, of subparagraph (g).

One member reserved his position as to the term "sovereignty" and as to explanatory note (b).

One member, while accepting the idea behind the words "as set out in this definition", said he would like to see these words redrafted.

It was furthermore felt that it was not necessary to specify that the territory of the State covers its territorial waters and air space, because this is a generally recognized concept in international law.

Article on "Questions of priority and aggressive intent"

There was no general agreement within the relevant contact group as to the text to be adopted.

Whereas many members expressed their willingness to consider this text as one which could be accepted, objections were expressed by some members as to the inclusion of the words "in contravention of the Charter" and the words "including, as evidence, the purposes of the States involved". Some amendments as to the drafting were also presented. One member proposed to replace the words "in contravention of the Charter" in the first line by the words "as set out in this definition".

Notwithstanding intensive negotiations, it was not possible to find at this stage a formula which would have been accepted by consensus.

Acts proposed for inclusion

As to the introductory sentence, it was suggested that this would have to be redrafted to ensure consistency with other provisions.

As to subparagraph (d), one member reserved his position on the words "marine and air fleets".

As to subparagraph (e), it was proposed that the words "beyond the termination of the agreement" be deleted and replaced by the following words: "after the agreement ceases to be in force".

One member reserved his position on the text as a whole.

As to subparagraph (f), one member reserved his position.

As to subparagraph (g), there was no general agreement but the text reproduced above was discussed during the last stages of consultations. It was proposed that the indirect use of force should rather be covered by a separate article than by inclusion as a subparagraph to the list of acts. The words "or its collaboration therein" were strongly opposed when they were first introduced at the end of the text and the objections remained as to the present wording: "or its open and active participation therein".

Other reservations were based on the view that the subparagraph was too narrow and omitted acts which should be covered.

Article on "The Right of peoples to self-determination"

There was no general agreement as to the text to be adopted. The text reproduced in the present document was considered in the final stages of consultations.

The following preambular paragraph was proposed in connexion with this paragraph:

"Reaffirming the duty of States not to use armed force to deprive peoples of their right to self-determination, freedom and independence."

Some members reserved their positions as to the above texts referring either to points of drafting or to the substance.

One member proposed that after the word "self-determination" in the second line the following words be added: ", sovereignty and territorial integrity".

Article on "Legal consequences of aggression"

With respect to the first paragraph, five various alternatives were considered as regards the brackets. These alternatives are as follows:

1. "a grave violation"
2. "a crime"
3. "criminal violation"
4. No provision on the legal consequences of aggression at all.
5. To insert instead of the present text of the paragraph, the text: "Aggression gives rise to responsibility under international law."

With respect to the second paragraph, one member of the relevant contact group supported the inclusion of the following text:

"The territory of a State is inviolable and shall not be the object, even temporarily, of military occupation or of other measures of force taken by another State on any grounds whatever and no territorial acquisitions as well as any other special advantages obtained by the use of force shall be recognized."

Another member reserved his position as to the words "special advantage".

It was furthermore proposed by one member that the following paragraph be included in the preamble of the definition of aggression:

"*Reaffirming* that the territory of a State is inviolable and that it shall not be the object, even temporarily, of military occupation or of other measures of force taken by another State in contravention of the Charter,".

Article on "Legal uses of force, including the question of centralization"

On behalf of the 13-Power group it was announced that the group had not taken a final decision on the question of the legal uses of force.

Additional text

One member reserved his position.

One member proposed the following text:

"No consideration of whatever nature, whether political, economic, military or otherwise, relating to the internal or foreign policy of a State, may serve as a justification for aggression as herein defined."

APPENDIX 4

DECLARATION OF PRINCIPLES OF INTERNATIONAL LAW CONCERNING FRIENDLY RELATIONS AND COOPERATION OF STATES (Res. 2625 (XXV))

Having considered the principles of international law relating to friendly relations and co-operation among states,

1. *Solemnly proclaims* the following principles:

The principle that states shall refrain in their international relations from the threat or use of force against the territorial integrity or political independence of any state, or in any other manner inconsistent with the purposes of the United Nations

Every state has the duty to refrain in its international relations from the threat or use of force against the territorial integrity or political independence of any state, or in any other manner inconsistent with the purposes of the United Nations. Such a threat or use of force constitutes a violation of international law and the Charter of the United Nations and shall never be employed as a means of settling international issues.

A war of aggression constitutes a crime against the peace, for which there is responsibility under international law.

In accordance with the purposes and principles of the United Nations, states have the duty to refrain from propaganda for wars of aggression.

Every state has the duty to refrain from the threat or use of force to violate the existing international boundaries of another state or as a means of solving international disputes, including territorial disputes and problems concerning frontiers of states.

Every state likewise has the duty to refrain from the threat or use of force to violate international lines of demarcation, such as armistice lines, established by or pursuant to an international agreement to which it is a party or which it is otherwise bound to respect. Nothing in the foregoing shall be construed as prejudicing the positions of the parties concerned with regard to the status and effects of such lines under their special régimes or as affecting their temporary character.

States have a duty to refrain from acts of reprisal involving the use of force.

Every state has the duty to refrain from any forcible action which deprives peoples referred to in the elaboration of the principle of equal rights and self-determination of their right to self-determination and freedom and independence.

Every state has the duty to refrain from organizing or encouraging the organization of irregular forces or armed bands, including mercenaries, for incursion into the territory of another state.

Every state has the duty to refrain from organizing, instigating, assisting or participating in acts of civil strife or terrorist acts in another state or acquiescing in organized activities within its territory directed towards the commission of such acts, when the acts referred to in the present paragraph involve a threat or use of force.

The territory of a state shall not be the object of military occupation resulting from the use of force in contravention of the provisions of the Charter. The territory of a state shall not be the object of acquisition by another state resulting from the threat or use of force. No territorial acquisition resulting from the threat or use of force shall be recognized as legal. Nothing in the foregoing shall be construed as affecting:

    (a) Provisions of the Charter or any international agreement prior to the Charter régime and valid under international law; or

    (b) The powers of the Security Council under the Charter.

All states shall pursue in good faith negotiations for the early conclusion of a universal treaty on general and complete disarmament under effective international control and strive to adopt appropriate measures to reduce international tensions and strengthen confidence among states.

All states shall comply in good faith with their obligations under the generally recognized principles and rules of international law with respect to the maintenance of international peace and security, and shall endeavour to make the United Nations security system based upon the Charter more effective.

Nothing in the foregoing paragraphs shall be construed as enlarging or diminishing in any way the scope of the provisions of the Charter concerning cases in which the use of force is lawful.

The principle that states shall settle their international disputes by peaceful means in such a manner that international peace and security and justice are not endangered

Every state shall settle its international disputes with other states by peaceful means, in such a manner that international peace and security and justice are not endangered.

States shall accordingly seek early and just settlement of their international disputes by negotiation, inquiry, mediation, conciliation, arbitration, judicial settlement, resort to regional agencies or arrangements or other peaceful means of their choice. In seeking such a settlement the parties shall agree upon such peaceful means as may be appropriate to the circumstances and nature of the dispute.

The parties to a dispute have the duty, in the event of failure to reach a solution by any one of the above peaceful means, to continue to seek a settlement of the dispute by other peaceful means agreed upon by them.

States parties to an international dispute, as well as other states, shall refrain from any action which may aggravate the situation so as to endanger the maintenance of international peace and security, and shall act in accordance with the purposes and principles of the United Nations.

International disputes shall be settled on the basis of the sovereign equality of states and in accordance with the principle of free choice of means. Recourse to, or acceptance of, a settlement procedure freely agreed to by states with regard to existing or future disputes to which they are parties shall not be regarded as incompatible with sovereign equality.

Nothing in the foregoing paragraphs prejudices or derogates from the applicable provisions of the Charter, in particular those relating to the pacific settlement of international disputes.

APPENDIX 5

CHARTER OF THE UNITED NATIONS: MAIN RELEVANT PROVISIONS
Chapter I
PURPOSES AND PRINCIPLES
Article 1

The Purposes of the United Nations are:

1. To maintain international peace and security, and to that end: to take effective collective measures for the prevention and removal of threats to the peace, and for the suppression of acts of aggression or other breaches of the peace, and to bring about by peaceful means, and in conformity with the principles of justice and international law, adjustment or settlement of international disputes or situations which might lead to a breach of the peace;

2. To develop friendly relations among nations based on respect for the principle of equal rights and self-determination of peoples, and to take other appropriate measures to strengthen universal peace;

3. To achieve international cooperation in solving international problems of an economic, social, cultural, or humanitarian character, and in promoting and encouraging respect for human rights and for fundamental freedoms for all without distinction as to race, sex, language, or religion; and

4. To be a center for harmonizing the actions of nations in the attainment of these common ends.

Article 2

The Organization and its Members, in pursuit of the Purposes stated in *Article 1*, shall act in accordance with the following Principles.

1. The Organization is based on the principle of the sovereign equality of all its Members.

2. All Members, in order to ensure to all of them the rights and benefits resulting from membership, shall fulfill in good faith the obligations assumed by them in accordance with the present Charter.

3. All Members shall settle their international disputes by peaceful means in such a manner that international peace and security, and justice, are not endangered.

4. All Members shall refrain in their international relations from the threat or use of force against the territorial integrity or political independence of any state, or in any other manner, inconsistent with the Purposes of the United Nations.

5. All Members shall give the United Nations every assistance in any action it takes in accordance with the present Charter, and shall refrain from giving assistance to any state against which the United Nations is taking preventive or enforcement action.

6. The Organization shall ensure that states which are not Members of the United Nations act in accordance with these Principles so far as may be necessary for the maintenance of international peace and security.

7. Nothing contained in the present Charter shall authorize the United Nations to intervene in matters which are essentially within the domestic jurisdiction of any state or shall require the Members to submit such matters to settlement under the present Charter; but this principle shall not prejudice the application of enforcement measures under Chapter VII.

.   .   .   .   .

Chapter VII
ACTION WITH RESPECT TO THREATS TO THE PEACE, BREACHES OF THE PEACE, AND ACTS OF AGGRESSION
Article 39

The Security Council shall determine the existence of any threat to the peace, breach of the peace, or act of aggression and shall make recommendations, or decide what measures shall be taken in accordance with *Articles 41* and *42*, to maintain or restore international peace and security.

Article 40

In order to prevent an aggravation of the situation, the Security Council may, before making the recommendations or deciding upon the measures provided for in *Article 39*, call upon the parties concerned to comply with such provisional measures as it deems necessary or desirable. Such provisional measures shall be without prejudice to the rights, claims, or position of the parties concerned. The Security Council shall duly take account of failure to comply with such provisional measures.

Article 41

The Security Council may decide what measures not involving the use of armed force are to be employed to give effect to its decisions, and it may call upon the Members of the United Nations to apply such measures. These may include complete or partial interruption of economic relations and of rail, sea, air, postal, telegraphic, radio, and other means of communication, and the severance of diplomatic relations.

Article 42

Should the Security Council consider that measures provided for in *Article 41* would be inadequate or have proved to be inadequate, it may take such action by air, sea, or land forces as may be necessary to maintain or restore international peace and security. Such action may include demonstrations, blockade, and other operations by air, sea, or land forces of Members of the United Nations.

Article 43

1. All Members of the United Nations, in order to contribute to the maintenance of international peace and security, undertake to make available to the Security Council, on its call and in accordance with a special agreement or agreements, armed forces, assistance, and

facilities, including rights of passage, necessary for the purpose of maintaining international peace and security.

2. Such agreement or agreements shall govern the numbers and types of forces, their degree of readiness and general location, and the nature of the facilities and assistance to be provided.

3. The agreement or agreements shall be negotiated as soon as possible on the initiative of the Security Council. They shall be concluded between the Security Council and Members or between the Security Council and groups of Members and shall be subject to ratification by the signatory states in accordance with their respective constitutional processes.

Article 44

When the Security Council has decided to use force it shall, before calling upon a Member not represented on it to provide armed forces in fulfilment of the obligations assumed under *Article 43*, invite that Member, if the Member so desires, to participate in the decisions of the Security Council concerning the employment of contingents of that Member's armed forces.

Article 45

In order to enable the United Nations to take urgent military measures, Members shall hold immediately available national air-force contingents for combined international enforcement action. The strength and degree of readiness of these contingents and plans for their combined action shall be determined, within the limits laid down in the special agreement or agreements referred to in *Article 43*, by the Security Council with the assistance of the Military Staff Committee.

Article 46

Plans for the application of armed force shall be made by the Security Council with the assistance of the Military Staff Committee.

Article 47

1. There shall be established a Military Staff Committee to advise and assist the Security Council on all questions relating to the Security Council's military requirements for the maintenance of international peace and security, the employment and command of forces placed at its disposal, the regulation of armaments, and possible disarmament.

2. The Military Staff Committee shall consist of the Chiefs of Staff of the permanent members of the Security Council or their representatives. Any Member of the United Nations not permanently represented on the Committee shall be invited by the Committee to be associated with it when the efficient discharge of the Committee's responsibilities requires the participation of the Member in its work.

3. The Military Staff Committee shall be responsible under the Security Council for the strategic direction of any armed forces placed at the disposal of the Security Council. Questions relating to the command of such forces shall be worked out subsequently.

4. The Military Staff Committee, with the authorization of the Security Council and after consultation with appropriate regional agencies, may establish regional subcommittees.

Article 48

1. The action required to carry out the decisions of the Security Council for the maintenance of international peace and security shall be taken by all the Members of the United Nations or by some of them, as the Security Council may determine.

2. Such decisions shall be carried out by the Members of the United Nations directly and through their action in the appropriate international agencies of which they are members.

Article 49

The Members of the United Nations shall join in affording mutual assistance in carrying out the measures decided upon by the Security Council.

Article 50

If preventive or enforcement measures against any state are taken by the Security Council, any other state, whether a Member of the United Nations or not, which finds itself confronted with special economic problems arising from the carrying out of those measures shall have the right to consult the Security Council with regard to a solution of those problems.

Article 51

Nothing in the present Charter shall impair the inherent right of individual or collective self-defense if an armed attack occurs against a Member of the United Nations, until the Security Council has taken measures necessary to maintain international peace and security. Measures taken by Members in the exercise of this right of self-defense shall be immediately reported to the Security Council and shall not in any way affect the authority and responsibility of the Security Council under the present Charter to take at any time such action as it deems necessary in order to maintain or restore international peace and security.

APPENDIX 6

DEFINITION OF AGGRESSION

(Resolution adopted by the General Assembly on the report of the Sixth Committee
(A/9890) A/Res/3314 (XXIX), 14 December 1974)

The General Assembly,

Having considered the report of the Special Committee on the Question of Defining Aggression, established pursuant to its resolution 2330 (XXII) of 18 December 1967, covering the work of its seventh session held from 11 March to 12 April 1974, including the draft Definition of Aggression adopted by the Special Committee by consensus and recommended for adoption by the General Assembly, 1/

Deeply convinced that the adoption of the Definition of Aggression would contribute to the strengthening of international peace and security,

1. *Approves* the Definition of Aggression, the text of which is annexed to the present resolution;

2. *Expresses its appreciation* to the Special Committee on the Question of Defining Aggression for its work which resulted in the elaboration of the Definition of Aggression;

3. *Calls upon* all States to refrain from all acts of aggression and other uses of force contrary to the Charter of the United Nations and the Declaration on Principles of International Law concerning Friendly Relations and Co-operation among States in accordance with the Charter of the United Nations; 2/

4. *Calls the attention* of the Security Council to the Definition of Aggression, as set out below, and recommends that it should, as appropriate, taken account of that Definition as guidance in determining, in accordance with the Charter, the existence of an act of aggression.

DEFINITION OF AGGRESSION

The General Assembly,

Basing itself on the fact that one of the fundamental purposes of the United Nations is to maintain international peace and security and to take effective collective measures for the prevention and removal of threats to the peace, and for the suppression of acts of aggression or other breaches of the peace,

Recalling that the Security Council, in accordance with Article 39 of the Charter of the United Nations, shall determine the existence of any threat to the peace, breach of the peace or act of aggression and shall make recommendations, or decide what measures shall be taken in accordance with Articles 41 and 42, to maintain or restore international peace and security,

Recalling also the duty of States under the Charter to settle their international disputes by peaceful means in order not to endanger international peace, security and justice,

Bearing in mind that nothing in this Definition shall be interpreted as in any way affecting the scope of the provisions of the Charter with respect to the functions and powers of the organs of the United Nations,

Considering also that, since aggression is the most serious and dangerous form of the illegal use of force, being fraught, in the conditions created by the existence of all types of weapons of mass destruction, with the possible threat of a world conflict and all its catastrophic consequences, aggression should be defined at the present stage,

Reaffirming the duty of States not to use armed force to deprive peoples of their right to self-determination, freedom and independence, or to disrupt territorial integrity,

Reaffirming also that the territory of a State shall not be violated by being the object, even temporarily, of military occupation or of other measures of force taken by another State in contravention of the Charter, and that it shall not be the object of acquisition by another State resulting from such measures or the threat thereof,

Reaffirming also the provisions of the Declaration on Principles of International Law concerning Friendly Relations and Co-operation among States in accordance with the Charter of the United Nations,

Convinced that the adoption of a definition of aggression ought to have the effect of deterring a potential aggressor, would simplify the determination of acts of aggression and the implementation of measures to suppress them and would also facilitate the protection of the rights and lawful interests of, and the rendering of assistance to, the victim,

Believing that, although the question whether an act of aggression has been committed must be considered in the light of all the circumstances of each particular case, it is nevertheless desirable to formulate basic principles as guidance for such determination,

Adopts the following Definition of Aggression:*

* Explanatory notes on articles 3 and 5 are to be found in paragraph 20 of the report of the Special Committee on the Question of Defining Aggression (*Official Records of the General Assembly, Twenty-ninth Session, Supplement No. 19* (A/9619 and Corr. 1)). Statements on the Definition are contained in paragraphs 9 and 10 of the report of the Sixth Committee (A/9890).

Article 1

Aggression is the use of armed force by a State against the sovereignty, territorial integrity or political independence of another State, or in any other manner inconsistent with the Charter of the United Nations, as set out in this Definition.

Explanatory note: In this Definition the term "State":

(*a*) Is used without prejudice to questions of recognition or to whether a State is a Member of the United Nations;

(*b*) Includes the concept of a "group of States" where appropriate.

Article 2

The first use of armed force by a State in contravention of the Charter shall constitute *prima facie* evidence of an act of aggression although the Security Council may, in conformity with the Charter, conclude that a determination that an act of aggression has been committed

---

1/ *Official Records of the General Assembly, Twenty-ninth Session, Supplement No. 19* (A/9619 and Corr. 1).

2/ General Assembly resolution 2625 (XXV), annex.

would not be justified in the light of other relevant circumstances, including the fact that the acts concerned or their consequences are not of sufficient gravity.

Article 3

Any of the following acts, regardless of a declaration of war, shall, subject to and in accordance with the provisions of article 2, qualify as an act of aggression:

(a) The invasion or attack by the armed forces of a State of the territory of another State, or any military occupation, however temporary, resulting from such invasion or attack, or any annexation by the use of force of the territory of another State or part thereof;

(b) Bombardment by the armed forces of a State against the territory of another State or the use of any weapons by a State against the territory of another State;

(c) The blockade of the ports or coasts of a State by the armed forces of another State;

(d) An attack by the armed forces of a State on the land, sea or air forces, or marine and air fleets of another State;

(e) The use of armed forces of one State which are within the territory of another State with the agreement of the receiving State, in contravention of the conditions provided for in the agreement or any extension of their presence in such territory beyond the termination of the agreement;

(f) The action of a State in allowing its territory, which it has placed at the disposal of another State, to be used by that other State for perpetrating an act of aggression against a third State;

(g) The sending by or on behalf of a State of armed bands, groups, irregulars or mercenaries, which carry out acts of armed force against another State of such gravity as to amount to the acts listed above, or its substantial involvement therein.

Article 4

The acts enumerated above are not exhaustive and the Security Council may determine that other acts constitute aggression under the provisions of the Charter.

Article 5

1. No consideration of whatever nature, whether political, economic, military or otherwise, may serve as a justification for aggression.

2. A war of aggression is a crime against international peace. Aggression gives rise to international responsibility.

3. No territorial acquisition or special advantage resulting from aggression is or shall be recognized as lawful.

Article 6

Nothing in this Definition shall be construed as in any way enlarging or diminishing the scope of the Charter, including its provisions concerning cases in which the use of force is lawful.

Article 7

Nothing in this Definition, and in particular article 3, could in any way prejudice the right to self-determination, freedom and independence, as derived from the Charter, of peoples forcibly deprived of that right and referred to in the Declaration on Principles of International Law concerning Friendly Relations and Co-operation among States in accordance with the Charter of the United Nations, particularly peoples under colonial and racist régimes or other forms of alien domination; nor the right of these peoples to struggle to that end and to seek and receive support, in accordance with the principles of the Charter and in conformity with the above-mentioned Declaration.

Article 8

In their interpretation and application the above provisions are interrelated and each provision should be construed in the context of the other provisions.

List of Abbreviations

A.J.I.L.	*American Journal of International Law.*
Ann.	Annexes.
Bourquin (ed.), *Collective Security*	M. Bourquin (ed.), *Collective Security*, A Record of the 7th and 8th International Studies Conferences, Paris, 1934—London, 1935 (International Institute of Intellectual Cooperation) (1936).
Bowett, "Reprisals"	D. W. Bowett, "Reprisals Involving Recourse to Armed Force" (1972) 66 *A.J.I.L.* 1-36.
Bull. EC	*Bulletin of the European Communities Commission.*
B.Y.B. Int. L.	*British Yearbook of International Law.*
Col. J. of Trans. L. *Colum. J. of Trans. L.*	*Columbia Journal of Transnational Law.*
Eastern Q.	*Eastern Quarterly.*
Ferencz, "Defining Aggression"	B.B. Ferencz, "Defining Aggression: Where It Stands and Where It's Going" (1972) 66 *A.J.I.L.* 491-508.
Ferencz, "The Last Mile"	B.B. Ferencz, "Defining Aggression—The Last Mile" (1973) 12 *Col. J. of Trans. L.* 430-463.
Ferencz, *Defining International Aggression* (1975) *Defining Aggression* (1975)	B.B. Ferencz, *Defining International Aggression: The Search For World Peace*, 2 Vols., 1975.
G.A.Res.	General Assembly Resolution.
Georgetown L.J.	*Georgetown Law Journal.*
G.A.O.R.	General Assembly Official Records (followed by the number of the session in Roman capitals. Unless otherwise indicated plenary meetings are referred to.)
Hague Recueil	Academy of International Law (The Hague), *Recueil des Cours.*
Harv. Int. L.J.	*Harvard International Law Journal.*
Int. and Comp. L.Q.	*International and Comparative Law Quarterly.*
I.C.J. Reports	Reports of the International Court of Justice.
Int. Lawyer	*The International Lawyer.*
I.L.C.	International Law Commission.
Indian J. of Int. L.	*Indian Journal of International Law.*
J. of Int. Law and Politics	*Journal of International Law and Politics.*
J.W.T.L. *Jo.W.T.L.*	*Journal of World Trade Law.*
Kunz, "*Bellum Justum*"	J. L. Kunz, "*Bellum Justum* and *Bellum Legale*" (1951) 45 *A.J.I.L.* 528-534.
L.N.O.J.	*League of Nations Official Journal.*
Lauterpacht, "The Pact of Paris"	H. Lauterpacht, "The Pact of Paris and the Budapest Articles of Interpretation" (1935) 20 *Trans. Grotius Soc.* 178.
Nederlands T. Int. R.	*Nederlands Tijdschrift voor Internationaal Recht (Netherlands International Law Review).*
Österreichische Z. für öff. R. (N.F.)	*Österreichische Zeitschrift für öffentliches Recht.*

Podrea, "L'Agression"	G. A. Podrea, "L'Agression. Ses Critères Déterminatifs et sa Définition" (1952) 30 R.D.I. 367-383.
Osteuropa	Osteuropa Recht.
Pompe, Aggressive War	C. A. Pompe, Aggressive War an International Crime (1953).
R.D.I.	Revue de Droit International.
Röling, "On Aggression"	B. V. A. Röling, "On Aggression, on International Criminal Law, on International Criminal Jurisdiction-I" (1955) 2 Nederlands T. Int. R. 167-196.
San Diego L. Rev.	San Diego Law Review.
Scelle, "L'Agression et la Légitime Défense"	G. Scelle, "L'Agression et la Légitime Défense dans les Rapports Internationaux" (1936) 16 L'Esprit International 372-393.
S.C.Res.	Security Council Resolution.
Schwebel, Aggression	S. M. Schwebel, "Aggression, Intervention and Self-Defence in Modern International Law", Hague Recueil 1972 (II) 419-497.
Slonim, South West Africa	S. Slonim, South West Africa and the United Nations: An International Mandate in Dispute (1973).
Stone, Aggression	Julius Stone, Aggression and World Order (1958).
Stone, Legal Controls	Julius Stone, Legal Controls of International Conflict (1954).
Stone, "International Justice"	Julius Stone, "Approaches to the Notion of International Justice" in R. A. Falk and C. E. Black, The Future of the International Legal Order, vol. 1 (1969) c. viii.
St. John's L. R.	St. John's Law Review.
Supp.	Supplement.
1956 Sp. Com. Rep.	Report of the Special Committee on the Definition of Aggression, 1956. G.A.O.R. XII, Supp. No. 16 (A/3574. A/AC. 77, 1.13).
Trans. Grotius Soc.	Transactions of the Grotius Society.
T.I.A.S.	Treaties and Other International Acts Series (U.S.).
U.N.C.I.O. Docts. Uncio Docts.	Documents of the United Nations Conference on International Organisation, San Francisco, 1945, 16 vols.
U.N.T.S.	United Nations Treaty Series.
U.N. Monthly Chronicle	United Nations Monthly Chronicle.
U.N. Doc. (or Doc. alone)	United Nations Document.
Y.B.I.L.C.	Yearbook of the International Law Commission.

FOOTNOTES TO PROLOGUE

[1] M. Klafkowski(Poland)A/C.6/SR.1472, p.7; cf. M. Bojilov(Bulgaria)A/C.6/SR.1472, p.17; M. Rassolko(Byelorussia)A/C.6/SR.1480, p.15; M. Coles(Australia)A/C.6/SR.1478, p.9.

[2] M. Klafkowski(Poland)A/C.6/SR.1472, p.8; cf. Chairman Broms,A/C.6/SR.1471, p.5; Sette Camara(Brazil)A/C.6/SR.1474, p.15, Jaipal(India)A/C.6/SR.1478, p.15.

[3] A/C.6/SR.1480, p.9.

[4] M. Reshetnyak(Ukraine)A/C.6/SR.1477, p.3.

[5] Rossides(Cyprus)A/C.6/SR.1479, pp.5-6.

[6] M. Ustor(Hungary)A/C.6/SR.1478, p.14.

[7] M. Klafkowski(Poland)A/C.6/SR.1472, p.7; cf. M. Bojilov(Bulgaria)A/C.6/SR.1472, p.17.

[8] Iguchi(Japan)A/C.6/SR.1473, p.9.

[9] See the exchanges of M. Güney(Turkey)A/C.6/SR.1480, pp.25-26, M. Rossides(Cyprus)*id.* pp.27-29, M. Güney,A/C.6/SR.1481, p.20, M. Rossides, A/C.6/SR.1481, p.20, M. Eustathiades(Greece)A/C.6/SR.1482, p.20, M. Rossides, A/C.6/SR.1482, pp.20-21, M. Güney,A/C.6/SR.1482, pp.24-25.

[10] A/C.6/SR.1473, p.6.

[11] A/C.6/SR.1475, p.10. Cf. *infra* Chs. 9-10 and references therein.

[12] A/C.6/SR.1473, p.2. Cf. *infra* Ch. 3, and Ch. 9, Sections X-XII.

[13] A/C.6/SR.1477, p.6.

[14] See, e.g., Rassolko(Byelorussia)A/C.6/SR.1480, p.15.

[15] A/C.6/SR.1480, p.12.   [16] A/C.6/SR.1482, pp.15-16.

[17] A/C.6/SR.1474, p.16.   [18] A/C.6/SR.1478, p.15.

[19] The Sri Lanka representative at A/C.6/SR.1478, p.17; the Pakistani at A/C.6/SR.1477, p.3.

[20] A/C.6/SR. 1479, pp.2-3,5.   [21] A/C.6/SR.1475, p.8.

[22] A/C.6/SR.1475, p.10.   [23] A/C.6/SR.1479, p.13.

[24] Madagascar,A/C.6/SR.1474, p.13.   [25] A/C.6/SR.1477, p.4.

[26] A/C.6/SR.1480, p.13.   [27] A/AC.134/SR.113, pp.43-46.

[28] *Id.* at p.43.   [29] *Id.* at p.44.   [30] *Id.* pp.44-45.

[31] *Id.* p.44.   [32] *Id.* p.44.   [33] *Id.* p.44.

[34] *Id.* p.45.   [35] *Id.* p.46.

[36] A/C.6/SR.1480, p.22.

FOOTNOTES TO CHAPTER 1

[1] The San Francisco Committee, indeed, explicitly stated "the entire decision" should be left to the Security Council "as to what constitutes a threat to the peace, breach of the peace or act of aggression". (Uncio.Docts.,vol.12(1945)p.505.) The reason given was that techniques of modern warfare made exhaustive listings impracticable, and that inexhaustive listing would (a) tempt an aggressor to resort to unlisted modes; (b) tempt the Security Council to make premature findings on such modes of aggression as were listed in a definition.

[2] See Stone, *Legal Controls of International Conflict* (1954)274-75.

[3] Cf. Stone, *Aggression and World Order* (1958, reprinted Greenwood Press, Westport, Conn. 1976)45-46,153-161, and *infra* Chs. 3 and 9, Sections Xff. To neglect this inspirational role of a hoped-for authoritative definition of aggression,

is to gloss over both the incompetence of the General Assembly itself to determine the existence of an act of aggression, and the need to secure *voluntary* cooperation of members. Mr. Ferencz's account ("Defining Aggression: Where It Stands and Where It's Going" (1972)66 *A.J.I.L.*491,493) is perhaps subject to this comment.

[4] In this instance, at least, the Israel representative made clear his recognition of the vacuity of the assumed definitional base.

[5] S. M. Schwebel, *Aggression* at 426.

[6] Schwebel,*op.cit.*428.   [7] Schwebel,*op.cit.*420.

FOOTNOTES TO CHAPTER 2

[1] See Resolution 2330(XXII) of Dec.18,1967; G.A.O.R.(XII),Supp.No.16 (A/6716), p.84.

[2] See J. Stone, *Aggression and World Order*(1958)48.

[3] For an analysis and documentation, see Stone, *op.cit.*50-62. (The figures "19" are coincidental, not error.)

[4] For analysis and documentation of the 1956 Committee, see Stone, *op.cit.* 55-77.

[5] See the account in Stone, *op.cit.*64-66.

[6] For an official summary of the work of these Committees, see Doc. A/AC.134/1, Mch.24,1968, *Survey of Previous U.N. Action on the Question of Defining Aggression.*

[7] See U.N.Doc.A/AC.134/SR.100/1974. For valuable essays on the work of the Fourth Special Committee 1967-74, see S. M. Schwebel, *Aggression* at 419-497, with Biblio. on 496-97; B. B. Ferencz, "Defining Aggression" (1972)66 *A.J.I.L.*491; *id.,* "A Proposed Definition by . . . Consensus" (1973)2 *Int. & Comp.L.Q.*407; *id.,* "The Last Mile" 430; *id.,* 1 *Defining International Aggression* 19-76. The bulk of these last 2 volumes is a useful compilation of League of Nations and U.N. documents.

[8] Doc.A/AC.134/L.12.

[9] Doc.A/AC.134/L.16 and Add. 1 and 2.

[10] A/AC.134/L.17 and Add. 1 and 2.

[11] B. B. Ferencz, *op.cit.*(1972) at 496.

[12] B. B. Ferencz, *op.cit.*(1972) at 504-505.

[13] G.A.O.R.(XXVIII)No.19 (A/9019), p.3.

[14] *The First Contact Group,* appointed on May 2,1973, consisted of Colombia, France, Ghana, Romania, Syria, Turkey, U.S.S.R. and U.S. to deal with the general definition of aggression including the terms "sovereignty" and "territorial integrity" (Art.1). It held 4 meetings to May 25,1973.

The Second Contact Group, appointed on May 8,1973, consisted of Bulgaria, Cyprus, France, Ghana, Romania, Syria, U.S.S.R. and two States sponsoring the (Western) Six-Power Draft. Its agendum covered the list of acts of aggression, indirect force and self-determination. It thus hints very clearly at the "put and take", "now we see it, now we don't" nature of the interrelations, e.g. between the "armed bands" provision (Art.3(g)) and the self-determination saving clause (Art.5). This Group held 11 meetings up to May 25,1973.

The Third Contact Group, also appointed on May 8,1973, consisted of Czechoslovakia, Egypt, France, Guyana, Mexico, Spain (later replaced by Ecuador), Turkey, U.S.S.R., and two States from sponsors of the (Western) Six-Power Draft. Its assignment was questions of priority and aggressive intent (i.e. Article 2). It held 8 meetings up to May 25,1973.

The Fourth Contact Group, appointed on May 15,1973, consisted of Czechoslovakia, France, Indonesia, Iraq, Romania, Spain, Turkey, Uganda, U.S.S.R. and two member States from sponsors of the (Western) Six-Power draft. This Contact Group was instructed to consider the legal uses of force and the legal consequences of aggression. It held 4 meetings.

A Drafting Group appointed on 23 May,1973, consisted of Chairman Broms, Canada, Egypt, France, Ghana, Iran, Spain, U.S.S.R. and U.S.A., to prepare a draft preamble and work with Groups on other drafting questions, and to prepare the Consolidated Text and related documents. It held two meetings.

15 See A/AC.134/L.42, and Corr.1 and Add.1, A/AC.134/SR.106-109, and G.A.O.R.(XXVIII) No.19 (A/9019) p.4, and Appendix A on pp.15-21, where the Consolidated Text is reprinted. This last document may here be cited as "A/9019(1973)".

16 See G.A.O.R.(XXVIII)No.19(A/9019) Appendix B, pp.22-28. The Consolidated Text had been preceded by a "comparative chart" prepared by the Secretariat staff for the 1970 General Session, setting out the differences and similarities of the main three proposed drafts (Doc.A/AC.134/L.22,24 July,1970).

17 See above cited Doc.A/9019(1973), p.4.

18 The last Session of the Special Committee met in New York from March 11 to April 12,1974. At its 110th meeting, on March 11,1974, a Working Group chaired by M. Broms of Finland was again established. This Working Group held nine meetings between March 12 and April 11,1974, its 2nd meeting (on March 12) being devoted to a reading of the Consolidated Text referred to above. On that day it also established Contact Group I (of 1974), chaired by M. Lamptey (Ghana), to consider Articles 1 and 2 of the Consolidated Text. At its 4th meeting, Mch.15, the Working Group established Contact Group II, chaired by M. Sanders (Guyana), to examine Articles 3, 4 and 5 of the Consolidated Text. Its 5th meeting, on March 20,1974, set up Contact Group III, chaired by M. Wang (Canada), to consider Articles 6 and 7. The Contact Groups included two representatives of the sponsors of each of the three main drafts; and each Contact Group worked through small negotiating teams which met regularly. At the 6th meeting of the Working Group, on April 1, an open-ended fourth Contact Group was established to prepare a new consolidated text. This new text was ready on April 11,1974, and was then referred by the Working Group to a Drafting Group, chaired by M. Broms, for final review. By the 112th meeting, on April 12, 1974, the Special Committee had before it the draft definition which was adopted by consensus of the Special Committee and later of the General Assembly. See the Special Committee Report, 11 March-12 April,1974, G.A.O.R.(XXIX),Supp. No.19(A/9619), pp.4-5.

It is unfortunate, in a scholarly sense, that the documents do not reveal in more detail the techniques and methods of persuasion used by the Contact Groups and their negotiating items. A number of aspects, including various pressures and non-consultation of troublesome viewpoints, were mentioned by representatives in their explanatory statements and will later be referred to in the appropriate context. An "oral history" from observers of the procedures would help. It is a pity that the most promising source of such an oral history, Mr. B. B. Ferencz's two volumes, discussed *infra* Ch.9, Section IX, include so little about the critical period. His article, "A Proposed Definition of Aggression: By Compromise and Consensus" (1973)22 *Int.& Comp.L.Q.*407, at 409-410, has some interesting comments but little on the methods of persuasion and negotiation used by the Negotiating Group.

19 See *infra passim,* esp. Chs.9 and 10.

20 See *infra* Ch.10, Section VI.

21 Cf. "Range of Crimes for a Feasible International Jurisdiction" in *Toward a Feasible International Criminal Court* (J. Stone and R. K. Woetzel, eds.)(1970) 315,326-330.

22 *Id.* at 327ff. For private juristic work in the meanwhile concerning a criminal court, see Draft Convention on International Crimes (1972) esp. Article 3(3)(a) in *The Establishment of an International Criminal Court* (1973). (Issued by the Foundation for an International Criminal Court, work of the (First) (Wingspread) Conference, Sept.1971, and the Second (Bellagio) Conference, Sept.1972). Article 3(3)(a) follows exactly the description of the aggressive war-

making count of the Charter of the International Military Tribunal at Nuremberg. The Foundation's final text, after the Fourth Conference at San Juan, Puerto Rico in January 1973, repeats the same provision in Article II(4)(a). These texts, of course, presuppose rather than contribute to an adequate definition of aggression.

23 On the even less sanguine mood of the participants in the preceding year, see B. B. Ferencz, op.cit.(1972)496,504-505.

24 See G.A.O.R.(XXVIII),Supp.No.19(A/9619), p.9.

FOOTNOTES TO CHAPTER 3

1 G.A.O.R.(VII)Ann.Item 54,Doc.A/2211.

2 See Sixth Committee Report, G.A.O.R.(IX)Ann.Item 51, pp.10ff.

3 A/Res.3314(XXIX) p.1.

4 On which see Stone, *Aggression and World Order* (1958)66-68,72-76, and *infra* Ch. 9, Sections Xff.

5 G.A.O.R.(IX)Supp.11, pp.5ff.

6 G.A.O.R.(IX)Supp.11, pp.8ff. Cf. in the Sixth Committee G.A.O.R.(IX) Ann.Item 51, p.11, where Preamble, para.4, and Art.55 were vouched in support.

7 *Id.* p.9.

8 G.A.O.R.(IX)Supp.11(A/2638) (Report of the Special Committee on the Question of Defining Aggression, 24 August-21 September, 1953), p.9, paras.76,77.

9 See the comment on the 1953 Committee's Report, G.A.O.R.(IX)Ann.Item 51, p.2. *Cf.* C. A. Pompe, *Aggressive War* 50-51,97, who dubs these proposals as "inflation" of the notion of aggression. "Dilution" might be a better term for the purpose of his argument that by this extension "the military element—the nucleus of the concept of aggression—has been completely lost". We may well agree with this, and yet add (see Stone, *op.cit.*(1958) at 69ff.,104ff.) that the core concept, as generally understood, has itself proved unworkable without the reference to the concomitant non-military components.

10 And see *infra* Ch.5.

11 1953 Committee Report, G.A.O.R.(IX)Ann.Item 51, pp. 9-10.

12 *Id.*10.

13 *Id.*11.

14 See *supra* Ch.1 and *infra* Ch.7.

15 The negative outcome in 1953 did not, of course, turn on this point. Probably more decisive was the consideration, well stated by M. Röling (Netherlands), that while the influence of any definition adopted by the Assembly upon the action of competent organs might be great if most States including the Permanent Members concurred in it, adoption by only a narrow majority, or without such concurrence, would have little value. See G.A.O.R.(IX)Ann.Item 51, p.10.

16 It is unnecessary to discuss separately in the text the legal standing of the asterisked footnote at the end of the Preamble to the Consensus Definition, indicating that certain "explanatory notes" on Articles 3 and 5 are to be found in the Special Committee's report (A/9619,para.20), and also other statements on the Definition in the Sixth Committee's Report (A/9890,paras.9 and 10). Clearly such "notes" or "statements" cannot have any greater or other legal effects than the resolution itself to certain parts of which they seek to give some shade of authoritative interpretation. They seem little different in this regard from the Explanatory Note concerning the meaning of the term "State" actually attached to Article 1 of the Definition. It seems better therefore to regard them, as I have done, as an attempt at authentic interpretation.

For the Peruvian argument (M. de Soto) that references in footnotes have the same legal value as inclusion in the body of the definition, see A/C.6/SR.1503, p.5.

[17] I.C.J. Reports, 1971, at p.58. See J. Stone, *Of Law and Nations* (1974)335; S. Slonim, *South-West Africa* 332-346.

[18] A/C.6/SR.1475, pp.7-8.

[19] A/C.6/SR.1472,Oct.9,1974, p.4.

[20] See respectively A/C.6/SR.1477, p.6, and A/C.6/SR.1480, p.22.

[21] German D.R., A/C.6/SR.1476, p.7.

[21a] They are also explicit in the Soviet Union's offered variant of the present Article 6; see G.A.O.R.(XXVII)Supp.No.19,Doc.A/8719, at pp.20-21. It was that (*inter alia*) "[a]cts undertaken in accordance with the Charter of the United Nations to maintain or restore peace, or in the exercise of the inherent right of individual or collective self-defence", and enforcement actions under Article 53 of the Charter, do not constitute aggression.

[22] A/C.6/SR.1477, p.4.   [23] A/C.6/SR.1474, p.5.

[24] A/C.6/SR.1473, p.4.   [25] M. Coles,A/C.6/SR.1478, p.10.

[26] A/C.6/SR.1482, p.16.

[27] A/C.6/SR.1480, p.22. Mr. Ferencz (*Defining International Aggression,* vol.2) succinctly observes as to the Security Council's legal authority, that Paragraphs 2 and 4 of the Preamble and Articles 2 and 4, as well as Article 6, of the Definition "left the subject the way they found it" (p.46, and see p.21).

[28] A/C.6/SR.1480, p.23.   [29] A/C.6/SR.1474, p.6.

[30] A/C.6/SR.1480, p.5.   [31] A/Res.3314(XXIX).

[32] A/C.6/SR.1472, p.10.

[33] *Id.*, p.11. Cf. M. Aleman,Ecuador,A/C.6/SR.1476, p.2.

[34] A/C.6/SR.1480, pp.19-20.

[35] E/CN.4/L.610(1962).

[36] A/C.6/SR.1480, p.20. He cited the definitive study on this matter of G. Arangio-Ruiz, *The Normative Role of the General Assembly of the United Nations and the Declaration of Principles of Friendly Relations* in *Hague Recueil*,1972-III, 421-742; *cf.* S. M. Schwebel, *Aggression, passim.*

[37] Guatemala,A/C.6/SR.1479, p.8.

[38] F.R. of Germany,A/C.6/SR.1478, p.7.

[39] See *infra.*   [40] A/C.6/SR.1483, p.10.

[41] It should also (he thought) have been in the emphatic form of a "declaration".(A/C.6/SR.1504, p.8.)

[42] A/C.6/SR.1483, p.5.   [43] A/C.6/SR.1480, p.7.

[44] A/C.6/SR.1478, p.12. So cf. M. Omar(Libya,A/C.6/SR.1477, p.5), who was sure that an act of aggression committed by one of the Permanent Members or its allies would not be recognised as such by the Security Council.

[45] A/C.6/SR.1472, pp.14-15.

[46] He also argued that such a power to abstain would be equivalent to a "power to absolve the aggressor". But this is either a mistranslation or it is simply wrong. Art.39 certainly provides for a power to absolve *in the sense of a negative determination.*

[47] A/C.6/SR.1483, p.10.   [48] A/C.6/SR.1480, p.4.

[49] A/C.6/SR.1479, p.9.   [50] Pakistan,A/C.6/SR.1477, p.2.

[51] A/C.6/SR.1474, p.8.   [52] A/C.6/SR.1473, p.3.

[53] A/C.6/SR.1474, p.10.

[54] See Stone, *Legal Controls* 243-246.

[55] A/C.6/SR.1472, p.11. Cf. probably the somewhat less clear remarks of M. Verosta(Austria,A/C.6/SR.1472, pp.13-14).

[56] A/C.6/SR.1476, pp.4-5.   [57] A/C.6/SR.1478, p.6.

[58] A/C.6/SR.1478, p.6.

[59] See Stone, *Legal Controls* 191-223,243-264.

[60] A/C.6/SR.1478, p.6.

[61] See Stone, *Aggression and World Order* (1958), esp. pp.154-57, and *supra* Ch.1. See also, for a perceptive analysis of the aggression debate against the background of the Uniting for Peace Resolutions and the Advisory Opinion Concerning

Certain Expenses of the U.N., I.C.J. Reports, 1962, p.151, S. M. Schwebel,*op.cit.* 473-76.

62 A/C.6/SR.1477, p.12.

63 See, e.g., M. Yasseen(Iraq,A/C.6/SR.1478, p.6) and M. Hassouna(Egypt, A/C.6/SR.1483, p.10).

64 S. M. Schwebel, *Aggression* 474-76,esp.476.

65 B. B. Ferencz,*op.cit.*(1972)496, points out that at one point of apparent deadlock in Working Group discussions, 20 non-aligned States threatened to stand pat on the Thirteen Power Draft.

66 A/C.6/SR.1479, p.14.

67 Resol.3236,U.N.Doc.A/5194.

68 See J. Stone, "Palestinian Resolution: Zenith or Nadir of the General Assembly" (1975) 1 *J. of Int. Law and Politics* 1-18,esp.6-7.

69 *Op.cit.*475-76.   70 *Op.cit.*475.

71 I.C.J. Reports, 1962, p.151.   72 U.N.Doc.A/8719, p.20.

73 S. M. Schwebel,*op.cit.*444-45.   74 *Id.* p.445.

FOOTNOTES TO CHAPTER 4

1 See Stone, *Aggression and World Order* (1958)137-146.

2 See Stone,*op.cit.* Ch.8,s.II. For earlier attempts to distinguish the definitional problems, see Q. Wright, "The Concept of Aggression..." (1935)29*A.J.I.L.*373, 376, who proposed a single definition for preventive, deterrent, and remedial as well as punitive purposes. But see *id.*389, where in the related context of international claims arising from responsibility for hostilities, he fully recognises the discrepant desiderata.

Differentiation of definitions for other purposes also was sometimes proposed in the League period, e.g., as between sanctions procedure and non-aggression treaties (Lord Lytton in M. Bourquin(ed.), *Collective Security,* 1936, at 329; C. A. W. Manning, *id.*338); or as between various regions (C. K. Webster, *id.*335).

3 See Stone,*op.cit.*(1958)Ch.3,s.III, also Ch.8,s.II, p.138. An "act of aggression" was to include certain acts, the character of which might otherwise be disputable, such as (for example) a threat to resort thereto, the preparation for the employment of armed forces, and the fomentation of civil strife in another State. It was *not* to include an act of collective self-defence, or an act done pursuant to decision or recommendation of a competent organ of the United Nations.

4 The term also appears, of course, in Arts.1(1) and 53.

5 See Stone,*op.cit.*(1958)134-35, and Ch.5,s.I. It has nevertheless often been assumed since that time that, by applying a definition, as compared with applying the notion undefined, action could be expedited. Even if a feasible and acceptable definition were found, however, this is doubtful. See *op.cit.*Ch.4,s.IV, and pp.154ff.

6 Report of the Special Committee on the Definition of Aggression, 1956, G.A.O.R.(XII)Supp.No.16(A/3574.A/AC.77,1.13).

7 *Cf.* C. A. W. Manning in Bourquin(ed.), *Collective Security* 338: "If you are going to compare war to murder, you should surely take account of the state of mind." Logically this need not be so, of course; liability might be absolute as in an expanding area of minor offences in municipal systems, e.g. contraventions of pure food and drug laws. This, however, could scarcely provide the correct analogy.

Cf. in general on the point in the text, G. G. Fitzmaurice, "The Definition of Aggression" repr.(1952)1 *Int.and Comp.L.Q.*137,140, objecting that the Soviet draft "leaves entirely out of account the subjective elements necessarily involved...." The question what are these "subjective" elements is of course a different one.

8 For the introduction of the term in the U.N. debates, see M. Spiropoulos in A/CN.4/44, pp.64ff. G. Scelle, *"L'Agression et la Légitime Défense..."* (1936) 16 *L'Esprit International* 372, at 379, squarely took the view that only the

factum of the use of force is material. So cf. as to the treacherous nature of contemporary expressions or other evidence of opinions and attitudes once hostilities have broken out, Q. Wright, "The Concept of Aggression . . ." (1935)29*A.J.I.L.* at 380.

M. Spiropoulos (and others) are not always clear as to whether they mean by "intention" mere deliberate commission of the *factum*, or a *mens rea* additional to the *factum*, e.g. that the act shall not have been done in legitimate defence. At moments he even suggested that there is a right of self-defence against a mere "aggressive intention". See G.A.O.R.(V) Sixth Committee, 279th Meeting, para. 10, 281st Meeting, para.13.

9 There is, indeed, an even deeper paradox whose relation to our subject cannot be explored here. This is the general assumption, in Sir J. Fischer Williams' words, that "aggression implies a moral stigma" (see his *Chapters on Current International Law and the League of Nations* (1934)119). Yet in psychological and even social psychological terms "aggressiveness" may be morally neutral. Lack of it may, indeed, be a defect, and even symptomatic (in extreme cases) of a mental deficiency. It may refer to ability to initiate what the international diplomat might well call "legitimate self-defence". J. L. Kunz observed (*"Bellum Justum . . ."*(1951)45*A.J.I.L.*528,530) that during the period when the *recta intentio* of the monarch directed to the supposedly known "just causes" of war was determinative of guilt, the just war doctrine remained perhaps necessarily "wholly ethical". In theory, under this doctrine, the exaction of terms unrelated to the "just cause" would render the war "unjust" *ab initio* through the *pax injusta*.

10 Cf. G. G. Fitzmaurice's view, *op.et.loc.cit.supra* n.7.

11 See J. W. C. Turner(ed.), *Kenny's Outlines of Criminal Law* (16 ed.,1952) s.50, pp.63ff.; R. Cross and P. A. Jones, *An Introduction to Criminal Law* (1953) 70.

12 See, e.g., the Consolidated Text of the Contact Groups and Drafting Group, App.A,G.A.O.R.(XXVIII)Supp.No.19(A/9019) Report of Special Committee, 25th April-30 May, 1973, pp.15-18,esp. p.16.

13 Doc.A/AC.134/L.17, and Add.1 and 2, repr. in G.A.O.R.(XXVIII)Supp. No.19(A/9019) pp.11-12.

13a See, e.g., B. B. Ferencz, *Defining International Aggression*(1975), vol.2, 33.

14 *Aggression* at 419,464.

15 *Id.*pp.466-470. Cf. Stone, *Aggression and World Order* (1958)69-72.

16 See Schwebel's convincing summation, *op.cit.*464-468, of the reasons why, even apart from provocation and self-defence, the priority principle cannot be automatically relied on. He instances *inter alia* the obscurations of the true course of events, as in Korea in 1950, the problems of the "chain of events" as with the Berlin Blockade, and anticipatory self-defence as in the 1967 Six Day War, and various frontier incidents.

Even where military measures are at their most overt, the inference from them may be concealed *ex post facto*. Though the Soviet and Nazi forces entered Poland simultaneously and in obvious concert in 1941, the Communist Government of Poland, for example, holds that while the Nazi entry was aggression, the Soviet entry was not, but was merely a preventive measure against total Nazi occupation. Professor Schwebel agrees with the present view, citing Stone, *op.cit.*(1958)71, that it is often not possible to confine a determination of aggression "to the occurrence of a precisely defined act, at a particular moment, in insulation from the broader context of the relations of the States concerned." And see, as to anticipatory self-defence and "preemptive strike" *infra* Section V.

17 See, e.g., G.A.O.R.(XXV)Supp.No.19,A/8019(1970), and Ferencz, "Defining Aggression" (1972)491,500.

18 With the insertion of the word "sovereignty", before "territorial integrity". This does not affect the point in the text. For the proposals to insert see A/C.6/SR. 1442, p.13(Yugoslavia); and p.15(Indonesia). Other States found the addition

superfluous, the reference to sovereignty being in any case implicit. Thus, M. Kolesnik for the Soviet Union thought that in context violation of sovereignty meant armed encroachment on the *territorial integrity* or political independence of a State. (See A/C.6/SR.1472, p.3, A/8019, p.57.) And see 2 Ferencz,*op.cit.* (1975)27.

[19] See Stone, *Of Law and Nations* (1974)1-38.

[20] D. P. O'Connell, "International Law and Contemporary Naval Operations" (1970)44 *B.Y.B.of Int.L.9* at 25. *Cf.* a similar early view in Stone, *Aggression and World Order* (1958)99-101, and *cf. id., Of Law and Nations* (1974)8-10. The Soviet Union itself acknowledged in the Fourth Committee debates that the automatic use of the priority principle, which it had advocated since 1933, could require States "to wait to be destroyed before they could legally respond to an attack." (As reported in B. B. Ferencz, "A Proposed Definition . . . by Consensus" (1973)22 *Int.& Comp.L.Q.*407, at 423-24.)

[21] Cf. M. S. McDougal and F. Feliciano, *Law and Minimum World Public Order* (1961)240.

[22] S. M. Schwebel, *Aggression* 467. At an early phase of the Fourth Committee's aggression debates, the U.S.S.R. proposed that "the use of nuclear, bacteriological or chemical weapons or any other weapons of mass destruction" be listed as an aggressive act (see G.A.O.R.(XXIV)Supp.No.20,Doc.A/7620 at 5 (A/AC.134,L.12 and Corr.)). This refers to a *"first* use", and would not thus forbid nuclear retaliation against nuclear first strike. It leaves quite unclear, however, whether the first use of nuclear weapons would be thus stigmatised, even if this use was in response to a prior use by the opponent of some other stigmatised act—e.g. invasion or attack by conventional armed forces. This would be very vital in relation to the possible use of tactical (as distinct from strategic) nuclear weapons in the defence of Europe. Indeed, the proposal is perhaps best understood as aimed against the attempts of Nato to compensate, by tactical nuclear weapons, for the Soviet superiority in conventional weapons in Europe.

[23] Tom Farer, "Law and War", in C. E. Black and R. A. Falk (eds.), *The Future of the International Legal Order,* Vol.III: *Conflict Management* (1971) 30-42,63-64. The quoted passages below are from pp.36-37.

[24] *Id.*39.

[25] *Op.cit.*36. And see the longer discussion of this basic aspect in Stone,*op.cit. supra* n.19,1-38 *passim.* And see *infra* Ch.9,Section XI.

[26] A/C.6/SR.1472, p.3. Cf. M. Bojilov of Bulgaria, *id.* p.16.

[27] A/C.6/SR.1472, p.13.   [28] A/C.6/SR.1477, p.7

[29] A/C.6/SR.1473, p.7. *Cf.* M. Orrego of Chile (A/C.6/SR.1474, p.7) who asserted flatly that under Article 2 the element of intent fell within "other relevant circumstances".

[30] A/C.6/SR.1483, p.3.   [31] A/C.6/SR.1482, p.19.
[32] A/C.6/SR.1482, p.18.   [33] A/C.6/SR.1473, p.3.
[34] A/C.6/SR.1479, p.4.   [35] A/C.6/SR.1479, p.11.
[36] A/C.6/SR.1479, p.14.   [37] A/C.6/SR.1474, p.8.
[38] A/C.6/SR.1483, p.10.   [39] A/C.6/SR.1472, p.6.
[40] A/C.6/SR.1479, p.6.   [41] A/C.6/SR.1477, p.11.
[42] A/C.6/SR.1478, p.16.   [43] A/C.6/SR.1477, p.13.
[44] A/C.6/SR.1474, p.18.

[45] Stone, *Legal Controls* 234-237, Stone, *Aggression and World Order* (1958) 94-103, Stone, *Of Law and Nations* (1974)1-38.

[46] A/C.6/SR.1478, p.4.

[47] G.A.O.R.(XXVIII)Supp.No.19(A/9019), p.9. The Consolidated Text, *id.* Appendix A, pp.15-18, wholly omitted it, but the comments thereto, *id.* 18-21, referred to the present wording of Article 5 (1) as a proposal by "one member", which the group had not decided where to place.

[48] See Stone, *Aggression and World Order* (1958)34-35. *Cf.* the briefer proposals of Mexico *et al.,* to the 1956 Special Committee (A/AC.77/L.10, repr. *id.*

203,205), and M. Yepes to the International Law Commission in 1951 (G.A.O.R. (VI)Supp.No.9(A/1858), p.9, A/CN.4/L.7, repr. Stone,*op.cit.*(1958)207).

[49] The Consolidated Text did not make this distinction in its Art.6, which left a blank where the words "a crime" now are. The non-aligned 13-Power Draft (para.9) proposed "crimes against international peace, giving rise to international responsibility". The Soviet draft (para.5) did distinguish "political and material responsibility of States" and "criminal responsibility" of individuals. But no draft made the distinction between "war of aggression" and "aggression".

[50] See, e.g., M. Bojilov of Bulgaria (A/C.6/SR.1472, p.17) rejecting the idea that, in Article 5, "aggression" as distinct from "war of aggression" gave rise only to some indeterminate form of responsibility.

[51] See Stone, *Legal Controls* 244; Stone, *Of Law and Nations* (1974)1-38.

[52] And see the immediately following paragraph.

FOOTNOTES TO CHAPTER 5

[1] S.C.Res.212, 22 U.N.S.C.O.R.1382nd meeting, pp.8-9.

[2] A. Lall, *The U.N. and the Middle East Crisis 1967* (1968)260-63; and see Stone, *No Peace-No War in the Middle East* (1970)32-38.

[3] Cf. the similar conclusions of W. V. O'Brien, "International Law and the Outbreak of War in the Middle East" (1967)11 *Orbis* 692,722-23; Henri Rolin, Sénat-Annales Parlementaires, No.58, *Séances de Jeudi 8 Juin 1967*, Brussels, pp.1535-36; N. Feinberg, *The Arab-Israel Conflict in International Law* . . . (1970) 114ff.; *id., On an Arab Jurist's Approach to Zionism and the State of Israel* (1971)96-98; T. M. Franck, "Who Killed Article 2(4)?" (1970)64 *A.J.I.L.*809,821; Y. Dinstein, "The Legal Issues of 'Para-War' and Peace in the Middle East" (1970)44 *St.John's L.R.*466,469-470; Stone, *The Middle East Under Cease-Fire* (1967)7-9; and (as to the Arab "armed attack"), Quincy Wright, "Legal Aspects of the Middle East Situation" (1968)33 *Law and Contemporary Problems* 5,27. Cf. for a balanced discussion of the bearing of Article 51 of the Charter on anticipatory self-defence, M. S. McDougal, *Law and Minimum World Public Order* (1961)233-38. On anticipatory self-defence see *supra* Ch.4, Section V, and Ch.9, Section XI.

[4] Cf. A. Lall, *op.cit.* 247, quoting Foreign Minister Eban in the Security Council, Nov.13,1967, S/PV 1375, p.28.

[5] And see *supra* Ch.6, Section II.   [6] Cf. *ibid.*

[7] Cf. B. B. Ferencz, *Defining International Aggression* (1975)23-24,45, as to the "redundancy" of both Preamble, para.7, and Article 5(3).

[8] The latter saving is no doubt intended to prevent attempts to reopen pre-Charter territorial settlements.

[9] G.A.O.R.(XXVIII)Supp.No.19(A/9019), p.10, repr. from A/AC.134/L.16 and Add.1 and 2. For good measure the Draft also included "military occupation, however temporary" and "forcible annexation" of territory *simpliciter,* as "acts of aggression", parallel to invasion or armed attack, in Paragraph 5(b).

[10] Romania and other States failed in a bid to delete the words "in contravention of the Charter" (see Document A/AC.134/WG 5/R.1), for only this clause made the text acceptable to other States. The United States, for example, pointed out that the military occupation of West Berlin rested on Article 107 of the Charter. Egypt's proposal that this could be covered by a footnote referring merely to Article 107, made it quite apparent that her preoccupation was with territories occupied by Israel, a matter of political warfare rather than the definition of aggression. See also 2 B. B. Ferencz,*op.cit.*(1975)23-24.

[11] G.A.O.R.(XXIX)Supp.No.19(A/9619),para.20.

[12] Canada, A/C.6/SR.1473, p.9. Cf. M.Jemiyo(Nigeria,A/C.6/SR.1474, p.2), M. Rakotoson(Madagascar,A/C.6/SR.1474, p.12) and (surprisingly) M. Jaipal(India, A/C.6/SR.1478, p.16) on Article 5(3).

Cf. on the point that the Definition adds no new guidance to the status of occupation or annexation, when not resulting from *injuria*, B. B. Ferencz,*op.cit.* (1975)34-35.

13 A/C.6/SR.1476, p.8.   14 A/C.6/SR.1483, p.4.
15 Democ.Yemen,A/C.6/SR.1479, p.10.
16 A/C.6/SR.1483, pp.10-12.   17 A/C.6/SR.1477, p.2.
18 A/C.6/SR.1478, p.16.   19 A/C.6/SR.1475, p.4.
20 Cf. the previous year, Paragraph 5 of the Palestine Resolution 3236 (XXIX).

FOOTNOTES TO CHAPTER 6

1 The earliest formal attempt is the Declaration on Inadmissibility of Intervention . . . 1965 (Resol.2131(XX)), which forbids "the use of force to deprive peoples of their national identity" as "a violation of their inalienable rights and of the principle of non-intervention" (Art.3) and declared that "all States shall respect the right of self-determination and independence of peoples and nations . . ." (Art.6). Consequently, all States should contribute to the complete elimination of racial discrimination and colonialism.

1a U.N.Doc.A/5746, p.42.

1b K. J. Skubiszewski, in M. Sørensen (ed.), *Manual of International Law* (1968)771. And see the comments by the present writer in (1969)63*A.J.I.L.*157, at 162.

1c It could, indeed, be expected that some colonial peoples would not want to seek self-government, as became recently clear in the France-Comoros conflict. In a French-sponsored referendum in the archipelago generally on Dec.22,1974, an overwhelming majority in the islands generally favoured independence, but two-thirds of the people of Mayotte voted against. France, in these circumstances, arranged for a referendum in Mayotte alone on February 8, 1976, and in due course this showed that 99.4% of the people there wished it to remain an integral part of France.

It is an ironic paradox that this scrupulous regard for the Mayotte people's wishes led, after the admission of Comoros to the U.N., to charges in the Security Council against France of interfering with the internal affairs of Comoros, and even of aggression. See the summary of debate in 13 *U.N. Monthly Chronicle* (March 1976,No.3) pp.5-14. And see other aspects of this case discussed *infra* Ch.9, Section VI.

1d See R. Rosenstock, "The Declaration of Principles of International Law Concerning Friendly Relations: A Survey" (1971)65*A.J.I.L.*713, at 732.

2 C. H. Alexandrowicz, "Reversion to Sovereignty . . ." (1967)45 *International Affairs* 465-480.

3 For the text of Paragraph 7 see Appendix.

3a G.A.Res.2625(XXV). For a commentary on the Declaration see R. Rosenstock,*op.cit.supra* n.ld, at 713-735.

3b G.A.Res.2734(XXV).   4 *Id*.para.18.

5 A/C.6/SR.1477, pp.9-10. This, in substance, was also the position of M. Bessou (France). Article 7 was "alien to the text" since not concerned with "aggression as defined in Article 1, i.e. between sovereign States." The text did *not* guarantee that States supporting self-determination struggles could not be guilty of aggression. See G.A.O.R.(XXIX)Supp.No.19(A/9619), p.22, repr. Ferencz,*op.cit.*1975, p.73. So also U.S. delegate Rosenstock, A/AC.6/SR.108, p.12; S.R.1480, p.24 (also in G.A.O.R.(XXIX)Supp.No.19(A/9619), p.24).

6 A/C.6/SR.1478, pp.13-14.

7 Soviet *bloc* spokesmen would no doubt justify the continued suppression of Baltic, Ukrainian and Jewish nationalist aspirations as "ordinary police action" in M. Ustor's term. The bland assumption that they can have it both ways is not

surprising if we recall that as to the ten States with which the Soviet Union made treaties containing a definition of aggression, she sooner or later committed acts against most of them clearly falling within the agreed definition. See S. Schwebel, *op.cit.*443, and cf. *infra* Ch.8, Sections IV-V.

8 A/C.6/SR.1478, p.3.   9 Spain, A/C.6/SR.1472, p.15.

10 B. B. Ferencz, "Defining Aggression" (1972)491,498.

11 A/C.6/SR.1475, pp.10-11.

12 A/C.6/SR.1473, p.6.

13 The Note would, if it meant what M. Lee said it meant, be similarly complaisant in relation to a use of armed force by the People's Republic of China against Taiwan, etc. But that is not so striking, since a similar result could be reached in that case by the more cogent meaning, relating to disputed boundaries, offered by New Zealand delegate Quentin Baxter.

It has perhaps a bearing on Explanatory Note (a) in this context (but one of uncertain import) that the Soviet delegate had pressed for the omission from Article 1 of the reference to "sovereignty" as distinct from "territorial integrity" and "political independence" and still insisted, even after its inclusion (M. Kolesnik, A/C.6/SR.1472, p.3), that Article 1 should be read as not adding anything to those two other notions.

14 A/AC.134/SR.111, pp.10-11.

15 A number of the varied drafts of the armed bands clause in U.N. Committee proceedings are collected in Stone, *Aggression and World Order* (1958) 201ff., including notably by Paraguay(202), Iran and Panama(203), Mexico(203), Dominican Republic,*et al.*(204-5), Bolivia(205), U.N.Sect. (quoted on p.205, from G.A.O.R.(IX)Supp.No.9(A/2693),c.iii, p.2), M. Yepes(207), M. Hsu(207), M. Cordova(207), China(208), Mr. Robert H. Jackson(216).

16 Collected in Report of the Special Committee ... G.A.O.R.(XXVIII)No. 19(A/9019), pp.7-28.

17 A/AC.134/L.16 and Add.1 & 2, repr. in A/9019, p.10. It would also have provided a substantial immunity for the territory of the aggressor State, as well as the insurgent or terrorist attackers. For the immediately succeeding Paragraph 8 roundly opens with the declaration that "the territory of a State is inviolable". This could easily have been argued (out of the context of its own paragraph) to constrain the measures which Paragraph 7 permits the victim State for safeguarding its existence, to those it could take *within its own territory*. As long ago as the *Caroline Case* the contrary rule has been widely acknowledged as international law.

Though Secretary of State Webster's classical formulation there in his letter of April 24, 1841 was in terms of "a necessity of self-defence, instant, overwhelming, and leaving no choice of means, and no moment for deliberation", the actual circumstances (smuggling of arms to rebels in the victim State) smacked more of the activities of armed bands operating across a frontier. The case established the victim State's right to cross the frontier in order to abate the activity where the above necessity arises. See 30 *British and Foreign State Papers* 193; J. B. Moore, 2 *Digest of International Law* (1906)409-414, esp.412. For a searching discussion, see R. Y. Jennings, "The Caroline and McLeod Cases" (1938)32 *A.J.I.L.*82-99, esp.88-92. That Author well observes on the paradox that "this *locus classicus* of the law of self-defence is a case which turned essentially *on the facts*" (92).

18 A/AC.134/L.17 and Add.1 & 2.

19 The phrase is from B. B. Ferencz, *Defining International Aggression* (1975) vol.2, p.38. Cf. more fully, Stone, *Aggression and World Order* (1958) 34-36,37-38,211-12.

20 Cf. B. B. Ferencz,*op.cit.*(1975)40; and see *id.* 41 as to issues of "proportionality".

21 A/C.6/SR.1479, p.6.   22 A/C.6/SR.1474, p.10.

23 A/C.6/SR.1473, p.8.

24 *Op.cit.* 1972, at 499,502. The shock of the antinomy later provoked Mr.

Ferencz (2 *Defining International Aggression* (1975)48-49) to his sharpest censure of the Consensus Definition. This was that its provision on this matter was such that the opposing parties might interpret it to their own advantage should the need arise. In the words of one of the delegates: "The definition had reached a sufficient level of abstraction to be acceptable." And cf. *id.* 22-23, on the "vexing dilemma" of "how to reaffirm the right to self-determination and still restrain the use of force."

25 *Op.cit.* at 471,472.

26 Grammatically, it is not clear what "to that end" refers to—presumably "the right of self-determination, etc."

27 So also, *mutatis mutandis,* with Article 3(e) stigmatising the use of one State's armed forces which are by agreement within the territory of another State, contrary to agreed conditions, or beyond the agreed term. This provision, which raised surprisingly little discussion, was proposed in the Six Power Draft (Para. IV.B(2). See A/AC.134/L.17 and Add.1 and 2, repr. A/9019(1973), pp.11-12.

Article 3(e) has other problems of its own. Since, unlike the original Six Power proposal (A/8019,Doc.18 at 58,60), Article 3(e) states the offence without any qualification as to the purpose or intent of transgression, the default stigmatised might be quite trivial and harmless. Cf. Ferencz, 1 *Defining International Aggression* 38. Presumably, of course, the Security Council could, under Article 2 of the Definition, refrain from stigmatising such trivia as aggression.

Article 3(e) situations which are not trivial might be thought to be caught in any case by Article 3(a), as a kind of retroactively constructive "invasion". *Sed quaere.*

28 A/C.6/SR.1477, p.6.

29 A/C.6/SR.1472, p.10. Cf. the Kenyan representative, A/C.6/SR.1474, p.9.

30 The Politis Report of 1933 (Conf.D./CG./108; Conf.D./C.P./C.R.S./9) observed that where the territorial State is not able to prevent or abate the activities of armed bands, it would not be regarded as responsible under international law. This, of course, is not necessarily inconsistent with the victim State's authority to take its own measures to abate the wrong.

31 See generally D. W. Bowett, "Reprisals Involving Recourse to Armed Force" (1972)66 *A.J.I.L.*1, and esp. 20.

The analysis in R. A. Falk, "The Beirut Raid and the International Law of Retaliation" (1969)63 *A.J.I.L.*415, esp. 434-38, is centrally affected by a certain haziness as to whether the incident in question there was to be judged according to peace-time reprisal rules, as Y. Z. Blum ("The Beirut Raid and the International Double Standard" (1970)64 *A.J.I.L.*73) points out (at 78). Other issues concern Professor Falk's disregard of authorities (including Lauterpacht-Oppenheim, Kelsen and the International Law Commission) asserting the international law responsibility of the host State in respect of operations of armed bands from its territory (see citations in Blum,*op.cit.*79-87); the question of fact whether Israel's prior warnings and requests to Lebanon sufficed (citations *id.* 87-89); and as to the application of the proportionality requirement (*id.* 89-90).

32 See the summaries of the above positions in G.A.O.R.(XXV),Supp.No.19, A/8019,Doc.18, pp.47-48, paras.131,133,132, and 134 respectively. And see on the Soviet position, A/AC.134/SR.97, p.4, and the British and American positions, A/AC.6/SR.63, p.5 (Mr. Schwebel) and A/AC.6/SR.74, p.8 (Mr. Steel), and 2 Ferencz, *Defining International Aggression* (1975)46.

The Soviet objection to any reference to proportionality was that it would place an unreasonable burden on the victim for the benefit of the aggressor (U.N. Doc.A/AC.134/SR.97, p.4).

33 Docs. of the Prep. Comm. for the Disarmament Conference, League of Nations, Series III, p.101. There is to be distinguished, of course, the requirement of proportionality in reprisals against illegality not involving use of armed force. China, for example, once proposed "that the employment of *comparable* methods in reprisal against an attack of unarmed force . . . is . . . lawful." (Working Paper

A/AC.66/L.7/rev.2, reproduced in the Report of the First Special Committee on the Question of Defining Aggression, A/AC.66/L.11.) Cf. also Secretary of State Webster's stipulation of proportionality for self-defence in *The Caroline* correspondence cited *supra* n.17.

[34] See A/9019(1973), pp.9-10.

[35] See G.A.O.R.(XXVII)Supp.No.19,A/8719, p.23. For general discussions on proportionality see D. W. Bowett, *Self-Defence in International Law* (1958)260; *id.*, "Reprisals..." (1973)66 *A.J.I.L.*1,11-12; M. S. McDougal and P. F. Feliciano, *Law and Minimum World Public Order* (1967) 217-260.

[36] Italy, A/C.6/SR.1472, p.11.   [37] A/C.6/SR.1476, p.6.

[38] A/C.6/SR.1473, p.5.   [39] A/C.6/SR.1477, pp.9-10.

[40] M. Rosenne of Israel (A/C.6/SR.1480, p.19) also thought that "Article 7 ... had little to do with a definition of aggression...".

[41] A/C.6/SR.1473, p.9. Cf. Canadian representative Wang, A/AC.134/SR. 113, p.45.

[42] Federal Republic of Germany, A/C.6/SR.1478, p.8.

[43] A/C.6/SR.1478, p.8. Cf. generally also M. Elias(Spain)A/C.6/SR.1472, p.15; M. Mahmud(Pakistan)A/C.6/SR.1477, p.3; M. Bracklo(F.R.G.)A/C.6/SR. 1478, p.8.

[44] A/C.6/SR.1480, p.24.   [45] A/C.6/SR.1480, p.19.

[46] Democ.Yemen,A/C.6/SR.1479, p.10.

[47] A/C.6/SR.1474, p.5.

[48] A/C.6/SR.1479, pp.11-13. Cf. M. Rakotoson(Madagascar)A/C.6/SR.1474, p.13.

[49] Cf., equally peremptorily, M. Njenga of Kenya (A/C.6/SR.1474, p.9).

[50] A/C.6/SR.1475, p.9. He invoked G.A.Resolutions 2649(XXV) and 3070 (XVIII).

[51] A/C.6/SR.1475, p.9.   [52] A/C.6/SR.1480, p.7.

[53] A/C.6/SR.1504, p.5.   [54] A/C.6/SR.1480, p.9.

[55] Ivory Coast, A/C.6/SR.1481, p.19.

[56] Other States claiming that Article 7 allowed use of "any means at their disposal" in self-determination struggles included China (M. An Chih-Yuan)A/C. 6/SR.1475, p.6; G.D.R. (M. Goerner)A/C.6/SR.1476, p.7; Congo (M. Ikouebe) A/C.6/SR.1478, p.12; Yugoslavia (M. Petric)A/C.6/SR.1479, p.4; Burundi (M. Nuyungeko)A/C.6/SR.1482, p.4; Tunisia (M. Gana)A/C.6/SR.1482, p.9; Venezuela (M. Alvarez Pifano)A/C.6/SR.1483, p.6; Egypt (M. Hassouna)A/C.6/SR. 1483, p.11.

[57] A/C.6/SR.1480, p.15.   [58] A/C.6/SR.1472, pp.3-4.

[58a] See 13 *U.N. Monthly Chronicle* (March 1976,No.3) at 5,64.

[58b] See on the rather calculatingly ambiguous scheme even of the Declaration on the issue whether armed force, as well as moral and political force, may be used to support a people's right of self-determination, R. Rosenstock,*op.cit.supra* n. 1d, at 732.

[59] A/C.6/S.R.1476, p.7.   [60] A/C.6/SR.1479, p.10.

[61] A/C.6/SR.1479, p.4.   [62] Of Cuba, A/C.6/SR.1479, p.14.

[63] A/C.6/SR.1477, p.1.   [64] A/C.6/SR.1477, p.5.

[65] Bangla Desh, A/C.6/SR.1478, p.3.

[66] Spain, A/C.6/SR.1472, p.15. In fact, M. Elias had proposed these words, "territorial integrity" for Article 7 itself, where they might have meant what he now asserted. They were inserted instead in the 6th preambular paragraph where they might apply only to States and not peoples. (See A/AC.134/SR.112, p.19.) These positions of Spain invite exploration in terms of that State's view of its Sahara dispute with Morocco.

[67] Democratic Yemen, A/C.6/SR.1479, pp.9,10.

[68] A/C.6/SR.1478, p.12.   [69] A/C.6/SR.1476, pp.9-10.

[70] A/C.6/SR.1475, p.6.

71 See, e.g. M. Kolesnik, U.S.S.R., A/C.6/SR.1472, p.3.
72 A/C.6/SR.1478, pp.13-14.   73 A/C.6/SR.1477, pp.2-3.
74 M. Mahmud, A/C.6/SR.1477, p.3.   75 A/C.6/SR.1477, p.12.
76 A/C.6/SR.1483, pp.10-11. The trampling of international law by this so-called "historical reality" expressed by manipulated majorities is already apparent in Security Council decisions. See, e.g., as to armed bands operating from Lebanon, L. Gross, "Voting in the Security Council and the P.L.O." (1976)70 *A.J.I.L.*470, 480-82.

FOOTNOTES TO CHAPTER 7

1 Cf. the discussion in S. M. Schwebel, *Aggression* 456-57.
2 Para.IV/B(6),(7),(8).
3 U.S. Representative J. L. Hargrove, 25 Mch.1969, quoted Schwebel,*op.cit.* 458.
4 And see the careful analysis on this point in Schwebel,*op.cit.*458-461, discussing also the Inter-American Treaty of Reciprocal Assistance, Sept.2,1947, T.I.A.S. p.1838, Art.6, and the views of the International Law Commission and the Secretary-General's Report of 1952.
5 Para.2.
6 See Stone, *Aggression and World Order* (1958)34-35,201-202, where the citations are noted.
7 League of Nations, Records of Conference for the Reduction . . . of Armaments, Series D,vol.5, p.11, repr. U.N.Sec.-Gen.'s Report, G.A.O.R.(VII)Ann. Agenda Item 54, pp.34ff. In the 1972 debates, Romania submitted a rather similar text to the Informal Negotiating Group. See G.A.O.R.(XXVII),Supp.No.19.
8 On which see the perhaps disputable interpretation in L. Schultz, "*Der Sowjetische Begriff der Aggression*" (1956) 2 *Osteuropa Recht* 274,282.
9 See the Bolivian view in the Sixth Committee, G.A.O.R.(VI), Sixth Committee, 293rd Meeting, para.30. And see the fuller discussion in text and notes in Stone,*op.cit.* (1958) at 58-60,66-68.
10 Resol.688(VII)Supp.20(A/2361), p.63.
11 See *supra* Ch.3, Section II, and Stone,*op.cit.* (1958) at 66ff.,72ff.
12 See Stone,*op.cit.* (1958)58ff., and 1956 Sp.Com.Rep.8.
13 It will be recalled that in earlier debates (see, e.g., as to the Kellogg-Briand Pact, Stone,*op.cit.* (1958)32, and as to the U.S. Proposal to the London Conference on the Nuremberg Charter, *id.* p.134) such a reaction of the victim of "aggression" was assumed to be permitted only in the context, however, of an armed aggression.
14 *1956 Sp.Com.Rep.*8 Cf. H. Thirring, "*Was is Aggression?*" (1952-53)5 *Österreichische Z. für öff. R.(N.F.)*238-240.
15 A view squarely taken in 1954 by Professor Röling ("On Aggression . . ." (1955)2 *Nederlands T.Int.R.*167,171).
16 The more revealing in the then Soviet draft, which substituted the term "attack" for "aggression" as to armed aggression, but preserved "aggression" for "economic" and "ideological" aggression. The Chinese representative pointed out that "armed attack" was the most obvious form of aggression, which stood least in need of definition (A/AC.77/SR.3, p.5), while subversion was far more dangerous. A definition limited to armed attack would, therefore, only create an illusion of definition. (A/AC.77/SR.14, pp.4-5, and *1956 Sp.Com.Rep.*25.) The Soviet focus on her expanded territorial interests led her to insist that the branding of armed attack was the principal task, and that disagreement about other forms of aggression, though their function was desirable, should not be allowed to impede it. See A/AC.77/SR.3, pp.10ff. And see Stone, *Aggression* . . . (1958)68, and Ch.6 *passim*.
17 It is important to add this observation to the conclusion of Mr. Pompe (*Aggressive War* 57) that "the mixture of military and non-military criteria makes

the problem of the determination of the aggressor in case of provoked aggression equal to that of the finding of a *Zirkelquadratur* to which Bismarck reduced the whole problem of aggression in a war". (The Bismarck reference is to 6 Lepsius *et al.* (eds.), *Die grosse Politik der europäischen Kabinette* 1871-1914.)

[18] On the distinctions in Soviet usage between "indirect", "ideological" and "economic" aggression, "indirect aggression" denoting generally "subversion", while "economic aggression" is also censured as a form of "direct aggression", and "ideological aggression" as an "aggression *sui generis*", see L. Schultz,*op.cit.supra* n.8, at 284. This writer observes that Soviet lawyers characterised the Marshall Plan as "economic aggression".

[19] See *supra* n.16, as to the Soviet use of "attack" in lieu of armed aggression.

[20] Cf., conversely, R. P. Gonzalez Muñoz, *Doctrina Grau* (1948)23ff., distinguishing the *values attacked* from the *method* or *motive* of attack.

[21] Insofar as Professor Wright ("The Prevention of Aggression" (1956)50 *A.J.I.L.*514,526-27; "Intervention, 1956" (1957)51*A.J.I.L.*257,268ff.) implies the contrary, we disagree with his view for reasons set out in Stone,*op.cit.*(1958)68, n.150. And cf. R. P. Gonzalez Muñoz,*op.cit.*67.

[22] See Stone,*op.cit.*(1958)Ch.9. Professor Röling in 1954 ("On Aggression ..." (1955)2 *Nederlands T.Int.R.*167,170) moved only part way to clarity when he observed: "[E]conomic measures have tremendous effects .... But we are not discussing the means to protect the political independence of a State, we are discussing the possibilities of eliminating war .... Other evils, other remedies; other vices, other dooms." (*Op.cit.*171.)

[23] See also on the active or passive capacity for aggression of non-State entities, the Iraqi draft (A/AC.77/L.8/rev.) and the Netherlands and Chinese comments in A/AC.77/SR.13, p.15, and SR.14, pp.4-5, and *1956 Sp.Com.Rep.*22, 23.

[24] This is constantly overlooked by the writers. See, e.g., R. Théry, *La Notion d'Agression* (1937)226-27, who insisted that without use of animus, we cannot identify either "aggression" or the "aggressor", that the very notion of the "criminality" of aggression is dependent on the possibility of finding "*l'intention agressive*". He thought, however (227), that no corresponding intent was necessary for "legitimate self-defence".

[25] Stone, *Aggression* ... (1958)19-21, and also *id.* Ch.7 as to the very limited area in which there is a core of determinacy in the aggression notion.

[26] See *infra* Ch.8, Section III, and more fully Stone,*op.cit.* (1958)118-133.

[27] Cf. the rather oversimple formulation in A. Denning, *The Road to Justice* (1955)4. And see H. Isay, *Rechtsnorm und Entscheidung* (1929). And cf. J. Stone, *The Province and Function of Law* (1950)368.

[28] This would follow from Art.4, insofar as the words "enumerated above" in that Article were taken to refer to all of Arts.1-3; and there seems no reason why they should not be so read. If those two words were limited, however, to the list of acts in Art.3 alone, this additional point would, of course, fall; for then Art.4 would not override the import of Arts.1 and 2, which name only aggression by "armed force". But, then, of course, as indicated in the text, the same authority of the Security Council to stigmatise "indirect" or "economic" aggression would still exist under the Charter.

[29] A/C.6/SR.1472, p.2. Cf. M. Broms,A/C.6/SR.1471, p.4; and see *infra* at n.32.

[30] A/C.6/SR.1474, p.3.

[31] M. Booh(Cameroon,A/C.6/SR.1483, p.5), Singh(Nepal,A/C.6/SR.1483, p.7) and Nicol(Sierra Leone,A/C.6/SR.1483, p.7), M'Bodj(Senegal,A/C.6/SR. 1480, p.6) spoke to similar effect.

[32] A/C.6/SR.1474, pp.8-9. Cf. M. Orrego(Chile)A/C.6/SR.1474, p.6.

[33] A/C.6/SR.1477, p.13.   [34] A/C.6/SR.1478, pp.11-12.

[35] A/C.6/SR.1478, p.16.   [36] A/C.6/SR.1480, p.11.

[37] A/C.6/SR.1480, p.11.   [38] A/C.6/SR.1477, p.5.

39 A/C.6/SR.1476, p.9.   40 A/C.6/SR.1471, p.4.

41 A/C.6/SR.1471, p.4. Cf. B. B. Ferencz, 2 *Defining International Aggression* (1975) pp.41-42, who, however, recognises wistfully the exclusive Security Council discretion both to inculpate and exculpate, not to speak of the inexorability of Great Power vetoes.

42 Cf. also, for this kind of argument, M. Kolesnik(U.S.S.R.),A/C.6/SR.1472, p.3.

43 A/C.6/SR.1472, pp.5-6.

44 M. Petric,Yugoslavia,A/C.6/SR.1479, p.5.

45 A/C.6/SR.1479, p.14.   46 A/C.6/SR.1476, p.4.

47 A/C.6/SR.1478, p.13.

48 This curious provision appears to be a vestige, rather mangled during verbal haggling, of the much clearer provision of the Soviet draft: "Armed aggression shall be an international crime against peace entailing the political and material responsibility of States and the criminal responsibility of the persons guilty of this crime" (Paragraph 5). The Thirteen Power Draft was also clearer, though different again: "Armed aggression . . . and the acts enumerated above, shall constitute crimes against international peace, giving rise to international responsibility". This latter text follows closely the Declaration . . . on . . . Friendly Relations . . . (Resol.2625(XXV),para.2 following Preamble).

B. B. Ferencz (2 *Defining International Aggression* (1975)43-44) makes the interesting (and somewhat incensed) criticism that the reference to "war" of aggression, rather than mere aggression, may have been designed to block criminal prosecution of guilty national leaders on the technical ground that the particular hostilities were not legally "war". On this kind of evasion under the League and the efforts to prevent it by the U.N. Charter, see Stone, *Legal Controls* 300,311ff. And see *ibid*. Mr. Ferencz's sharp criticism of the clause concerning "international responsibility".

50 A/C.6/SR.1474, pp.11-12.

51 On the legal relation of the Definition to the Charter, see *supra*, Ch.3.

52 M. Tabio(Cuba),A/C.6/SR.1479, p.14.

53 See text at n.43.

54 See, e.g., M. Rydbeck(Sweden),A/C.6/SR.1472, p.5; M. Wehry(Netherlands),A/C.6/SR.1475, pp.4-5; Van Brusselen(Belgium),A/C.6/SR.1476, p.4. And it was mostly China and various Third World States which condemned its omission. See, e.g., M.An Chih-yuan(China), A/C.6/SR.1475, p.6; M. Tabio (Cuba),A/C.6/SR.1479, p.14; M. Perez de Cuellar(Peru),A/C.6/SR.1474, p.3; M. Orrego(Chile),*id.*, p.6, M. Njenga(Kenya),*id.*, pp.8-9; M. Omar(Libya),A/C.6/SR.1477, p.5; M. Ikouebe(Congo),A/C.6/SR.1478, pp.11-12; M. Jaipal(India),*id.*, p.16; M. M'Bodj(Senegal),A/C.6/SR.1480, p.6; M. Bamba(Upper-Volta),*id.*, p.11; M. Bararwerekana(Ruanda),*ibid.*; M. Booh(Cameroon),A/C.6/SR.1483, p.5; M. Singh(Nepal),*id.*, p.7; M. Nicol(Sierra Leone),*ibid.*

55 See Stone,*op.cit.* (1958)59,67.

56 See B. B. Ferencz, "Defining Aggression" (1972) at 500, esp. statement quoted in n.65.

57 See A/C.6/SR.1475, p.6.

58 As late as 1972, the year before the Consolidated Draft, the word was still bracketed, as not an agreed part of the draft for discussion. See G.A.O.R.(XXVII) Supp.No.19(A/8719), p.14.

59 A/C.6/SR.1442, p.13; Doc.A/9411,Doc.25, p.7.

60 A/C.6/SR.1442, p.15.

61 Doc.A/8019,Doc.18, p.56. The Declaration on Principles of International Law Concerning Friendly Relations and Cooperation Among States characteristically straddles these contraries by asserting that the principle of sovereign equality includes the elements "territorial integrity" and "political independence", implying possibly that it is broader than these. See G.A.Res.2625(XXV)(1970); see also 6 U.N.C.I.O.,Doc.457.

[62] Cf. the Yugoslav claim that the additional reference to sovereignty is "particularly important to smaller countries". A/C.6/SR.1442, p.13.

[63] G.A.O.R.(IX) Supp.11(A/2638) 8ff. M. Adamiyat(Iran) also saw the essence of "economic aggression" as "coercive economic and political measures taken against a State . . . designed to impede the exercise of its *sovereignty* over its natural resources or its efforts towards economic development." (See *id.*, p.9.) And see *infra* Ch.8, Section VIII, as to the bearing of G.A.Resol.1803,(XVII) of 1962, concerning each State's "sovereignty" over its natural resources.

[64] A/C.6/SR.1472, p.3. Clearly the debate was only very remotely related to Hans Kelsen's thesis ("Sovereignty and International Law" (1960)48 *Georgetown L.J.*627-640) that "sovereignty in the sense of supreme authority can be nothing else but the quality of a legal order" (628), and the problem of "the sovereignty of the State" is only the problem of the sovereignty of the national legal order in its relation to the international legal order.

FOOTNOTES TO CHAPTER 8

[1] See Stone, *Aggression and World Order* (1958)78-79,esp.85.

[2] See Stone,*op.cit.supra* n.1, at 119-133.

[3] *Theory and Reality in International Law* (transl.Corbett,1968) at 303.

[4] *Y.B.I.L.C.*1951,vol.2, pp.67-68.

[5] This is especially clear when we address the question of criminal punishment of individuals for instigating aggression. An illustration is perhaps the Soviet attitude to the International Military Tribunal at Nuremberg. General Nikitchenko, Vice-President, Soviet Supreme Council, observed in his well-known statement in 1945 that "(t)he fact that Nazi leaders are criminals has already been established. The task of (Nuremberg) Tribunal is only to determine the measure of guilt . . ." and to inflict punishment. See Intern.Conf. on Military Trials (1945) 303 *Dept.of State Publ.* 3080, quoted Ferencz, "Defining Aggression . . ." (1972)491,493.

[6] It is not to question the sincerity of the scholars concerned to observe on the views so sternly restrictive of resort to force taken by a number of French publicists in the 'thirties. P. Bastid, indeed, in M. A. F. Frangulis, 3 *Dictionnaire Diplomatique* (*sine anno,* after 1933, but before World War II), *sub voce* "*Aggression*", drew attention to the relation of this view to the protection of the *status quo.* And he interpreted opposition to the Soviet-French *rapprochement* in the London Convention of 3 July, 1933, to demands for the redistribution of territories. Cf. Y. de la Brière,*ibid.* So in 1936, W. Komarnicki (in Bourquin(ed.), *Collective Security* 314-16) pressed for a rigorous "territorial" criterion in which aggression = invasion. On *de facto* control of territory in this context see the view of N. Politis discussed by M. Amado in I.L.C. A/CN.4/L.6, p.4, in relation to the Chaco, Leticia and Vilna Affairs.

[7] See Stone,*op.cit.*(1958),Ch.2,s.I.

[8] Cf. on the tactical changes in Soviet attitudes, L. Schultz,*op.cit.supra* Ch.7, n.1d, at 275 and *passim.* Even at the 1933 stage the favourable propaganda effect of the Soviet initiative upon dependent nations was obviously present to Litvinov's mind, when he called the Soviet draft a "Charter of Freedom of Nations". See Litvinov's 1935 publication on Soviet foreign policy, in Russian, cited by Schultz at 275. Soviet reaction to rejection of the draft was to charge "reactionary" circles in the West with encouraging aggression against the Soviet Union, and even with responsibility for World War II. (See the article by G. Tunkin, on the definition of aggression, cited Schultz,*op.cit.*277.) So cf. the reversal of Soviet attitudes on the veto. See Documents Relating to . . . Application of the Principles of the Covenant, *L.N.O.J.*Sp.Supp.No.154,Nov.1936.

[9] *1956 Sp.Com.Rep.,*Ann.II, pp.30-31. It was first introduced in the precise form in 1954, and has of course a long prior history. See Stone,*op.cit.* (1958)34-36, 46-53,201-202.

[10] While leaving the Soviet Union with the apparent lack of inhibition which enabled her to absorb some States to whom she was bound by non-aggression treaties embodying the Soviet draft definition of 1933. See Stone,*op.cit.* (1958)Chs. 2,n.5, and 4,nn.31-32.

Stephen Schwebel (*Aggression* 443) has done well to recall in the context of the current consensual definition the historical reality that the Soviet Union in 1933 concluded conventions reproducing the Politis definition of aggression, with Afghanistan, Czechoslovakia, Estonia, Finland, Iran, Latvia, Poland, Romania, Turkey and Yugoslavia. Of these ten States, five were in due course invaded by the Soviet Union; portions of four were incorporated into the Soviet Union; two were annexed *in toto* by the Soviet Union; one was subject to overstay of Soviet troops. Only one of the ten, he concludes, was spared from one or other of the types of aggression listed by the Soviet definition.

[11] M. François (U.N.Doc.A/CN.4/5 SR.93,para.19) has pointed to the loopholes in the landing of forces provision in the Soviet definition for manipulation by the aggressor of the consent of the victim Government.

It seems clear that there was a movement of Soviet troops into Hungarian territory in November 1956 to participate in the displacement of the Nagy Government of Hungary. Yet, under the Soviet definition of aggression (Clause 1(d)) aggression includes the landing or leading of forces inside the boundaries of another State without the permission of the government of the latter. Did the Nagy Government invite the Soviet forces in to destroy itself? The Soviet argument that her entry was in reaction to "indirect" aggression of other States against Hungary seems also inconsistent with her view on the question whether armed reaction to indirect aggression should be permitted. And see Stone,*op.cit.* (1958)67,nn.145,147.

[12] "Surely," G. G. Fitzmaurice (repr. "The Definition of Aggression" (1952) 1 *Int.and Comp.L.Q.*137,140) has observed, "it depends on the nature of the treaty whether a violation of it justifies another State in going to war or not."

[13] This is an important point to be added to the very proper comments of G. G. Fitzmaurice,*op.cit.*140 on this part of the Soviet proposal.

[14] See *supra* Ch.5.

[15] *Cf.* M. Vennemoe(Norway) in A/AC.77/SR.6, p.9: "Lack of support for the idea of defining aggression did not mean, as some people seemed to suggest, a lack of appreciation of the seriousness of the crime of aggression."

[16] Cf. the U.S. representative (J. Maktos) in the Sixth Committee on Jan. 10, 1952; and cf. his article, "*La Question de la Définition de l'Agression*" (1952) 30 *R.D.I.* 5,8: "*Je crois que cette définition est en réalité un piège destiné à servir des desseins autres que les desseins de ceux qui l'accepteraient de bonne foi. Il pourrait s'agir d'un instrument de propagande destiné à porter de fausses accusations qui causeraient d'irreparables dommages.*"

Cf., even if overstated, a main point of J. Poniatowski, "War and Aggression in Western Eyes" (1953)6 *Eastern Q.*27-32,esp.29-30, as to the relation of Soviet "peace campaigns" of the late '40s and early '50s, to the time needed for military strengthening of the Soviet Union and China, to the greater susceptibility of democratic electorates to pacifist appeals, and to the special strategic advantages of surprise in warfare with the new weapons.

[17] On the bearing (if any) of "logical" "codifying", or "pragmatic" "case-by-case" traditions, see H. Lauterpacht, "The Pact of Paris ..." (1935)20 *Trans. Grotius Soc.*178,190; C. Jordan, in Bourquin(ed.), *Collective Security* 301; and for an opposed view, C. A. W. Manning,*id.*338. The Soviet Union and the satellite countries are, of course, neither of these latter, though most of them have codes. Some code States, e.g. Norway, Germany, and the Netherlands, have usually opposed definition; and at least one State (Hungary), whose system is analogous to a common law one, has steadily supported definition. Of course, even common lawyers accept as inevitable the careful statutory definition of numerous municipal law offences. Even if the correlation were stronger, however, this would not discount the factors discussed in the text, nor prove the feasibility of definition.

¹⁸ Soviet political thinking has long taken it as self-evident that aggression is characteristic of the West, as deeply rooted in capitalism. Orthodox communist doctrine also denies that any Soviet war could be a war of aggression, aggressive attitudes contradicting the structure of the socialist society. At the same time "wars of liberation" from "capitalist exploitation", being always just, cannot be "aggressive". See e.g. Stalin, *Geschichte der KPdSU(B), Kurzer Lehrgang* (1952) 210; and E. Korowin, *Die Grundprinzipien der Aussenpolitik der UDSSR.* (1953) 38, quoted in L. Schultz,*op.cit.supra* n.8. Cf. the formulation of W. Komarnicki, *De la Définition de l'Agresseur* (1949)75 *Hague Recueil* 5-103, at 6, who treats the matter in more traditional terms.

So cf. in United Nations proceedings, M. Vyshinsky's account on Nov.3, 1950 (G.A.O.R.(V) First Committee, 380th Meeting, p.223) of the official Leninist doctrine: "In the case of a liberating war, only a traitor could shirk his duty by pleading the horrors of war . . . . Only a person devoid of all culture could fail to understand the Leninist concept of the just war; . . .".

At the 383rd Meeting (p.242), after chastising those "who seemed unable to grasp the most elementary ideas", he pointed out that "the U.S.S.R. did believe that a war against capitalist slavery, indeed a war against any form of slavery, was a just war. But how could it be said that that opened the door to Soviet Union intervention in a struggle against the capitalist regime in any country?" The present writer has long been among those unable to grasp the "elementary idea" that this kind of exposé *dispels* all fear that the Soviet concept of aggression "made intervention in support of a rising against any capitalist regime possible".

Cf. the statement by M. Morozov, G.A.O.R.(V) Sixth Committee, 234th Meeting, p.157; and of M. Krylov cited in B. Meissner, *Die Sowjetunion, die baltischen Staaten und das Völkerrecht* (1956)166ff., and the observations of Professor Röling in A/AC.77/SR.3, p.8.

¹⁹ In the rather different power setting of 1924, the Soviet position had been dramatically different from what came to be regarded as her traditional position. In commenting on the League-sponsored Draft Treaty of Mutual Assistance (see *L.N.O.J.*,Sp.Supp.No.26, p.138), the Soviet Government denied "the possibility of determining in the case of every international conflict which State is the aggressor and which is the victim . . . ."

"[I]n the present international situation", it continued, "it is impossible in most cases to say which party is the aggressor. Neither the entry into foreign territory nor the scale of war preparations can be regarded as satisfactory criteria. Hostilities generally break out after a series of mutual aggressive acts of the most varied character." It went on to point out that in its view the Japanese attack on the Russian Fleet at Port Arthur in 1904, though "aggression" from a technical point of view, was "politically speaking" a reaction to Czarist aggressive policy.

So cf. Mr. Maktos' explanation (G.A.O.R.(VI) Sixth Committee, 286th Meeting, para.36) of the U.S.'s reversal of its former support of definition, on grounds that its hope of international cooperation had been disappointed: "The United States delegation had not obeyed a whim; it had adopted a position which was diametrically opposed to the stand it had taken in 1945 and had done so in view of international developments." See Stone,*op.cit* (1958)132-33.

²⁰ See Stone,*op.cit.* (1958)18,U.N.Doc.A/AC.77/SR.13, p.7.

²¹ Austria, A/C.6/SR.1472, p.11.

²² A/C.6/SR.1478, p.6.

²³ A/C.6/SR.1475, p.6.

²⁴ A/C.6/SR.1475, pp.10-11.

²⁵ Paraguay, A/C.6/SR.1483, p.3.

²⁶ See *supra* Ch.2, Section III; cf. Ch.6, Section III.

²⁷ A/C.6/SR.1483, p.3.

²⁸ They were not content with the view of some that Article 3(d) would not reach attacks on individual vessels fishing illegally, but only massive attacks on fleets (see A/C.6/SR.1442, p.19). The main citations for the States asserting the

freedom of action of coastal States are in the A/C.6/SR. series as follows: SR. 1473, p.8 (Mr. Lee, Canada); SR.1474, p.7 (M. Orrego, Chile); SR.1474, p.12 (M. Rakotoson, Madagascar); SR.1474, p.16 (M. Sette Camara, Brazil); SR.1474, pp.18-19 (M. Zuleta, Colombia); SR.1475, p.7 (Mr. An Chih-yuan, China); SR. 1475, p.9 (M. Siage, Syrian Arab Republic); SR.1475, p.11 (Mr. Quentin Baxter, New Zealand); SR.1476, pp.5-6 (M. van Brusselen, Belgium); SR.1477, p.2 (Mr. Mahmud, Pakistan), pp.5-6 (M. Omar, Libya), and pp.8-9 (Mr. Steel, U.K.); SR. 1478, p.5 (M. Yasseen, Iraq); SR.1478, p.18 (Mr. Jaipal, India); SR.1479, p.9 (M. Obadi, Yemen); SR.1479, p.15 (M. Alvarez Tabio, Cuba); SR.1480, p.6 (M. Dabiri, Iran); SR.1480, p.7 (M. M'Bodj, Senegal); SR.1480, p.21 (M. Tellefsen, Norway), and p.23 (Mr. Rosenstock, U.S.); SR.1481, p.19 (M. Essy, Ivory Coast); SR.1482, p.2 (M. Rios, Panama); SR.1482, p.6 (M. Guerrero, Philippines); SR.1482, p.6 (MM. Guerrero, Philippines and Ballesteros, Uruguay); SR.1482, pp. 10-11 (M. Valera, Costa Rica); SR.1482, p.12 (M. Wisnoemoerti, Indonesia); SR. 1482, p.13 (M. Al-Haddad, Yemen); SR.1482, p.14 (M. Soglo, Dahomey); SR. 1483, pp.2-3 (M. Rosales, El Salvador); SR.1483, pp.3-4 (M. Godoy, Paraguay); SR.1483, p.6 (M. Alvarez Pifano, Venezuela); SR.1483, p.7 (M. Nicol, Sierra Leone); SR.1483, p.8 (M. Balde, Guinea); SR.1483, p.13 (M. de Soto, Peru).

[29] A/C.6/L.988. Cf. M. Garcia Ortiz, Ecuador, A/C.6/SR.1504, p.2.

[30] A/C.6/SR.1483, p.13.

[31] A/C.6/SR.1477, pp.8-9. His further argument that to qualify Article 3(d) implied that other articles of the definition should be similarly qualified, is hard to follow (if not also far-fetched) in the context.

[32] A/C.6/SR.1480, p.23. He drew the point, of course, from the fact that the whole listing in Article 3 was expressly "subject to and in accordance with Article 2," and that Article 2 expressed the requirement of contravention of the Charter.

[33] Sixth Committee Report, Doc.A/9890, p.1,para.10. Cf. on the speciousness of this solution, Ferencz, 2 *op.cit.*(1975)36-37.

[34] El Salvador, A/C.6/SR.1483, pp.2-3. Cf. M. Nicol (Sierra Leone) A/C.6/ SR.1483, p.7; M. Balde (Guinea) A/C.6/SR.1483, p.8.

[35] Cited *supra* n.34.

[36] A/C.6/SR.1477, p.4.

[37] A/C.6/SR.1480, p.9. Cf. Mme. Ulyanova(Ukraine),A/C.6/SR.1504, p.7.

[38] A/C.6/SR.1479, p.18 and 1488, p.8.

[39] See A/C.6/SR.1477, p.14. The question had already been raised by Canada in 1950 as an objection against the then Soviet draft definition, similarly limited to blockade of ports or coasts.

[40] Working Paper A/C.6/L.990.

[41] As Pakistan thought (of course in 1974, after landlocked East Pakistan became Bangla Desh!) they should, to avoid encroachment on the transit State's sovereignty. See A/C.6/SR.1504, p.3.

[42] Note to the Definition in Sixth Committee Report Doc.A/9890(A/C.6/SR. 1502),para.9. Cf. with the present view as to this Note, Ferencz, 1 *Defining International Aggression,* 35,67.

[42a] The above outcome is the more striking since the basis for asserting any rights of transit of landlocked states is at best rather hazardous under customary law, and the main conventional provisions relevant to the existence of such rights are problematical, either as to their meaning or their legal operativeness. Article 7 of the Convention and Statute on Freedom of Transit (Barcelona, 20 April 1921, League of Nations Treaty Series, No.171) while enouncing "the principle of freedom of transit . . . to the utmost possible extent", does not expressly refer to landlocked States. Article 5(2) of the General Agreement on Tariffs and Trade, 1947, is in similarly general terms. Landlocked States *are* expressly referred to in G.A. Res.1028(XI)(1957) on Landlocked Countries and the Expansion of International Trade; in Principle 5(1) of the Principles Enunciated by the Preliminary Conference of Landlocked States (1958) drawn up by the International Conference of Plenipotentiaries to examine the Law of the Sea, par.3 (summoned under G.A.Res.

1105(XI)(1957)); and in the eight principles referred to in the request of the 1964 Unctad Conference for the drafting of a convention on this very matter. These documents, however, have in themselves no operative legal force. While the Convention on Transit Trade of Landlocked Countries of 1965 which ensued lacks the ratifications by transit countries necessary to give it any practical legal effect. See 597 U.N.T.S.42.

See also the Convention on the High Seas (29 April,1958),Art.3,450 U.N.T.S. 82; Third Law of the Sea Conference, 1973-75,esp.Doc.A/Conf.62/C.2/L.29,Doc. A/AC.138/93,Doc.A/Conf.62/L.8/Rev.1; Draft Convention on the Sea Bed and the Ocean Floor and the Sub-soil thereof beyond the Limits of National Jurisdiction, Doc.A/Conf.62/W.P.8. And see generally, M. I. Glassner, *Access to the Sea for Developing Landlocked States,* 1970 (this book contains an extensive bibliography at 280-293);*id.,* "Developing Land-locked States and the Resources of the Seabed" (1974)11 *San Diego L.Rev.*633-655; P. Childs, "The Interests of Land-locked States in the Law of the Seas" (1971)9 *San Diego L.Rev.*701-732; R. T. McKinnell, "Land-locked Countries: A Test for UNCTAD III?" (1972)6 *Jo.W.T.L.*227-236; R. Makil, "Transit Rights of Land-locked Countries: An Appraisal of International Conventions" (1970)4 *Jo.W.T.L.*35-51; A. H. Tabibi, *The Right of Transit of Landlocked Countries* (1970).

[43] I may mention, in the hope of representing the diverse approaches rather than exhausting the literature, R. N. Gardner, S. Okita and M. J. Udink, "A Turning Point in North-South Domestic Relations", *Report of the Trilateral Task Force on Relations with Developing Countries,* Brussels, June 23-25,1974,esp.11ff.; R. N. Gardner, "The Hard Road to World Order" (1974)52 *Foreign Affairs* 556-576; Th. de Montbrial, "For a New World Economic Order" (1975)54 *Foreign Affairs* 61; R. White, "New International Economic Order" (1975)24 *Int.and Comp. L.Q.*542; C. N. Brower, "Charter of Economic Rights and Duties of States: A Reflection or Rejection of International Law?" (1975) 9 *Int.Lawyer* 295; P. Chandrasekhara Rao, "Charter on Economic Rights and Duties of States" (1975)15*Indian J. of Int.L.*351; R. D. Hansen, "The Political Economy of North-South Relations: How Much Change?" (1975) 29 *International Organization* 921; U. Wassermann, "Key Issues in Development—Interview with Unctad's Secretary-General" (1975) *Jo.W.T.L.*17; T. J. Farer, "The United States and the Third World: A Basis for Accommodation" (1975) 54 *Foreign Affairs* 79; M. Dumas, "*Qu'est-ce que le nouvel ordre économique international?*" (1976) *Tiers Monde* 265; J. de Bandt, "*Les produits de base dans le nouvel ordre économique mondial*" (1976) *Tiers Monde* 339; B. Gosovic and J. G. Ruggie, "On the Creation of a New International Economic Order: Issue Linkage and the Seventh Special Session of the U.N. General Assembly" (1976) 30 *International Organization* 300. And see the Seminar on "Use of 'Economic Force' by States with near Monopoly of Special Resources and new Economic World Order" (University of Delhi Faculty of Law, 26-28 March 1976) (mimeographed materials).

[44] See, e.g., Res.1706(XVI),1961; Res.1707(XVI),1961; Res.1710(XVI), 1961; and the Agreed Conclusions of the Special Committee on Trade Preferences of 1970 (U.N.Docs.TD/B/329/Add.5 and TD/B/AC.3/36); Res.2626(XXIV), 1970; Res.3515(XXX),1975.

[45] Res.3201(S-VI),1974.

[46] Res.3202(S-VI),1974.

[47] Res.3281(XXIX),1974, of which the principles were reaffirmed in the Seventh Special Committee's Declaration on Development and Economic Cooperation (Res.3362(S-VII),1975).

[48] See Doc.A/CN.9/122 of 7.4.1976 and Res.3362(S-VII),1975,par.7 of the Preamble.

[49] Th. de Montbrial,*cit.supra* n.43, at 65.

[50] *Id.* at 66.

[51] See par.4(j) of Res.3201(S-VI),1974, which reads in part as follows: "Just and equitable relationship between the prices of raw materials . . . imported by

them with the aim of bringing about sustained improvement in their unsatisfactory terms of trade and the expansion of the world economy."; Res.3202(S-VI),I,1(d) and I,3(a)(viii); Res.3281(XXIX), Article 28.

[52] See Res.3202(S-VI),s.I,3(a)(xi). The proposal to set up buffer stocks was vehemently opposed by the developed countries during the Unctad IV Conference in Nairobi (5-31May 1976), because it would undermine the global economic system and the operation of market forces.

[53] See Res.3362(S-VII),s.II,3. Cf. the related proposals canvassed in G. Bird, "The Role of S.D.R.'s in Financing Commodity Stabilization" (1976)11 *Jo.W.T.L.* 372-379.

[54] See Res.3202(S-VI),I,3(a)(ii); Res.3281(XXIX),Art.18.

[55] For example, the "Third Window" between the World Bank and the International Development Association (IDA), for the benefit of borrowing nations not eligible for soft loans, and too hard-pressed to meet the Bank's normal terms, where interest charges are subsidized on financing for development programmes. See *Bulletin of the European Communities Commission* 9-1975, at 23-24 and *id.* 1-1976, at 19 (meetings of September 1-5,1975) (hereinafter cited as *"Bull.EC"*). The International Monetary Fund has also established a trust fund for economic development, financed through gold sales. See *Bull.EC* 1-1976, at 17-18 (January Meeting, Jan.7-9,1976).

[56] See Res.3281(XXIX),par.4 of the preamble; Res.3202(S-VI),s.VI; Th. de Montbrial,*op.cit.supra* n.43, at 66-67.

[57] The principle of sovereignty was reaffirmed in many other resolutions, e.g. 1515(XV),1960; 2158(XXI),1966; 2386(XXIII),1968; 2692(XXV),1970; 3016 (XXVII),1972; 3171(XXVIII),1973; 3175(XXVIII),1973.

[58] Cf. J. J. Paust and A. P. Blaustein, "The Arab Oil Weapon—A Threat to International Peace" (1974)68*A.J.I.L.*410, at 422.

[59] Opec does extend some aid to developing countries. See E. el Hadj, "OAPEC's Aid to Less Developed Countries", *Euromoney* (September 1975) at 123-125. Its effectiveness has been questioned as mostly channelled to Arab countries, especially Egypt and Syria. Benefits to developing States generally such as "selective pricing of oil" or "oil-aid grants" have been rejected by OPEC countries. See M. Williams, "Where OPEC Aid Is Going in the Third World", *Euromoney* (March 1976) at 69. There is also debate as to whether, in view of heightened oil revenues, the scale of OPEC aid should not be more comparable to that of developed countries. Should earnings from oil be treated differently from earnings of other commodities? See, as to the effects of the Arab oil embargo on the food reserves and population trends in developing countries, J. J. Paust and A. P. Blaustein,*op.cit.supra* at 433-437.

[60] R. D. Hansen,*cit.supra* n.43, at 927-928.

[61] On the legality of the oil embargo, from an Arab standpoint, see I. F. I. Shihata, "Destination Embargo of Arab Oil: Its Legality Under International Law" (1974)68 *A.J.I.L.*591. And see the critique of this article in J. J. Paust and A. Blaustein, "The Arab Oil Weapon: A Reply and Reaffirmation of Illegality" (1976)15 *Col.J.of Trans.L.*57-73.

[62] I can here only note some of the complex economic problems of "cartelization" namely: (1) prerequisites of successful collective bargaining; (2) backfire from soaring prices (for example by accelerating search for alternative commodities); (3) consolidation of the stances of the affected nations. See *Bull.EC* 2-1974, at 13-22, and H. Simonet, "Energy and the Future of Europe" (1975)53 *Foreign Affairs* at 453-454, as to mutually protective measures and mechanisms such as oil-sharing in emergencies and financial solidarity.

After the oil boycott, the developed nations sought a stable price-supply relationship in global petroleum sales (The Conference on Energy and Related Economic Problems, April 7-15,1975,Paris.) Dialogue with oil-producers failed because Algeria and Fourth World States pressed the "New World Economic Order" notion for indexing the price of basic commodities generally to the prices of manufactured goods. See *Bull.EC* 4-1975, at 18-21 and Th. O. Enders, "Opec and the Industrial Countries: The Next Ten Years" (1975)53 *Foreign Affairs*625. A preparatory meeting for a new international Conference on Energy, Raw Materials and Development was held in Paris (13-16 October, 1975), leading to a Conference on International Economic Co-operation (The North-South dialogue) in December 1975, on ministerial level. That conference set up commissions on energy, raw materials, development and finance to meet throughout 1976. See *Bull.EC*10-1975, at 7-11; *Bull.EC*12-1975, at 11-17; *Bull.EC* 2-1976, at 18-19.

62a Cf. Stone, *Of Law and Nations* (1974)364-365.

63 See Z. Brzezinski, "U.S. Foreign Policy: The Search for Focus" (1973)51 *Foreign Affairs* 708-727.

64 See Stone, "International Justice" 372-460, esp.403-424,430-452.

65 Stone,*op.cit.supra* n.64, at 452-460.

FOOTNOTES TO CHAPTER 9

1 A/C.6/SR.1472, p.2.

2 As M. M'Bodj of Senegal resoundingly prophesied. (A/C.6/SR.1486, p.7.)

3 On the even less sanguine mood in the preceding year, see Ferencz, "Defining Aggression" (1972)496,504ff. And cf. *supra*,Ch.2, Section II.

4 A/9019(1973) p.9.

5 G.A.O.R.(XXVIII)Supp.No.19(A/9019) p.23. There is a deceptive implied reference here to this phrase as used in the prohibition of Art.2(4) of the Covenant. But, of course, it is there *not forbidden simpliciter,* but only as used "against the territorial integrity or political independence", etc. See Stone, *Of Law and Nations* (1974)23-38,esp.23.

6 See *supra* Ch.7.   7 See Stone,*op.cit.*(1974)18,23.

8 See Stone, *Aggression and World Order* (1958)139ff.

9 For a full consideration of this in relation to the 1974 Definition, see *supra* Ch.4.

10 E.g., Mexico, G.A.O.R.(XXVIII)Supp.No.19(A/9019), p.25. The positions of the various States are considered *supra* Ch. 4, Sections III-IV.

11 Algerian proposal, G.A.O.R.(XXVIII)Supp.No.19(A/9019), p.23.

12 *Id.* at p.23.   13 See *supra* Ch.4.

14 Now included in Art.5(1) of the Consensus Definition. See A/C.6/SR.1472, p.5 (M. Rydbeck for Sweden); A/C.6/SR.1479, p.5 (M. Petric for Yugoslavia); A/C.6/SR.1476, p.4 (M. van Brusselen for Belgium). Romania proposed this as paragraph 3 of Article 1. See A/AC.134/SR.111.

15 1973 Report, G.A.O.R.(XXVIII)Supp.No.19(A/9019), p.18.

16 See on this matter *supra* Ch.7.

17 This seems to be how Uruguay would have understood the Note. See G.A.O.R.(XXVIII)Supp.No.19(A/9019), p.27.

18 A/9019(1973), p.19.

19 The sixth preambular paragraph of the Consolidated Text stated the duty of States not to use armed force to deprive peoples of their right to "self-determination, freedom and independence". In the final draft of the Consensus Definition there was added—"or to disrupt the territorial integrity". This might be read to imply either that any licence to support self-determination ceases at the point when such support would disrupt the territorial integrity of a State. This would support the Western view of the final Article 6. Or it might, with more difficulty, be taken to imply that a State's territorial integrity is protected only if the State complies with the right to self-determination of its peoples. See for fuller discussion *supra* Ch.6.

19a See the record of debate in 13 *U.N. Monthly Chronicle* (March 1976,No. 3)5-14, and the historical discussion in J. Binet, *"Les Comores au seuil de l'indépendance", Afrique Contemporaine* (No.84,March-April 1976)16-20,esp.19-20.

20 G.A.O.R.(XXVIII)Supp.No.19(A/9019), p.22.

21 *Id.* p.23.   22 *Id.* pp.24,27.

23 Comment of the Contacts and Drafting Groups, *id.* p.19.

24 *Id.,* p.19.

25 See Sixth Committee Report, G.A.O.R.(XXIX)Doc.A/9890,Para.10, as to national maritime jurisdiction. Cf. *id., Para.9,* as to the analogous problem of landlocked States.

26 See Stone, "International Justice", and generally *supra* Ch.8.

27 See the works cited *supra* Ch.2,n.7.

28 Ferencz, *Defining International Aggression* (1975). Vol.2 is the one here concerned, pp.19-76 being commentary and pp.79-614 the texts of various documents. Vol.1 similarly introduces and collects the documents of the League period.

29 Ferencz, "The Last Mile" (1973)430,463.

This kind of aphorism is, of course, related to the view often expressed in the last half-century that any agreed definition however "imperfect" would be more conducive to justice than "no definition at all". See, e.g. the Yugoslav representative in A/AC.77/SR.7, p.8, and *1956 Sp.Com.Rep.13.* Cf. the Peruvian views, A/AC.77/SR.18, p.9. Some "imperfect" definitions could certainly have the effect of constantly protecting the unjust and punishing the just.

It is not necessary to run to the extreme opposite position which at moments was suggested in the Chinese (Taiwan) view, that "a defective definition would only have a confusing effect and would therefore be harmful and dangerous. The adoption of such a definition could only be detrimental to the prestige of the United Nations". (A/AC.77/SR.14, p.5, and *1956 Sp.Com.Rep.13.) Within limits* imperfection of definition may be tolerable, so far as trusted adequate arbiters and procedures for its application exist. The present strictures, as the text indicates, turn on grossness and centrality of the imperfections of the 1974 Consensus Definition, and inadequacy of the likely arbiters, namely, the General Assembly as at present constituted.

30 See n.28 *supra.*

30a See Stone, Book Review, 70 *A.J.I.L.*(October,1976); *id.,* "Hopes and Loopholes in the 1974 Definition of Aggression", 71*A.J.I.L.* (April 1977).

31 Ferencz,*op.cit.*(1975)51.

32 *Id.*52.   33 *Ibid.*

34 Many volumes have been written on the problematics of the limits of lawful force under the Charter. See the discussion and basic literature in Stone, *Legal Controls* 165-284,324-334; Stone, *Of Law and Nations* (1974)Chs.1,18, and authorities there cited.

35 I.C.J. Reports, 1971, at pp.53 and 58.

36 G.A.O.R.(XXVIII)Supp.No.19(A/9019), pp.22-28, at p.27.

37 Stone, *Aggression and World Order* (1958)Ch.5 (Aggression and the Charter); Stone, *Of Law and Nations* (1974)Ch.1.

38 A/9019(1973), p.20.

39 G.A.O.R.(XXVIII)Supp.No.19(A/9019), p.11.

40 See *supra* Ch.4, Section V.

41 Cf. *id.* Ch.3, Section IV.

42 Ferencz, 1 *Defining International Aggression* (1975)49, illustrates well, by reference to the placement of Article 7 in the Definition, the epidemic nature of the fever of unreduced conflicts among the provisions of the Definition. Protagonists of wars of liberation wanted to exalt Article 7 by placing it last. Opposed States wanted it to be followed by the present Article 6 preserving the present range of Charter provisions as to lawful use of force. The compromise was to place Article 7 after the present Article 6, but then to add the above final Article 8! The learned writer aptly observes upon the inferences and interrelations "tucked away in the dark shadows of the various ambiguous clauses".

FOOTNOTES TO CHAPTER 10

[1] Such a determination was made against South Africa on March 31, 1976, in relation to Angola, significantly no Permanent Member except the Soviet Union concurring. (S.C.Res.387(1976).) China did not participate in the vote, and France, Italy, Japan, the U.K. and the U.S. abstained, leaving the resolution carried by the minimum of 9 votes. China expressly and the others implicitly found unacceptable a resolution which did not also determine aggression by the Soviet Union and Cuba. This latter would certainly have been vetoed by the Soviet Union. See the account in "South Africa Condemned for Aggression against Angola; Full Compensation Demanded" (1976)13 *U.N.Monthly Chronicle* 5-13,61-65, and esp. M. Huang Hua (China) at 6-7,64; Mr. Richard (U.K.) at 64, and Mr. Scranton (U.S.) at 63. See generally J. A. Marcum, "Lessons of Angola" (1976)54 *Foreign Affairs* 407, and for a Soviet interpretation, K. Uralov, "New Advances in Angola" *International Affairs* (Moscow, August 1976) 76-80.

[2] Cf. the related point of R. B. Pal, *International Military Tribunal For the Far East* (1953) that "even now questions of very great weight in the life of States are left *outside* the system and no State would agree to make them justiciable . . . ." (56, and see also 58-59). And cf. J. L. Kunz (*"Bellum Justum* . . ." (1951)45*A.J.I.L.*528,530), who pointed out that "just war" according to the classical doctrine was "a reaction against a wrong," a procedure either in restitution or compensation for torts, or broken guarantees, or in punishment for crimes.

This is no mere "perfectionism", as Professor Röling implies in his delightful quip that "if the Lord God had been such a perfectionist, He would never have succeeded in formulating the Ten Commandments." (B. V. A. Röling, "On Aggression . . ." ((1955)2 *Nederlands T.Int.R.*167,177.) For the Author of the Ten Commandments did not just single out one part of man's duties and leave all the rest to barbarous anarchy. He offered, for that time, a rounded statement of all the main duties of men. Nor did He proceed, within the rounded Code, to support one part by the direst penalties, and leave enforcement of the rest to chance or animus.

[3] So cf. R. B. Pal (*op.cit.*115-116), who observed that "emphasis on an arbitrarily fixed *status quo* would certainly not lead us to any understanding of the real conditions of peace . . . . A trial conducted on this basis may . . . shut out the essential facts responsible for the world trouble and may, at the same time, afford ample opportunity for a collective expression of retributive and aggressive sentiment."

[4] And including, as Pompe (*Aggressive War* 177) well pointed out in relation to Nuremberg, not only the full circumstances of starting the war, but the gravity of the consequences thereof, for example, the war crimes and mass murders of the war waged by the Axis Powers. Cf. also G. Podrea, "*L'Agression* . . ." (1952) 30 *R.D.I.*367,369; Komarnicki, 43.

The above result coincides with the first of the conceivable classes of tests detected by the late Quincy Wright, "The Concept of Aggression . . ." (1935)29 *A.J.I.L.*373,378ff. The difficulties, that authority pointed out, arise "whether we centre our interest on legal rights, or in the military field, and ask who was responsible for starting an armament race, or in the psychological field and ask who had a spirit of aggrandizement, or in the procedural field and ask who has refused to accept reasonable proposals of pacific settlement." (379.)

[5] Cf. on the intractability of this question in the context of the old "just war" doctrine, J. L. Kunz, "*Bellum Justum* . . ." (1951)45*A.J.I.L.*528,531ff. And see Stone,*op.cit* (1958)104-105,n.3.

[6] One of the best analyses is still that of Quincy Wright,*op.cit.* (1935) at 380ff., who after pointing out the difficulties of full evaluation of the *preceding* history, adds that "tests confining attention to events which occurred at the time fighting began, conform less to the usual conception of justice, and still raise (though to a lesser degree) difficulties of proof, and objective evaluation,

especially in view of the tension at the moment of crisis". "The difficulties," he thinks, "are similar whether we inquire who first invaded someone else's territory, committed other acts of war, or omitted legal formalities in the initiation of hostilities; who first issues a mobilization or other military order rendering an offensive movement inevitable; who, at the moment hostilities began, wanted war and who did not; who, at that moment was ready to arbitrate or conciliate, and who was not." (379.) These difficulties, he admits, render this class of tests "seldom capable of providing the rapid and precise conclusions which a war prevention procedure demands". Cf. Stone,*op.cit.* (1958) Ch.9 *passim.*

While agreeing that these difficulties affect tests based on the outbreak of hostilities, we are unable (for reasons given in Stone,*op.cit.* (1958)108-110) to share Professor Wright's greater optimism as to tests based upon events after fighting is in progress. That writer thinks that these tests may make use of events such as a cease-fire order, and the parties' attitudes thereto, which are prepared or observed with the purpose of providing a test of aggression, thus relying on "experimental" rather than "historical" evidence. As shown in Stone,*op.cit.* (1958) 28ff. modern wars make it even more impossible to support Professor Wright's definition of an aggressor as "a State which is under an obligation not to resort to force, which is employing force against another State, and which refuses to accept an armistice proposed in accordance with a procedure which it has accepted to implement its no-force obligation" (381). As to whether League Council practice under Art.11 of the Covenant really warrants (as the learned writer assumes) his above inferences, see Stone,*op.cit.* (1958)38-40, and the classical work of T. P. Conwell-Evans, *The League Council in Action* (1929)esp.35ff.

[7] J. Maktos, "*La Question de la Définition de l'Agression*" (1952)30 *R.D.I.* 5,6: "*Il ne s'agit pas de la définition du terme 'agression' dont il est facile de donner non pas une, mais plusieurs définitions. Il s'agit du développement du droit international.*" (This article was a summary of the author's remarks as U.S. representative on the Sixth Commission in the debate of Jan. 10, 1952, on the Report of the Third Session, International Law Commission.)

[8] Cf. D. Sidjanski and S. Castanos, "*L'Agresseur et l'Agression au Point de Vue Idéologique et Réel*" (1952)30*R.D.I.*44,45, who, for reasons similar to those in the text, conclude: "*Ainsi, si la définition de l'agression peut être utile, voire necessaire en tant qu'orientation, rigide et automatique, elle sera lourde de consequences néfaste. La question est beaucoup plus complexe qu'on ne désire la croire. Une simple définition ne saurait la resoudre.*" We agree in substance with this position. And cf. J. Maktos,*op.et loc.cit.*, and Komarnicki,*op.cit. supra* Ch.8, n.18, at 43.

[9] It is thus, in the actual world, self-contradictory to lay down as concurrent conditions of peace *both* the demand for change conformable to justice, *and* the demand for a precise automatically operating definition of aggression, as was common in the League period. See e.g. A. B. Plaunt in Bourquin(ed.), *Collective Security* 295, C. Jordan, *id.* 301-304. So also with demands for a definition which shall simultaneously embrace "every act contrary to law and justice", *and also* be "a solid base" for collective security. See e.g. A. Derying in Bourquin(ed.), *Collective Security* 325.

[10] Ferencz, 1 *op.cit.* (1975)51.

[11] *Supra* Ch.2, Section I and Chapter 4, Sections I-II. For a full examination, see Julius Stone and Robert K. Woetzel(eds.), *Towards a Feasible International Criminal Court* (1970) (here cited as "Stone-Woetzel, *International Criminal Court*") Ch.26(Stone)315-341, esp.323-336; cf. *id.*, Ch.28(Graven)206-222, esp. 219-221.

[12] Res.898(IX). And see Sixth Committee Report, A/2827 and Corr.1.

[13] A/AC.134/SR.110-113, p.4. Professor Suy's exposition (*ibid.*) proceeded, of course, on the basis that the Court to be established would have jurisdiction over the crime of aggression, and the Definition would form a basis for decision by it.

14 A/C.6/SR.1473, p.5.

15 There is evidence that even during the debates on definition, still at a great distance from application by an International Criminal Court, both Communist and Western representatives were somewhat preoccupied with the implications of the Definition for criminal charges against their leaders. There were objections, for example, in the Sixth Committee from the German Democratic Republic, to any implication of collective responsibility which might be drawn from Explanatory Note (b) to Article 1 stating that the term "State" "includes the concept of a 'group of States'." (See SR.1441, p.5. Cf. SR.1443, p.20(Hungary), A/AC.134/ WG.5/R.4(Japan).) The concluding words "where appropriate" were then added.

So, too, with regard to Article 5, paragraph 2 of the Consensus Definition, which states that "(A) war of aggression is a crime against international peace. Aggression gives rise to international responsibility." As to the meaning of "war" in this context, the United States urged that the war must have been *declared* as a prerequisite for criminal liability of individuals. This was directed presumably to the possibility that American prisoners in North Vietnamese hands might be put on trial on this count.

16 R. L. Perret, "Doctrinal Bases for International Penal Jurisdiction" in Stone-Woetzel, *International Criminal Court* 154.

17 See J. Stone,*op.cit. supra* n.11, esp. at 335-336.

18 Cited in n.11 *supra*.   19 A/C.6/SR.1472, p.9.

20 A/C.6/SR.1478, p.7.   21 A/C.6/SR.1478, p.14.

22 Wang(Canada),A/AC.134/SR.113, p.43.

23 A/C.6/SR.1480, pp.17-18.   24 A/C.6/SR.1504, p.2.

25 A/C.6/L.993.   26 A/C.6/SR.1504, p.6.

27 For Peru, A/C.6/SR.1474, p.4.

28 I have given reasons (*supra* Ch.9, Section III, and Sections I and II of the present Chapter) why it may also well be uncompletable.

29 A/C.6/SR.1488, p.8.

30 Cf. M. Godoy of Paraguay (A/C.6/SR1488, p.9); and as to 30 landlocked States and blockade, A/C.6/L.990. And see the Statement on National Waters and Landlocked States, A/C.6/I/L.988,L.990.

31 A/C.6/SR.1504, pp.2-3.   32 A/C.6/SR.1504, p.5.

33 A/C.6/SR.1472, pp.2,4.   34 Belgium, A/C.6/SR.1476, p.4.

35 A/C.6/SR.1471, p.3.

36 Per M. Fuentes Ibañez, Bolivia, A/C.6/SR.1477, p.13.

37 A/C.6/SR.1471, p.3.

38 A/C.6/SR.1479, p.11.

39 A/C.6/SR.1479, p.12.

40 A/C.6/L.993; and see M. Prieto, Chile, *et al.,* A/C.6/SR.1503, and discussion thereon on pp.2-8, and A/C.6/SR.1504, pp.9-17, A/C.6/SR.1505, pp.15-18.

41 If, in rather Alice-in-Wonderland fashion, some participants' claims about the achievements of the Definition in real control of aggression are taken at face value, the conflict between the General Assembly and the Security Council may be seen as an obstacle to the objectives of the Definition. Alden Abott, *et al.,* "The Definition of Aggression" (1975)16 *Harv.Int.L.J.*589-612, esp.593-94 and notes, and 604-605, almost enters this wonderland.

42 Res.377(V),G.A.O.R.(V)Supp.20(A/1775), p.10. And see Stone, *Legal Controls* 266-284.

43 Stone, *Aggression and World Order* (1958)164.

44 It has been a main theme of my work, however, since the books cited in nn.42 and 43 *supra*.

45 The Writer, therefore, welcomes the initiative and general orientation of the *Ad Hoc* Group on United States Policy Toward the United Nations, "comprising scholars professionally concerned with international affairs, former U.S. delegates to the U.N. and nongovernmental organization delegates". See the

Memorandum "A New United States Policy Towards the United Nations", March 1976 (mimeographed), and the report in *New York Times,* April 21, 1976, p.3. The *Ad Hoc* Group includes Professor Richard N. Gardner, former Deputy Assistant Secretary of State for International Organization, Rita Hauser, formerly member of the Human Rights Commission, Professors Thomas M. Franck, Hans Morgenthau and Thomas Buergenthal, Charles W. Maynes, Secretary, Carnegie Endowment for International Peace, Norman Cousins, publisher and writer, and others.

Of course, a withdrawal policy is but the lesser of two evils. The greater evil is now very patent in General Assembly majoritarian pressures to outflank the legal basis of Security Council decisions. See on this matter, L. Gross, "Voting in the Security Council and the P.L.O." (1976)70 *A.J.I.L.*470-491, esp. at 476-480. This writer observes that "the unprincipled majoritarianism of the Soviet and Third World blocs which all too often has come to prevail in the Assembly has found a second home in the Security Council" (484).

Index of Names

Index of Subjects

A

ACQUISITION OF TERRITORY, 57-65, 125-28, 199(n.10). See also *Int. L., M.E. Crisis, M.E. Res.* 242.

ACTUS REUS, 40, 45. See also *Animus Aggressionis, Ag., Int. Cr. Ct., Int. Cr. L., Priority P.*

AFGHANISTAN, 118, 166

AFRO-ASIAN STATES, 11-12, 37, 173; anti-colonialism and, 11. See also *Bounds., Trespass of; Colonialism, Third W., Fourth W., Redistr. of R., Oil B., G.A., Aut. Majorities*

AGGRESSION, "act of", 2, 5, 7, 9, 191(n.1), 196(n.3); as fact-value complex, 96, 108, 109, 114; desirability of def., 17; "ec. ag.", "ideol. ag.", etc. See under these rubrics; as emotive symbol, 192(n.3); ethical elements in, 14; flow of time and, 13, 136; legal meaning or results of, 39, 192(n.14); loopholes in def. of, 123-152, 165-171; *mens rea.* See *Animus Aggressionis;* military and non-military, 194(n.9); moral approval and, 2, 10, 55; Nur. and S.F. Charters and, 42; State to State relation, 71-72, 133,

graphy and, 15-16, 105ff., 154;
peaceful change and, 216(n.9);
Pentateuch and, 13; politico-military
role, 40-43; prescriptive functions
of, 15, 106; rational enquiry and,
13; subjective elements in, 196(n.7);
taxonomy and, 15-16, 105ff.
See also *Animus Aggressionis, Armed
F., Cons. Def., Ind. Ag., Pol. War.*
DEMOCRATIC YEMEN, 32, 83,
200(n.15), 203(n.46), 210(n.28);
on Art.2 of the Def., 32
DÉTENTE, 1, 19, 129, 153. See also
Helsinki Declaration, U.S., U.S.S.R.
DEVELOPMENT. See *Aid Pro-
grammes*
DOMINICAN REPUBLIC, 201
(n.15)
DRAFT CODE OF OFFENCES
AGAINST ... MANKIND, 17, 20,
42, 159. See *Int. Cr. Ct., Int. Cr. L.*
DUE PROCESS, 108

E

ECONOMIC AGGRESSION, 23-25,
52-54, 64, 87-103, 110, 115, 116,
119, 123, 127-131, 149, 174, 204
(n.16), 205(n.28), and 207(n.63);
Latin-American and Soviet proposals 1953, 23; sovereignty and,
103-04, 207(n.63)
See also *Ag., Ind. Ag., Oil B., Redistr.
of R., World E.O.*
ECONOMIC COERCION. See
*Armed F., Ec. Ag., Oil B., Re-
distr. of R., Unequal Treaties*
ECUADOR, 165, 166, 195(n.33),
210(n.29)
EGYPT, 52, 58-60, 64, 86, 126-28,
138, 170, 171, 174, 196(n.63),
212(n.59); on Art.2 of the Def.,
30, 32; on acquisition etc. by law-
ful force, 57-65, 125-28, 199(n.10)
See also *Acquisition of Territory, Ind.
Ag., M.E. Crisis, Pol. War., Pol.
War. Dr., Six Day War*
EL SALVADOR, 210(nn.28, 34)
ESTONIA, 208(n.10)
EQUAL RIGHTS PRINCIPLE, 67,
69, 121, 122, 143; and sovereignty,
103-04; and natural resources,
119-122
See also *Decl. ... Concerning Friendly
Relations ..., Charter (U.N.)*
EX INIURIA MAXIM, 58-63, 126.

See also *Ag., Military Occupation,
Self-D., Six Day War, Uti Possidetis*
EXPRESSIO UNIUS MAXIM, 118

F

FINLAND, 193(n.18), 208(n.10)
FORCE. See under *Armed Bands,
Armed F.*, Charter limits on,
Charter (U.N.), Art.2(4), *Cons.
Def.* Consolidated Text, *Decl.* ...
*Friendly Relations, Ec. Ag., Ind.
Ag., Self-D.*
FOURTH WORLD, 104, 212(n.62).
See also *Ec. Ag., Oil B., Redistr. of
R., States, Third W., World E.O.*
FRANCE, 11, 33, 76, 83, 92, 110,
135, 154, 200(n.1c), 215(n.1);
crossing frontiers criterion, 11,
109-10; security of, and tests of ag.,
11, 109-10; views on def., Art.2, 33;
Art.3(g), 76; Art.7, 200(n.5)
See also *France-Comoros Affair,
Princ. Dr., Pol. War. Dr.*, and see
particular rubrics
FRANCE-COMOROS AFFAIR, 134-
36, 200(n.1c). See also *France,
Ind. Ag., Self-Det.*
FREE TRADE, 119. See also *Ec. Ag.,
Redistr. of R., World E.O.*
FREEDOM of the press etc. and
ideol. ag., 24. See also under *Civil
War, Ideol. Ag., Ind. Ag., Self-Det.*

G

GATT. See *Landlocked States*
GENERAL ASSEMBLY (U.N.), ag.,
competence to define, 192(n.3);
aut. majorities in. See under that
rubric; auto-interpretation by, 34,
37-38; creation of Int. Cr. C. and,
160, 161; decls. of. See under
particular Decls.; emergency session
of, 8; force authorised by, attitudes
to, 37, 143-151; functions of, con-
trasted with S.C., 8, 25-26, 146,
172-75; normative role of, 195
(n.36); peace enf. and, 8, 13, 14,
30, 23, 35-41, 155, 168; political
influence of, 37; powers of, 25-29,
37, 56, 175; power to bind Members, 25, 27; power to bind S.C.,
26-28
RESOLUTIONS; Res. 377 (V),
217(n.42); Res. 898 (IV), 218
(n.12); Res. 1028 (XI), 210(n.42a);
Res. 1105 (XI), 211(n.42a); Res.